W9-BFV-010

Advance Praise for *Awe*

"Twenty years of insight about awe. *Whoa!* On every continent and in every imaginable religion. *Wow.* Intensely personal, recognizably collective, and utterly universal, Keltner's stories and science of awe are inspired. Awe merges us with systems larger than self—nature, music, art, spirit, morality, collectives, life, and death. We are better for Keltner's account. Read it. *Aahhh.*"

— Susan T. Fiske, coauthor of *Social Cognition: From Brains to Culture* and author of *Envy Up, Scorn Down: How Status Divides Us*

"A researcher who has taught us new ways to think about generosity and cooperation has turned his attention to one of the most understudied emotions of all, Awe. Eye-opening and mind-expanding."

— Sarah Blaffer Hrdy, author of *Mother Nature* and *Mothers and Others: The Origins of Mutual Understanding*

"Our troubling times, our clickbait media, even our own habits of mind, blanket our consciousness with the negative and threatening in life. This book is a counterforce. Powerful, erudite, rooted in brilliant research, but always fascinatingly accessible, it uplifts the wonderful in life. From the beauty of movement in sports to the moral courage of a friend, it's a guide to how to see and experience the wonder that is always all around us. It balances consciousness. It has been a long time since I've read anything as inspiring. I'd say race to read it. You won't be disappointed."

— Claude M. Steele, Lucie Stern Professor Emeritus of Psychology at Stanford University

"Dacher Keltner has written a deeply personal, scientifically brilliant treatise on an emotion he convinces us we need to experience more often in our daily lives."

— Richard E. Nisbett, author of *Mindware: Tools for Smart Thinking*

Awe

ALSO BY DACHER KELTNER

The Power Paradox
Born to Be Good

Awe

The New Science of

EVERYDAY WONDER

and How It Can

TRANSFORM YOUR LIFE

. . .

DACHER KELTNER

PENGUIN PRESS

NEW YORK

2023

PENGUIN PRESS
An imprint of Penguin Random House LLC
penguinrandomhouse.com

Copyright © 2023 by Dacher Keltner
Penguin Random House supports copyright. Copyright fuels
creativity, encourages diverse voices, promotes free speech,
and creates a vibrant culture. Thank you for buying an authorized
edition of this book and for complying with copyright laws by
not reproducing, scanning, or distributing any part of it in any
form without permission. You are supporting writers and
allowing Penguin Random House to continue to publish
books for every reader.

"There's a certain Slant of light" from EMILY DICKINSON'S
POEMS: AS SHE PRESERVED THEM, edited by Cristanne
Miller, Copyright © 2016 by the President and Fellows of Harvard
College. Copyright © 1998 by the President and Fellows of
Harvard College. Copyright © 1951, 1955 by the President and
Fellows of Harvard College. Copyright © renewed 1979, 1983 by
the President and Fellows of Harvard College. Copyright © 1914,
1918, 1919, 1924, 1929, 1930, 1932, 1935, 1937, 1942 by Martha
Dickinson Bianchi. Copyright © 1952, 1957, 1958, 1963, 1965 by
Mary L. Hampson. Used by permission. All rights reserved.

"Letter of gratitude," copyright © Yuyi Morales, on page 84 is
reprinted courtesy of Yuyi Morales.

"Poem of awe" on pages 205–8 is reprinted courtesy of Yuria
Celidwen.

Illustration credits appear on page 253.

LIBRARY OF CONGRESS CATALOGING-IN-PUBLICATION DATA

Names: Keltner, Dacher, author.
Title: Awe: the new science of everyday wonder and
how it can transform your life / Dacher Keltner.
Description: New York: Penguin Press, 2022. |
Includes bibliographical references and index.
Identifiers: LCCN 2022002707 (print) | LCCN 2022002708 (ebook) |
ISBN 9781984879684 (hardcover) | ISBN 9781984879691 (ebook) |
ISBN 9780593653012 (international edition)
Subjects: LCSH: Awe. | Wonder.
Classification: LCC BF575.A9 K45 2022 (print) |
LCC BF575.A9 (ebook) | DDC 152.4—dc23/eng/20220921
LC record available at https://lccn.loc.gov/2022002707
LC ebook record available at https://lccn.loc.gov/2022002708

Printed in the United States of America
1st Printing

Designed by Amanda Dewey

For Rolf Keltner

From wonder into wonder,
existence opens.

· LAO TZU ·

SECTION IV

Living a Life of Awe

Contents

Introduction

I have taught happiness to hundreds of thousands of people around the world. It is not obvious why I ended up doing this work: I have been a pretty wound-up, anxious person for significant chunks of my life and was thrown out of my first meditation class (for laughing while we chanted "I am a being of purple fire"). Life can surprise us, though, in giving us the work we are here to do. So nearly every day in classrooms of different kinds, from kindergarten circle rugs to lecture halls in Berkeley, from the apses of churches to inside prisons, from sterile conference rooms in hospitals to gatherings in nature, I've taught people about finding the good life.

What we are seeking in such inquiry is an answer to a perennial question, one we have been asking in different ways for tens of thousands of years: How can we live the good life? One enlivened by joy and community and meaning, that brings us a sense of worth and belonging and strengthens the people and natural environments around us? Now, twenty years into teaching happiness, I have an answer:

FIND AWE.

Awe is the emotion we experience when we encounter vast mysteries that we don't understand. Why would I recommend that you find happiness in an emotion that is so fleeting and evanescent? A feeling so elusive that it resists simple description? That requires the unexpected, and moves us toward mystery and the unknown rather than what is certain and easy?

Because we can find awe anywhere. Because doing so doesn't require money or the burning of fossil fuels—or even much time. Our research suggests that just a couple of minutes a day will do. Because we have a basic need for awe wired into our brains and bodies, finding awe is easy if we just take a moment and wonder. Because all of us, no matter what our background, can find our own meaningful path to awe. Because brief moments of awe are as good for your mind and body as anything you might do.

My hope for you in reading this book is simple—it is that you will find more awe.

In the service of this aim, I will need to tell you four stories.

The first is the new science of awe. In ways I am beginning to understand, I was raised to study awe with the tools of science. My mom taught poetry and literature at a large public university, and in how she lived her life she taught me about the wisdom of the passions and to speak truth to power. My dad painted in the horrifying and beautiful style of Francisco Goya and Francis Bacon and suggested that life is about seeking the Tao with your Zen mind, beginner's mind. I grew up in wild Laurel Canyon,

California, in the late 1960s, with the Doors and Joni Mitchell as neighbors, and then in the hardscrabble foothills of the Sierras, where a poor, rural wildness prevailed. The soaring ideas of the times—civil rights, antiwar protests, women's rights, sexual and artistic revolution, Watergate—filled the conversations at our dinner table and posters on the walls of our home.

I spent unusual amounts of time as a child looking at art and hearing about great scenes and characters in novels, poems, paintings, and films. But I showed no early talents, to my chagrin, for literary analysis or writing fiction, nor painting or drawing, for that matter. Instead, I was awestruck by dinosaurs, natural history museums, sports statistics, basketball, the Beatles, the biological life of ponds and creeks, and being near mountains, rivers, and wide-open, star-filled skies. Given the passion-filled home and the passionate era I was raised in, I guess it makes sense that I would devote my career to mapping emotions with science, first at the University of Wisconsin–Madison and then at University of California, Berkeley.

Early in my career, I spent hundreds of hours in a basement lab discerning in frame-by-frame video analysis the expressions of embarrassment and shame—fitting for the paranoid young professor that I was. With the arrival of two daughters and the delights of family life filling my days, I would turn to the wonders of laughter, how we express love in the face and body, the vocalizations and physiological patterns of compassion, and how with simple acts of touch we can express gratitude. This work was animated by the thesis that emotions like compassion, gratitude, and love are the glue of social relations, which I summarized in my book *Born to Be Good: The Science of a Meaningful Life.*

What about awe, though? Is awe a fundamental emotion, a

universal core to who we are, like fear, anger, or joy? How would one study awe scientifically? Measure feelings that seem beyond words? Could we bring awe, so mysterious in how it arises, reliably into the lab?

Fifteen years ago, my PhD students and I as well as other scientists around the world began to find awe in the lab. We charted this elusive emotion with new measures of the brain and body, physical responses like tears and piloerection (the contraction of small muscles surrounding hair follicles), sensations like the chills, and demonstrations of how awe transforms the ways we think and act. We have studied how we feel awe near great trees and in looking out at panoramic views. At sporting events, punk rock shows, and in the flowing effervescence of dance. In mystical experiences in prayer, meditation, yoga, and during psychedelic trips. In peak experiences with music, visual art, poetry, fiction, and drama. Science found awe, producing the first story of awe I will tell.

Before science, humans were making sense of awe in forms of culture. The second story we will hear, then, is how culture archives awe. This is a story of how we create music, visual art, religion, fiction, and film to share in experiences of awe, so that we may understand the vast mysteries we face together in a culture we call our own. Awe animates the stories, ceremonies, rituals, and visual designs of Indigenous peoples dating back tens of thousands of years. You might think of these as our first awe technologies. Awe structures the legends, myths, temples, and sacred texts of religions. It jumps out of paintings, photographs, and films, from Goya to Berlin street artists to the films of Miyazaki. And you can sense it in your body and feel its form in nearly every kind of music, from the sounds of the kora of West Africa to an Indian raga to Nicki Minaj.

Science tends toward generalization. Cultural forms aspire to idealization, and often some perfection of form. There is a third story of awe we need to hear, the personal and first-person. This became clear to me when I asked people this question and listened to the stories they told:

> What is an experience of awe that you have had, when you encountered a vast mystery that transcends your understanding of the world?

If you have a spare moment, you might think of an awe story of your own.

The stories I heard people tell reveal timeless truths about awe. About the awe of watching a quadriplegic person, a former Olympic athlete, take his first steps while recovering from a devastating injury to his spine. Or being in the front row of a Coltrane concert when he was just breaking big. Or from a woman in the CIA at Abu Ghraib, who discovered her pacifism in looking at the currents of the Euphrates River.

Moved by these narratives, I gathered personal stories of awe from doctors, combat veterans, professional athletes, prisoners, writers, environmentalists, poets, musicians, artists, photographers, filmmakers, ministers, Indigenous scholars, spiritual pilgrims, midwives, and hospice workers. Stories about the courage of people who suffer with disease and how nature transforms the traumas of combat. Of how music allows us to find home in a strange land. About what it is like to nearly die, and how we make sense of such extraordinary experiences. These personal stories revealed first-person truths in a particularity, metaphor, image, and vernacular that science simply cannot capture, and that cultural forms only approximate.

These three stories of awe—the scientific, the cultural, and the personal—converge on an understanding of how we can find awe. Where do we find it? In response to what I will call the eight wonders of life, which include the strength, courage, and kindness of others; collective movement in actions like dance and sports; nature; music; art and visual design; mystical encounters; encountering life and death; and big ideas or epiphanies. These wonders are all around us, if we only pause for a moment and open our minds. There are so many opportunities for everyday awe.

How does awe transform us? By quieting the nagging, self-critical, overbearing, status-conscious voice of our self, or ego, and empowering us to collaborate, to open our minds to wonders, and to see the deep patterns of life.

Why awe? Because in our distal evolution as very social mammals, those individuals who united with others in awe-like patterns of behavior fared well in encounters with threats and the unknown. And because in the more proximal calculus of thriving in the present, awe brings us joy, meaning, and community, along with healthier bodies and more creative minds.

There is one last story of awe that led me to write this book, one I had no interest in being part of. That story began on a blustery January day in 2019.

On that day, I stepped off a handball court, sweaty and unburdened, having finished a tough game with my longtime partner, Isaac. I looked at my iPhone on my gym bag. Two texts.

From my brother's wife, Kim:

Can you come here as fast as possible?

Fifteen minutes later from my mom:

It's over. Rolf took the cocktail. He is leaving us.

Rolf is my younger brother, born a year after me in a small clinic in Jalisco, Mexico. The "cocktail" was the combination of end-of-life opiates he took, which usually ends a human life in an hour or two.

I called Kim, who summarized.

It was a bright morning with a blue sky. Rolf and Lucy [their fourteen-year-old daughter] sat outside and had a long talk in the sun. Rolf came in and said he was ready. He took it at three p.m. He wandered around the kitchen. Checked the fridge. Rambled. I told him it was time to lie down. . . . So we lay down in his bed. After a while he fell asleep. He's snoring. Here, listen . . .

Kim put the phone up to Rolf's mouth. I heard the deep, rhythmic vibration of his vocal cords—his death rattle.

My parents are here. Your dad and Nancy are on their way. Can you bring your mom?

We'll get there as soon as we can, I replied. Thank you, Kim.

I picked up my wife, Mollie, and our daughters, Natalie and Serafina, in Berkeley, then my mom in Sacramento. We arrived at Rolf and Kim's home in the foothills of the Sierras at ten p.m.

Rolf was lying in a bed downstairs, which he had retreated to in his last weeks. He lay on his stomach and right cheek, his head tilted slightly upward. My dad held his foot. I leaned in near his midsection. My mom was at the head of the bed, stroking his thin hair.

Rolf's face was full and flushed. The sunken eyes and gaunt cheeks caused by colon cancer were gone; the tightened, sagging skin around his mouth smoothed. His lips curled upward at the corners.

I rested my right hand on his left shoulder, a rounded protrusion of bone. I held it the way I would the smooth granite stones we used to find near the rivers we swam in as young brothers.

Rolf . . . This is Dach . . .
You are the best brother in the world.

My daughter Natalie laid her hand lightly on his shoulder blades:

We love you, Rolf.

The cycle of his breathing slowed. He was listening. Aware.

Listening to Rolf's breath, I sensed the vast expanse of fifty-five years of our brotherhood. Roaming Laurel Canyon in the late '60s, spying on rock-and-roll neighbors and skateboarding through Volkswagen-lined streets. In our adolescence, walking the wild foothills of the Sierras, and playing Little League on the Penryn A's, me pitching, Rolf, a long-haired lefty, on first, a mischievous light in his eyes saying *Man, this is fun!* As young adults, on wild trips to Mexico, dancing in clubs, wandering in the high Sierras. And then in graduate school, buying wedding suits and being each other's best man, becoming teachers and fathers to daughters.

I sensed a light radiating from Rolf's face. It pulsated in concentric circles, spreading outward, touching us as we leaned in with slightly bowed heads. The chatter in my mind, clasping words about the stages of colon cancer, new treatments, lymph nodes, and survival rates, faded. I could sense a force around his body pulling him away. And questions in my mind.

What is Rolf thinking?
What is he feeling?
What does it mean for him to die?

A voice in my mind said:

I feel awe.

My feeling in that overwhelming moment shared some essence with experiences of awe from my past, both big (for example, seeing Nelson Mandela speak after his twenty-seven years of captivity with fifty thousand other people) and small (seeing the dusk light on an oak tree, listening to my young daughters' duets of laughter). Watching Rolf pass, I felt small. Quiet. Humble. Pure. The boundaries that separated me from the outside world faded. I felt surrounded by something vast and warm. My mind was open, curious, aware, wondering.

A couple of weeks after Rolf's passing, Kim brought together friends and family to tell our stories of Rolf. We talked about his fascination with clowns and magic tricks, and how he loved to cook for crowds of friends and enthrall neighborhood kids with his over-the-top Halloween costumes. From his coworkers came stories of how he calmed the most difficult boys at a little mountain school where they taught. And then the stories tapered off and we fell into a silence. A church bell rang, stirring a spiral of blackbirds out of the trees, rising into a sky heavy with dark gray clouds. We shook hands and hugged and then walked quietly out of Rolf and Kim's home to return to our lives, mine with a Rolf-sized hole in it.

In the grief that followed, I would regularly jolt awake before dawn, gasping. My body ran hot. I ached physically. I dreamed dreams unlike anything I'd experienced before. In one, I was walking up a dark, winding dirt road to an illuminated Victorian that resembled our childhood home in Penryn. Rolf burst around a corner in yellow shorts, running in his high school miler strides. He stopped, smiled, waved, and moved his lips, uttering words he knew I could no longer hear. I experienced the hallucinations that Joan Didion describes in *The Year of Magical Thinking*. I saw the outline of Rolf's face in the shifting boundaries of neighboring clouds. On one walk on the Berkeley campus, I saw his chemo-exhausted eyes in the spiraling bark of a redwood tree. I heard his voice in the rustling of leaves, his sigh in the wind. On two occasions I was so convinced I had seen him that I followed strangers whose shoulders, foreheads, freckles, and jawlines looked like his.

Our minds are relational: we see life patterns through our shared experiences with others, sense life's significant themes in the sounds of others' voices, and feel embraced in things larger than the self through others' touch. I saw the wonders of the world through Rolf's eyes. With his passing, I felt *aweless*. And my companion in awe was no longer around to help me make sense of the vastest mystery I had encountered in my fifty-seven years of living.

A loud voice called out:

FIND AWE.

Knowing of awe's many benefits, and that we can find it all around us, I went in search of awe. I took a moment each day to be open to the awe-inspiring around me. I sought out places of importance in the history of awe. I engaged in open-ended conversations with people I consider awe pioneers. I immersed myself as a newcomer in various wonders of life. These explorations led to personal experiences, memories, dreams, and insights that helped me make sense of losing my brother. They brought me to the conviction that awe is almost always nearby, and is a pathway to healing and growing in the face of the losses and traumas that are part of life.

There are four stories of awe, then, for us to consider together— the scientific, the personal, the cultural, and one about the growth that awe can bring us when we face hardship, uncertainty, loss, and the unknown. I have organized this book accordingly. The first three chapters traverse the scientific story of awe. We consider what awe is, the contexts in which it arises, how it differs from fear and beauty, and how it feels in our everyday lives (chapter 1). We follow how awe transforms our sense of self, our thought, and our relation to the world (chapter 2). And we take an evolutionary journey back in time to ask: Why awe? Jane Goodall, a hero of mine, believed that chimpanzees feel awe and have a sense of spirituality grounded in a capacity Goodall describes as *being amazed at things outside yourself.* Animated by this mystery, we will investigate where our chills, tears, wide-open eyes and mouths, and *wow*s and *whoa*s come from in our mammalian evolution, and what this tells us about the primordial meaning of awe (chapter 3).

In the second section of the book, we turn to personal stories of awe. We will hear stories about the transcendent power of others' moral beauty and its place in prisons and more life-enhancing institutions like libraries and hospitals (chapter 4). About finding collective effervescence in ecstatic dance and professional basketball and in the collective movements of our daily lives (chapter 5). About nature and how it can help heal the traumas of combat, loneliness, and poverty (chapter 6).

The third section shifts to a treatment of how culture archives awe in different forms. We will consider the place of awe in music (chapter 7), visual art (chapter 8), and religion and spirituality (chapter 9). These are large tasks indeed but illuminating once we narrow in on the place of awe in these creative forms of culture.

The last section of the book returns to how awe helps us grow when we face loss and trauma, and more generally when we face the unknowns and uncertainties of life. It was striking for me to learn how central awe is in how we grapple with life and death and their ever-repeating, species-shaping cycle (chapter 10). And how across the eight wonders of life, awe reveals big insights to us about the point of our lives in our continual search for meaning (chapter 11).

In teaching happiness for more than twenty years, I have seen how much health and well-being we gain by *being amazed at things outside ourselves*. By finding awe. From our first breath to our last, awe moves us to deepen our relations with the wonders of life and to marvel at the vast mysteries that are part of our fleeting time here, guided by this most human of emotions.

A Science
of Awe

EIGHT WONDERS OF LIFE

An Awe Movement Begins

*The strange thing about life is that though the
nature of it must have been apparent to
every one for hundreds of years, no one has left
any adequate account of it. The streets of
London have their map; but our passions are
uncharted.*

· VIRGINIA WOOLF

The last time the word "awe" hit me with the force of personal epiphany, I was twenty-seven years old. I was in Paul Ekman's living room, having just interviewed for a fellowship in his lab to study emotion. Ekman is well-known for his study of facial expression, and a founding figure in the new science of emotion. At the conclusion of his querying, we moved to the deck off his home in the San Francisco hills. We were embraced by a view of the city. Thick fog moved through the streets toward the Bay Bridge and eventually across the bay to Berkeley.

Stretching for conversation, I asked Paul what a young scholar might study. His answer was one word:

Awe.

At that time—1988—we knew very little scientifically about emotions: what they are, how they influence our minds and bodies, and why we experience them in the first place.

Psychological science was firmly entrenched in a "cognitive revolution." Within this framework, every human experience, from moral condemnation to prejudice against people of color, originates in how our minds, like computer programs, process units of information in passionless ways. What was missing from this understanding of human nature was emotion. Passion. Gut feeling. What Scottish philosopher David Hume famously called the "master of reason," and Nobel Prize winner Daniel Kahneman, in *Thinking, Fast and Slow*, termed "System 1" thinking.

Emotions have long been viewed as "lower" and animalistic, disruptive of lofty reason, which is often considered humanity's highest achievement. Emotions, so fleeting and subjective, others observed, cannot be measured in the lab. Our passions were still very much uncharted some seventy years after Virginia Woolf's musing.

Ekman, though, would soon publish a paper—now the most widely cited in the field—that would push the scientific pendulum firmly toward emotion. In this essay, a field guide really, he detailed the *what* of emotions: They are brief feeling states accompanied by distinct thoughts, expressions, and physiology. Emotions are fleeting, shorter-lived than moods, like feeling blue, and emotional disorders, such as depression. He outlined *how* emotions work: they shift our thought and action to enable us to adapt to our present circumstances. To approach the *why* of emotions, Ekman took a cue from Charles Darwin: Emotions enable us to accomplish "fundamental life tasks," such as fleeing peril, avoiding toxins, and finding nutritious food. Emotions are central to our individual survival and our evolution as a species.

A young science had a field guide, and scholars promptly went exploring. First, scientists mapped anger, disgust, fear, sadness, surprise, and joy, the emotions whose facial expressions Ekman had documented in the hills of New Guinea in the early 1960s. Next to appear in the lab were the self-conscious emotions— embarrassment, shame, and guilt. Studies charted how these states arise when we make social mistakes, and how blushes, head bows, awkward appeasing smiles, and apologies restore our standing in the eyes of others. Sensing that there is more to the mind, brain, and body than negative emotions, and more to the delights of life than "joy," young scientists then turned to studies of states like amusement, gratitude, love, and pride. My own lab got into the act with studies of laughter, gratitude, love, desire, and sympathy.

An emotion revolution in reaction to the cognitive revolution was underway, moving psychological science beyond its dry and cool cognitivist account of the mind and inattention to the body. Neuroscientists were mapping "the emotional brain." Studies alerted those interested in the secrets of love to the finding that marriages dissolve when partners express contempt to one another. Our culture wars over abortion, race, class, and climate crises could be traced back to gut feelings about the moral issues of our times. For faring well in life, emotion scientists determined that we are better served by cultivating our "emotional intelligence," or EQ, than our IQ. Today we are still in the midst of "an age of emotion" in science, one that shapes every corner of our lives.

One emotion, though, would not get the call for this revolution, an emotion that is the provenance of so much that is human—music, art, religion, science, politics, and transformative insights about life. That would be awe. The reasons are in part method-ological. Awe seems to resist precise definition and measurement, the bedrock of science. In fact, how would a scientist study awe in a lab? How could scientists lead people to feel it on cue and mea-sure its near-ineffable qualities, or document how awe transforms our lives, if, indeed, it does?

There were theoretical barriers as well. As the science of emo-tion got off the ground, it did so in a theoretical zeitgeist that held that emotions are about *self*-preservation, oriented toward minimiz-ing peril and advancing competitive gains for the *individual*. Awe, by contrast, seems to orient us to devote ourselves to things outside of our individual selves. To sacrifice and serve. To sense that the boundaries between our individual selves and others readily dis-solve, that our true nature is collective. These qualities did not fit neatly within the hyperindividualistic, materialistic, survival-of-the-selfish-genes view of human nature so prominent at the time.

One cannot help but suspect that personal hesitations were at play as well. When people talk about experiences of awe, they often mention things like finding their soul, or discovering what is sacred, or being moved by spirit—phenomena that many believe to be beyond measurement and the scientific view of human nature.

Emotion science had a field guide, though, a road map for charting the what, how, and why of awe. What awe needed first was a definition, the place where all good scientific stories begin. What is awe?

Defining Awe

With emotion science turning its attention to the varieties of positive emotion, in 2003 my longtime collaborator at New York University Jonathan Haidt and I worked to articulate a definition of awe. At the time, there were only a few scientific articles on awe (but thousands on fear). There were no definitions of awe to speak of.

So we immersed ourselves in the writings of mystics about their encounters with the Divine. We read treatments of the holy, the sublime, the supernatural, the sacred, and "peak experiences" that people might describe with words like "flow," "joy," "bliss," or even "enlightenment." We considered political theorists like Max Weber and their speculations about the passions of mobs whipped up by demagogues. We read anthropologists' accounts of awe in dance, music, art, and religion in faraway, remote cultures. Drawing upon these veins of scholarship, we defined awe as follows:

> Awe is the feeling of being in the presence of something vast that transcends your current understanding of the world.

Vastness can be physical—for example, when you stand next to a 350-foot-tall tree or hear a singer's voice or electric guitar fill the space of an arena. Vastness can be temporal, as when a laugh or scent transports you back in time to the sounds or aromas of your childhood. Vastness can be semantic, or about ideas, most notably when an epiphany integrates scattered beliefs and un-knowns into a coherent thesis about the world.

Vastness can be challenging, unsettling, and destabilizing. In evoking awe, it reveals that our current knowledge is not up to the task of making sense of what we have encountered. And so, in awe, we go in search of new forms of understanding.

Awe is about our relation to the vast mysteries of life.

What about the innumerable variations in awe? How awe changes from one culture to another, or from one period in history to another? Or from one person to another? Or even one moment in your life to another?

The content of what is vast varies dramatically across cultures and the contexts of our lives. In some places it is high-altitude mountains, and in others flat never-ending plains with storms ap-proaching. For infants it is the immense warmth provided by par-ents, and when we die, the enormous expanse of our lives. During some historical periods it is the violence humans are capable of, and during other times protests in the streets against the machines and institutions that perpetrate violence. The varieties of vastness are myriad, giving rise to shifts in the meaning of awe.

"Flavoring themes," Jon and I reasoned, also account for variations in awe. By flavoring themes, we meant context-specific ways in which we ascribe meaning to vast mysteries. For example, you shall learn that extraordinary virtue and ability can lead us to feel awe. Conceptions of virtue and ability vary dramatically ac-cording to context: whether, for example, we find ourselves in combat or at a meditation retreat, whether we are part of a hip-hop performance or a chess club, whether we live in a region of religious dogma or one governed by the rules of Wall Street. How we conceptualize virtue and ability within our local culture gives rise to variations in awe.

Another flavoring theme that shapes the experience of awe is supernatural belief systems—beliefs, for example, about ghosts, spirits, extraordinary experiences, gods, the Divine, heaven, and hell. These beliefs imbue experiences of awe with culturally specific meanings. For example, for many people across history, experiences of awe in encounters with mountains, storms, winds, the sun, and the moon have been flavored with local stories and beliefs about the Divine. For others, those same mountains, storms, winds, the sun, and the moon stir a different kind of awe, one more grounded in a sense of what is sacred about nature but lacking the sense of the Divine.

Perhaps most pervasively, perceived threat also flavors experiences of awe, and can layer fear, uncertainty, alienation, and terror into our experience of the emotion. Perceptions of threat explain why people in certain cultures—such as the Japanese or Chinese—feel more fear blended with awe when around inspiring people than people from less hierarchical cultures do. Why psychedelic experiences with LSD, MDMA, or ayahuasca inspire pure awe for some and are flooded with terror for others. Why encounters with the Divine are filled with fear in some cultures, whereas in other cultures that lack ideas about a judgmental God they are defined by bliss and love. Why dying is oceanic and awe-filled for some and horrifying for others. And why cultural symbols like the American flag can move some to tears and chills, and others to shudder in the sense of threat and alienation.

In awe we encounter the vast mysteries of life, with flavoring themes like conceptions of virtue, supernatural beliefs, and perceived threat giving rise to near-infinite variations.

Eight Wonders of Life

Emotions are like stories. They are dramas that structure our day, like scenes in a novel, movie, or play. Emotions unfold in actions between people, enabling us, for example, to comfort someone in need, show devotion to a loved one, redress injustice, or belong to a community. Having defined awe, our answer to the question "What is awe?" needs next to move to people's own stories of the emotion.

When William James, a founding figure in psychology, went in search of understanding mystical awe at the turn of the twentieth century—an exploration we will consider later—he did not have people rate their feelings with numbers. He did not do experiments. He did not measure physiological reactions or sensations, which had long fascinated him. Instead, he gathered stories: First-person narratives, utterly personal, about encounters with the Divine. Religious conversions. Spiritual epiphanies. Visions of heaven and hell. And in discerning the patterns in these stories, he uncovered the heart of religion: that it is about mystical awe, an ineffable emotional experience of being in relation to what we consider divine.

Guided by this approach, Professor Yang Bai, a longtime collaborator of mine, and I gathered stories of awe from people in twenty-six countries. We cast our net broadly because of the scientific concern about "WEIRD" samples: those composed disproportionately of people who are Western, Educated, Individualist, Rich, and Democratic. Our participants were anything but WEIRD. Participants included adherents to all major religions—many forms of Christianity, Hinduism, Buddhism, Islam, and Judaism—as well as denizens of more secular cultures (e.g., Holland). Our participants varied in terms of their wealth and education. They lived within democratic and authoritarian political systems. They held egalitarian and patriarchal views of gender. They ranged in their cultural values from the more collectivist (e.g., China, Mexico) to the more individualistic (e.g., the United States).

In our study, people were provided with the definition of awe you have considered: "Being in the presence of something vast and mysterious that transcends your current understanding of the world." And then they wrote their story of awe. Speakers of twenty languages at UC Berkeley translated the 2,600 narratives. We were surprised to learn that these rich narratives from around the world could be classified into a taxonomy of awe, the eight wonders of life.

What most commonly led people around the world to feel awe? Nature? Spiritual practice? Listening to music? In fact, it was *other people's courage, kindness, strength, or overcoming.* Around the world, we are most likely to feel awe when moved by *moral beauty,* the first wonder of life in our taxonomy. Exceptional physical beauty, from faces to landscapes, has long been a fascination of the arts and sciences, and moves us to feelings of infatuation, affection, and, on occasion, desire. Exceptional virtue, character, and ability—moral beauty—operate according to a different aesthetic, one marked by a purity and goodness of intention and action, and moves us to awe. One kind of moral beauty is the courage that others show when encountering suffering, as in this story from the United Kingdom:

> The way my daughter dealt with the stillbirth of her son. I was with her at the hospital when he was delivered and her strength in dealing with this left me in awe. My little girl grew up overnight and exhibited awesome strength and bravery during this difficult time.

The courage required in combat is another time-honored source of awe. This is a stirring theme found in Greek and Roman myths, gripping scenes in films like *Saving Private Ryan*, and war stories veterans tell, as in this story from South Africa:

> I was in the Angolan war. One of our soldiers got shot. An officer risked his life and fears to drag the soldier to safety. In the process the officer was wounded but continued saving the soldier's life. I came out of hiding and secured the area for enough time in order for the officer to drag the soldier to safety.

Horrific acts also occasioned awe, but much less commonly, and most typically in epiphanies found in art, as in this example from Sweden:

> The first time I saw *Schindler's List* back in 2011. The music and the performance of the main actor were insanely powerful. And the grim truth of human nature. All I wanted to do, and all I did the next few hours, was cry.

Human atrocities captivate our imagination, but are more aptly deemed the provenance of *horror*, a different state than awe. And art, we shall see, so often provides a space in our imagination for contemplating human horrors, giving rise to aesthetic experiences of awe.

A second wonder of life is *collective effervescence*, a term introduced by French sociologist Émile Durkheim in his analysis of the emotional core of religion. His phrase speaks to the qualities of such experiences: we feel like we are buzzing and crackling with some life force that merges people into a collective self, a tribe, an oceanic "we." Across the twenty-six cultures, people told stories of collective effervescence at weddings, christenings, quinceañeras, bar and bat mitzvahs, graduations, sports celebrations, funerals, family reunions, and political rallies, as in this one from Russia:

> At the parade of victory, the city and entire country were with me. There was a procession called "Immortal Regiment" with portraits of soldier participants of the war. I felt pride for my country and people.

A third wonder of life should not surprise. It is *nature*. Often what inspired natural awe was a cataclysmic event—earthquakes, thunderstorms, lightning, wildfires, gale-force winds, and tsunamis, or for one participant from China, watching a flood rip through her village. Many mentioned night skies, whose patterns of stars and illumination were an inspiration of Greek, Roman, and Mesoamerican imaginings of the gods. Many worry today about how the dimming of the night sky in this era of light pollution is harming our capacity to wonder. Experiences in mountains, looking at canyons, walking among large trees, running through vast sand dunes, and first encounters with the ocean brought people awe, as in this example from Mexico:

> The first time I saw the ocean. I was still only a child, listening to the waves and wind, feeling the breeze.

Common to experiences of natural awe is the sense that plants and animals are conscious and aware, an idea found in many Indigenous traditions and attracting scientific attention today. In this story of wild awe translated from Russian, notice how the participant remarks upon the awareness of trees, which seem to be looking at something alongside them:

> Five years ago, collecting mushrooms in the forest, I bumped into an uncommon hole in the ground. Around it all the trees stood in a circle as if gazing into the hole.

Music offered up a fourth wonder of life, transporting people to new dimensions of symbolic meaning in experiences at concerts, listening quietly to a piece of music, chanting in a religious ceremony, or simply singing with others. In this story from Switzerland, the individual feels connected to something larger than the self, a defining theme of awe:

> It was at around Christmas several years ago. I was away on a trip to different monasteries in west Switzerland with fellow students. We were in a Dominican monastery. It was snowing outside and it was freezing cold. The Romanesque church was only dimly lit and you could hear Gregorian songs—the acoustics were unparalleled. A feeling of reverence for

something bigger and at the same time a feeling of comfort came over me.

Musical awe often arose in response to favorite rock groups, virtuosos, and, perhaps most poignantly, children, as in this story from Ireland:

When my seven-year-old daughter went in front of a couple hundred people and played the tin whistle with such determination and I was in awe of her courage to do that. She got an applause after her performance. We were attending her communion in the local church with her brothers and extended family. I felt nervous for her before her performance but was in awe at the way she did her performance so well and the way she handled herself at such a young age. I gave her a big hug and kiss after and told her she was great.

So much for booming electric guitars; give me a tin whistle any day.

Visual design proved to be a fifth wonder of life. Buildings, terracotta warriors in China, dams, and paintings appeared in stories of awe from around the world. So too did more surprising kinds of visual design, as in this example from South Africa:

I went to a customer factory for a machine inspection on a pharmaceutical sorting line. The machine's capabilities were astounding—mind-blowing. I was in complete awe with the functionality, speed, and design of the machine. This happened roughly one year ago inside my customer's factory and I was with my colleague (designer of the machine).

In his book *The Doors of Perception*, Aldous Huxley suggested that the visual design of jewels opens our minds to the mystic's way of perceiving the world. The awe we feel in relation to visual design allows us to locate ourselves within cultural systems that we may be part of. You may feel this in relation to Haussmann's grand boulevards in Paris, a Mayan pyramid, the graffiti of Barcelona, and for some, a machine that sorts pills.

Stories of *spiritual* and *religious* awe were a sixth wonder of life. These weren't as common as you might imagine, given our perennial search for nirvana, satori, bliss, or samadhi. Some experiences of mystical awe were classic conversion stories like that of Saint Paul on the road to Damascus or the Buddha under the bodhi tree, as in this example from Singapore:

When the Holy Spirit of God came upon me at a Life in the Spirit Seminar organized by the Catholic church. It was so powerful I could not stand and instantly collapsed but I was conscious of my surroundings and as my eyes were closed I could only see a very bright white light. Before the event I felt that the world had rejected me, that no one cared. When the event happened, I immediately felt lifted but most important of all I felt loved.

Other stories like this one from Canada mix mystical awe with sexual desire, a timeless blending of the sacred and the profane.

I met a man at our local farmers market who opened my eyes about meditation and the power of one's body and emotions. With one touch of my shoulders he was able to see through me (in a sense). His presence and knowledge let me want to learn more. . . . Therefore I started to take meditation classes with him on a weekly basis. I learned so much about my body, mind, and spirit.

We shall see how often the sensations that arise during mystical awe, and all encounters with the wonders of life, involve touch, feeling embraced, a warm presence, and an awareness of being seen—clues, perhaps, to the deep origins of the emotion.

Stories of *life and death*, the seventh wonder of life, were common around the world. We are awestruck by how, in an instant, life comes out of the womb. And on the other end of the life-death cycle, when a person makes the transition from being a breathing physical being to some other form of existence, as I observed that night in watching Rolf die. Here is a cycle-of-life narrative from Indonesia, revealing how in grief our minds turn to ideas about the ways the departed remains with us:

> That time around six years ago at the Sardjito hospital in Yogya-karta, me along with my father and other siblings waited for my mother who was sick, she had been hospitalized for one week and hadn't regained consciousness. That time we were waiting until Mother met her maker, we were extremely heart-broken and sad at that time, however we realized that we shouldn't drown in too much sorrow. Our future is still long. It was only after Mom left us that we realized how important is a mother and a wife, that now all of us have grown to appreciate and love our wives who are the mothers of our children.

This story leads us to *epiphanies*—when we suddenly understand essential truths about life—which were the eighth wonder of life. Around the world, people were awestruck by philosophical insights, scientific discoveries, metaphysical ideas, personal realizations, mathematical equations, and sudden disclosures (such as a wife leaving her husband for his best friend) that transform life in an instant. In each instance, the epiphany united facts, beliefs, values, intuitions, and images into a new system of understanding. Here is an epiphany from Japan that delighted me, because I had found awe in my childhood in art and natural history museums and later in Darwin's theory of evolution:

> Just before I was twelve, I saw a science museum exhibit and understood the evolution of biology. I realized that human beings are undoubtedly only one species of many creatures (not particularly advantageous compared to other creatures).

We can find awe, then, in eight wonders of life: moral beauty, collective effervescence, nature, music, visual design, spirituality and religion, life and death, and epiphany. If you are offended that your favorite form of the sublime did not make this periodic table of awe, the Eight Wonders of Life Club, perhaps you'll find solace in this: our "other" category encompassed 5 percent of the responses worldwide. This category included stories about incredible flavors, video games, overwhelming sensations (for example, of color or sound), and first experiences of sex.

It also merits considering what was *not* mentioned in stories of awe from around the world. Money didn't figure into awe, except in a couple of instances in which people had been cheated out of life savings. No one mentioned their laptop, Facebook, Apple Watch, or smartphone. Nor did anyone mention consumer purchases, like their new Nikes, Tesla, Gucci bag, or Montblanc pen.

Awe occurs in a realm separate from the mundane world of materialism, money, acquisition, and status signaling—a realm beyond the profane that many call the sacred.

A Space of Its Own

The etymology of the word "awe" traces back eight hundred years to the middle English "ege" and Old Norse "agi," both of which refer to fear, dread, horror, and terror. The legacy of this etymology is deep. If I asked you now to answer our current question—*What is awe?*—you might define it in terms related to fear. Remember, though, that when "ege" and "agi" emerged in the spoken word some eight centuries ago, it was a time of plagues, famines, public torture, religious inquisition, war, and short life expectancy; what was vast and mysterious was violence and death.

When we use the word "awe" today, are we describing an experience similar to fear, or a variant of feeling threatened and seeking to flee?

Another question is this: Do our experiences of awe differ from our feelings of beauty? We feel beauty in response to all manner of things that can bring us awe, from skies to music to vibrant neighborhoods in cities. Is awe just a more intense feeling of beauty?

Up until recently, the science of emotion had no answers to these questions. The study of emotional experience had largely focused on those six states Paul Ekman had studied in the 1960s, eliciting emotions like fear and disgust with images of horrifying, repulsive things—spiders, snarling dogs, bloody gore, feces—and, for sensory pleasure or joy, photos of chocolate cakes, tropical beaches, beautiful faces, and bucolic nature scenes. No study had sought to inspire awe in its participants. Had it done so, it still would have failed to capture that experience, since the most widely used emotional experience questionnaire, which measures these positive states—*active, interested, proud, excited, strong, inspired, alert, enthusiastic, determined, attentive*—makes no mention of awe or beauty (or amusement, love, desire, or compassion, for that matter). The experience of awe was uncharted.

To map the experience of awe, I was fortunate to carry out the following study with my computationally minded collaborator Alan Cowen, a math prodigy well versed in new quantitative approaches to mapping the structures of human experience. Alan first scoured the internet, locating 2,100 emotionally rich GIFs, or two-to-three-second videos. The GIFs our participants viewed extended far beyond the images and videos relied on in the past to elicit Ekman's six emotions, to include things like dog pratfalls, awkward social encounters, a moving speech by Martin Luther King Jr., delicious-looking food, couples kissing, scary images of hairy spiders, terrifying car crashes, rotting food, weird and transfixing geometric patterns, beautiful landscapes, baby and puppy faces, amusing mishaps of cats, parents hugging infants, dramatic storm clouds, and so on. After viewing each GIF, our participants rated their experience on more than fifty emotional terms, including, most germane to our present interests, awe, fear, horror, and beauty.

One day Alan dropped by my office with a data visualization of his results, which I present on the following page. What in the world are we looking at? That's what I first asked Alan. After detailing the new statistical analyses he derived to produce such an image, he explained that each letter refers to a GIF in our study, and each GIF is placed spatially in terms of which emotion it

predominantly evoked. The overall distribution of emotions is called a semantic space. The streets of London have their maps, and so too do our emotional experiences.

You will notice right away how rich our emotional experience is; in this study, people felt twenty-seven distinct kinds of emotions. Many emotional experiences, this visualization reveals, are emotion blends, or mixtures of emotions, for example, of sadness and confusion, love and desire, or awe and horror. Emotional experience is complex.

Where does awe fall in this semantic space of emotion? Is it simply a kind of fear? No, not by any stretch of the imagination. As you can see, our feelings of awe, toward the bottom, are far away from fear, horror, and anxiety. This in part is what astonished me so in watching Rolf die: that despite the horrors of cancer and the profound losses in his leaving, the vastness of his passing and the mysteries it unearthed in my mind left me in awe.

Instead, feelings of awe are located near admiration, interest, and aesthetic appreciation, or feelings of beauty. Awe feels intrinsically good. Our experiences of awe, though, clearly differ from feelings of beauty. The GIFs evocative of the feelings of beauty were familiar, easier to understand, and more fitting with our expectations about our visual world—images of oceans, forests, flowers, and sunsets. The awe-inspiring GIFs were vast and mysterious—an endless river of cyclists in a road race; an undulating, spiraling swarm of birds; the time-lapsed changes of a star-filled sky in the desert; a video of flying through the Alps as seen through a bird's-eye camera; a trippy immersion in Van Gogh's *Starry Night.*

In subsequent mapping studies with similar methodologies, Alan and I documented other ways in which awe is distinct from fear, horror, and feelings of beauty (for relevant emotion maps, go to alancowen.com). The sounds we use to express awe with our voices sound different from our vocalizations of fear (and closer to vocalizations of emotions we experience when learning new things, like interest and realization). Our facial expressions of awe are easily differentiated from those of fear. The music and visual art that leads us to feel awe differs from that which evokes horror and beauty. Our experiences of awe take place in a space of their own, far away from fear and distinct from the familiar and pleasing feelings of beauty.

Everyday Awe

With stories from around the world and maps of emotional experience, we have begun to chart the what of awe. Perhaps, though, you have reservations. When we recall stories of awe—the core methodology of the twenty-six-culture study—we likely call to mind more extreme, once-in-a-lifetime experiences—saving a stranger's life, being one of the millions at the festival of Guadalupe in Mexico City, visiting the Grand Canyon, watching a mother die. Artistic portrayals of what brings us awe—GIFs, music, paintings in our awe-mapping studies—are stylized and idealized representations. Neither method captures what awe is like in our daily lives—if there is even such a thing.

In search of everyday awe, Yang Bai, University of Michigan professor Amie Gordon, and I carried out several studies in different countries with a method known as the daily diary approach. This method brings into the lab the very human tendency to write and journal about our emotions, to translate feelings into words. In one study, people in China and the United States wrote about daily experiences of awe—if they occurred—each night for two weeks. Here is a story from China, which speaks once again to the power of museums to bring us awe:

> In the national museum, I saw the exhibition of bronze wares in Shang dynasty, the exhibition of Picasso's art works, and the exhibition of statues of Mao Zedong. . . . I was blown away by the delicate statues, the refined shapes of the hands, the structures of males' and females' nudes of Picasso's art works, and the story, revealed by bronze wares, of the female warrior Fu Hao. I was in awe.

Fu Hao was a female general who fought to preserve the Shang dynasty some three thousand years ago—moral courage from Chinese history. And this study participant is not alone in appreciating the marvels of the hand: the sculptor Rodin saw hands as spiritual parts of our body, and in his sculpture *The Cathedral*, two right hands point upward, creating a mysterious sense of light and space one would find in a forest or cathedral.

A Berkeley student felt awe in learning about the causal processes of chemistry, that fundamental, invisible layer of life underlying visible reality:

> I was at work in the lab and was taught a new process that I had no experience with until today. The effects of very subtle changes in temperature on the outcome of the process was awesome in the literal sense. The actual tool that was used for the process was also awesome.

Another found awe in thinking about the vastness of big data:

> It was in my sociology class about social media. I was awe-struck and humbled by the vastness of data and the power it exerts over each and every one of our lives, whether we choose to ignore it or not. Social media and technology amass so much data about our lives that is hard to comprehend—to the point where our every heartbeat can be timestamped.

The results from these daily diary studies dovetailed with what we learned from our twenty-six-culture study: In our daily lives, we most frequently feel awe in encounters with moral beauty, and secondarily in nature and in experiences with music, art, and film. Rarer were everyday awe experiences of the spiritual variety (although had we done the study at a religious college, this no doubt would have been different). We also confirmed, as in our mapping studies, that most moments of awe—about three-quarters—feel good, and only one-quarter are flavored with threat.

Culture shaped awe in profound ways. Students in Beijing more commonly found awe in moral beauty—inspiring teachers or grandparents and virtuosic performances of musicians. For the U.S. students, it was nature. And here is a cultural difference that left us shaking our heads: the individual self was twenty times more likely to be the source of awe in the United States than in China. U.S. students could not help but feel awe at getting an A in a tough class, receiving a competitive fellowship, telling a hilarious joke, or, for those true narcissists, posting a new photo on Tinder.

Sometimes the most important finding in a scientific study is a simple observation, free of any hypothesis or pitting of theoretical perspectives against one another. And this was true in our daily diary research: people experience awe two to three times a week. That's once every couple of days. They did so in finding the extraordinary in the ordinary: a friend's generosity to a homeless person in the streets; the scent of a flower; looking at a leafy tree's play of light and shadow on a sidewalk; hearing a song that transported them back to a first love; bingeing *Game of Thrones* with friends.

Everyday awe.

Great thinkers, from Walt Whitman to Rachel Carson to Zen master Shunryu Suzuki, remind us to become aware of how much of life can bring us awe. It is a deep conviction in many Indigenous philosophies from around the world that so much of the life that surrounds us is sacred. Our daily diary findings suggest that these great minds and cultures were onto something: the wonders of life are so often nearby.

Transcendent States in 1,372 Slides

With stories of awe from around the world, twenty-first-century emotion-mapping techniques, and hearing people's reports of everyday awe, we can now offer an answer to the question "What is awe?" Awe begins in encounters with the eight wonders of life. The experience of awe unfolds in a space of its own, one that feels good and differs from feelings of fear, horror, and beauty. Our everyday lives offer so many occasions for awe.

As Rolf's colon cancer reduced his body from a broad-shouldered

210 pounds to a frail, starving 145, the future of his life was increasingly clear. And so I sought to look to the past, to distill the story of our brotherhood.

On my second-to-last visit with Rolf, about ten days before he passed, we took in 1,372 photos from the fifteen years our family had been together before our parents divorced. They were mostly black-and-white slides tucked away in small, yellowing cardboard boxes. They hadn't been looked at for years. They dated from 1963—our shared baby years in Mexico—to 1978, our last days as an intact family in England.

Rolf, my mom, and I looked over the photos, proceeding year by year. From the early 1960s: photos of us held aloft in our young parents' arms as babies, cheeks pressing into cheeks, adult hands cupping fuzzy heads. Slides from the late 1960s chronicled our Laurel Canyon years and wandering summer vacations in our blue Volkswagen bus. Peering out of tents in the Rockies, surrounded by aspens. Climbing down rocky, wild coastal cliffs off Highway 1 near Mendocino, California. At art shows of my dad's. Late '60s music festivals and renaissance fairs and Fourth of July communal celebrations in the mountains. Long-haired collective effervescence everywhere.

The 1970s brought a move to the foothills of Northern California, a new VW bus, and a Huck Finn–like freedom of early adolescence on our five acres with a pond. Shooting hoops on the basketball court my dad had built in a star-thistly pasture. Inner tubing and rafting down rivers. A bicentennial trip across the United States in 1976—vast plains of cornfields out the windows of the bus, my brother and I spoofing and mugging at Monticello.

And then our last year as an intact family, on our way to

England, where our parents would part ways. Rolf and I at revered sites—the Alhambra, the Louvre, and Notre Dame—as teens, sneering and mocking, and on occasion solemn and moved.

As we looked at the slides, Rolf drifted in and out, and with an inviting finger asked for more. Before finally falling into a deep sleep, he observed: "We had fun."

Fun, like awe, is one of several *self-transcendent* states, a space of emotions that transport us out of our self-focused, threat-oriented, and status quo mindset to a realm where we connect to something larger than the self. *Joy*, the feeling of being free, for the moment, of worldly concerns, is part of this space, as is *ecstasy* (or *bliss*), when we sense ourself to dissolve completely (in awe we remain aware, although faintly, of our selves). And fun, the *mirth* and lighthearted delight we feel when imagining alternative perspectives upon our mundane lives we so often take too seriously.

Gratitude is part of this transcendent realm of feeling, the reverence we feel for the gifts of life. I felt it acutely that day amid waves of sadness and anxiety, surveying those 1,372 slides. My parents had allowed my brother and me to wander, locating us in a world of wonders. Rolf and I had lived a brotherhood of awe.

Knowing now a bit more about the what of awe, where we find it, how it feels, and how it is part of a broader space of transcendent states, it is time to turn to how awe works. How does awe transform our minds, our sense of self, and our way of being in the world?

TWO

AWE INSIDE OUT

How Awe Transforms Our Relation to the World

The most beautiful experience we can have is the mysterious. It is the fundamental emotion which stands at the cradle of true art and science.

· ALBERT EINSTEIN

A sense of wonder so indestructible it would last throughout life, as an unfailing antidote against the boredom and disenchantments of later years, the sterile preoccupation with things that are artificial, the alienation from the sources of our strengths.

· RACHEL CARSON

On a bustling day in 2010, I was working in my office when I received a call from Pete Docter, whose film *Up* had just won an Academy Award. He was calling to ask if I would talk with his team about his next film. The main characters, he continued, would be five emotions inside the mind of Riley, an eleven-year-old girl. The film was tentatively titled *Inside Out.*

On my visits to Pixar's campus, Pete would take me to a se-
questered room where he and his cocreator, Ronnie del Carmen,
passed the hours drawing storyboards for *Inside Out* (a typical film
is based on 70,000 to 120,000 storyboards). I had prepared for questions of a technical nature: What does the face look like during
envy? What color best conveys disgust? Instead, we tackled questions about *how* emotions work. How does feeling shape thought?
How do emotions guide our actions?

Like great novels and films so often do, *Inside Out* dramatizes
two central insights about how emotions work. The first is this:
emotions transform how we perceive the world—the "inside" of
Inside Out. For example, studies find that if you are feeling fear,
you will perceive more uncertainty in your romantic partnership,
think it more likely you will die from a weird disease or terrorist
attack, remember more readily harrowing moments from your
teens, and detect more quickly an image of a spider on a computer
screen. During fear, our mind is attuned to danger. Each emotion
is a lens through which we see the world.

The "out" of *Inside Out* refers to how emotions animate action.
In the film, it is the five emotions that move Riley to action. As
eighteen-month-old Riley dodges an electrical outlet, Bill Hader's
voice of Fear narrates the action. When Riley plays hockey with
sharpened elbow ferocity, Lewis Black's Anger moves her forceful
actions forward on the ice. Emotions are much more than fleeting
states in the mind; they involve sequences of actions between individuals as they negotiate social relationships.

Let's turn to the Inside Out of awe: How does awe transform
how we see the world? And what actions do experiences of awe
lead us to take upon encountering the vast mysteries of the eight
wonders of life?

Something Larger Than the Self

Our experiences of awe seem ineffable, beyond words. But you might have noticed an irony at play: awe's ineffability hasn't stopped people from telling stories of awe in journaling, writing poems, singing, composing music, dancing, and turning to visual art and design to make sense of the sublime. In our narration of experiences of awe in these symbolic traditions, a clear motif emerges: our individual self gives way to the boundary-dissolving sense of being part of something much larger.

For hundreds of years, awe has been a central character in spiritual journaling, in which people write—to this day—about their encounters with the Divine. Fourteenth-century mystic Julian of Norwich had sixteen visions of Jesus's compassionate love. These stories of awe became *Revelations of Divine Love*, one of the first books written by a woman in the English language, and influential in shifting Christian theology toward an emphasis on a compassionate, love-based faith. Julian of Norwich used the phrase "I am nothing" throughout to express her feelings of awe in relation to Christ's love.

Some of the most influential passages in nature writing in the global West, those of Wordsworth, Emerson, Thoreau, and Carson, portray the self as dissolving during experiences of natural awe. This dissolving of the self would transform early feminist Margaret Fuller, a central force in American transcendentalism, an editor at the influential magazine *The Dial*, and author of the bestselling treatise *Woman in the Nineteenth Century*, all remarkable achievements during a deeply sexist time. At the age of twenty-one, Fuller had an experience of awe that began in the pews of a

church and then continued outdoors under "sad clouds" and a cold
blue sky:

> I saw there was no self; that selfishness was all folly, and the
> result of circumstance; that it was only because I thought self
> real that I suffered; that I had only to live in the idea of the
> all; and all was mine.

Awe freed Fuller of the very gendered self of the early nineteenth century to go in search of "the all," a life of expanding
freedom and empowerment.

The vanishing self, or "ego death," is also at the heart of psychedelic experiences. In a story of awe, modern author Michael
Pollan choked down a piece of a magic mushroom containing psilocybin, and then lay down with eyeshades on, listening to music.
He saw his self, represented as a sheaf of papers, disappear::

> a sheaf of little papers, no bigger than Post-its, and they were
> being scattered to the wind . . .

Pollan perceives his self to expand in ways fitting for a food
writer married to a painter:

> I looked and saw myself out there again, but this time spread
> over the landscape like paint, or butter, thinly coating a wide
> expanse of the world with a substance I recognized as me.

The personal always imbues the transcendent.

What exactly vanishes during awe? Aldous Huxley called it
"the interfering neurotic who, in waking hours, tries to run the

show" in making sense of what disappeared during his experiences with mescaline. This is a pretty good approximation of how psychological science makes sense of the *default self*. This self, one of many that makes up who you are, is focused on how you are distinct from others, independent, in control, and oriented toward competitive advantage. It has been amplified by the rise of individualism and materialism, and no doubt was less prominent during other time periods (e.g., in Indigenous cultures thousands of years ago). Today, this default self keeps you on track in achieving your goals and urges you to rise in the ranks in the world, all essential to your survival and thriving.

When our default self reigns too strongly, though, and we are too focused on ourselves, anxiety, rumination, depression, and self-criticism can overtake us. An overactive default self can undermine the collaborative efforts and goodwill of our communities. Many of today's social ills arise out of an overactive default self, augmented by self-obsessed digital technologies. Awe, it would seem, quiets this urgent voice of the default self.

How would one study the vanishing self of awe? In our first effort, Yang Bai camped out in Yosemite National Park. Over the course of a few days, she approached more than 1,100 travelers from forty-two countries at a lookout at the side of State Route 140. That lookout offers an expansive view of Yosemite Valley, a natural wonder that led Teddy Roosevelt to observe:

> It was like lying in a great solemn cathedral, far vaster and more beautiful than any built by the hand of man.

As a measure of their sense of self, participants were asked to draw themselves on a sheet of graph paper, and write "me" next to their drawing. In a control condition, travelers were asked to do the same thing at Fisherman's Wharf in San Francisco, a place more evocative of light-hearted, carefree joy. Other research has found that simple measures—the size of the drawn self and how large you write "me"—are pretty good measures of how self-focused the individual is. Below are randomly selected drawings from this study: to the left is one from Fisherman's Wharf, and to the right, a drawn self in Yosemite eight squares from the left.

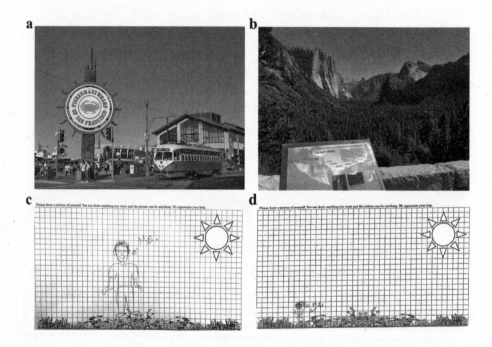

Simply being in a context of awe leads to a "small self." We can quiet that nagging voice of the interfering neurotic simply by locating ourselves in contexts of more awe.

In related work with Yang Bai, we found that the "small self" effect of awe arises in all eight wonders of life, and not just vast nature. Finding awe in encounters with moral beauty, for example, or music, or when struck by big ideas, quiets the voice of that interfering and nagging neurotic. We also found that awe leads to a vanishing self when this elusive construct is measured by other means, like simple self-report measures (e.g., "I feel small"; "my personal concerns are insignificant").

What about other core convictions of the default self, of being distinct, independent, in control, and seeking to prevail over others? To explore how awe expands our sense of self from feeling independent to feeling part of something larger, Arizona State University professor Michelle Shiota and I carried out the following study. We took college students to a paleontology museum and had them stand facing an awe-inspiring model of a *T. rex* skeleton. In the control condition, participants stood in the same location but looked down a fluorescent-lit hallway. Participants then filled in this sentence stem twenty times: "I AM _____". People in the control condition defined themselves in terms of distinct traits and preferences, in the spirit of individualism and its privileging of distinctness over common humanity. People feeling awe named qualities they shared with others—being a college student, belonging to a dance society, being human, being part of the category of all sentient beings.

Another pillar of the default self is that we are in control of our lives. This conviction in agency and freedom has many benefits but can blind us to a complementary truth: that our lives are shaped by vast forces, like the family, class background, historical period, or culture we happen to be born into. To test whether awe opens our minds to the vast forces that shape our lives, University of Toronto collaborator Jennifer Stellar and I took college students up to the observation deck of the Campanile tower on the UC

Berkeley campus, opened in 1914. It is 220 feet in the air and provides students with an expansive view of the Bay Area: its bay, bridges, cities, arteries of roads, and fog-laced, ever-changing skies. When eighteenth-century Europeans floated above the ground at about this height in the first hot-air balloons, one early balloonist perceived "the earth as a giant organism, mysteriously patterned and unfolding, like a living creature." Many astronauts experience a scaled-up version of this sensation, known as the overview effect, when looking at Earth from out in space. Here is astronaut Ed Gibson in 1964 offering his own story of awe from space:

> You see how diminutive your life and concerns are compared to other things in the universe. . . . The result is that you enjoy the life that is before you. . . . It allows you to have inner peace.

In our study, participants enjoying an expansive view also reported a greater sense of humility, and that the direction of their lives depended on many interacting forces beyond their own agency.

Awe's vanishing self has even been charted in our brains. The focus in this work has been the default mode network, or DMN, regions of the cortex that are engaged when we process information from an egocentric point of view. In a nuanced study from Japan, one group of participants watched videos of awe-inducing nature (footage of mountains, ravines, skies, and animals from BBC's *Planet Earth*). Other participants viewed more threat-filled awe videos of tornadoes, volcanoes, lightning, and violent storms. Both led to reduced activation in the DMN. This finding would suggest that when we experience awe, regions of the brain that are associated with the excesses of the ego, including self-criticism, anxiety, and even depression, quiet down.

The positive form of awe, though, led to increased connections between the DMN and a region of the brain (the cingulate cortex) involved in our sense of reward. Threat-based awe led to increased connections between the DMN and the amygdala, which activates fight-or-flight physiology—more evidence of the flavoring of awe by threat. It is worth noting now that sources of mystical awe—meditation, prayer, and psilocybin—also reduce activation in the DMN. The same is likely true of other wonders of life.

As our default self vanishes, other studies have shown, awe shifts us from a competitive, dog-eat-dog mindset to perceive that we are part of networks of more interdependent, collaborating individuals. We sense that we are part of a chapter in the history of a family, a community, a culture. An ecosystem. For Walt Whitman, this transformation of the self felt like a song:

> I celebrate myself, and sing myself,
> And what I assume you shall assume,
> For every atom belonging to me as good belongs to you.

Feeling part of something much larger than the self is music to our ears. This transformation of the self brought about by awe is a powerful antidote to the isolation and loneliness that is epidemic today.

Wonder

In *The Age of Wonder*, Richard Holmes details how awe transformed science during the eighteenth and first half of the nineteenth centuries. One example of this transformative power of awe is the scientist William Herschel, who as a young man was awestruck by how the moon hovered in the sky, surrounding him in its light, during his nighttime walks. He would be moved by awe to build the largest telescope in the world and painstakingly map, with his sister Caroline, the movements of stars and comets in the sky. Their discoveries put to rest the "fixed stars" thesis, that a two-dimensional pattern of a couple thousand stars revolved around Earth in unchanging ways. Instead, they opened the world's eyes to a near-infinite, ever-changing, three-dimensional space of billions of stars. This epiphany led the philosopher John Bonnycastle to this story of awe:

> Astronomy has enlarged the sphere of our conceptions, and opened to us a universe without bounds, where the human imagination is lost. Surrounded by infinite space, and swallowed up in an immensity of being, man seems but as a drop of water in the ocean, mixed and confounded with the general mass. But from this situation, perplexing as it is, he endeavors to extricate himself; and by looking abroad into Nature, employs the powers she has bestowed upon him in investigating her works.

Like so many stories of awe, Bonnycastle's about the vast mysteries of space reveals the emotion's unfolding pattern. It begins with vastness—"universe without bounds"—and mystery—"human imagination is lost." What follows is the vanishing of the self—"drop of water"—and the sense of being related to something larger—"immensity of being." And as the default self fades, the mind opens to intellectual questioning and searching that awe inspires ("investigating her works"). Or wonder.

———

Wonder, the mental state of openness, questioning, curiosity, and embracing mystery, arises out of experiences of awe. In our studies, people who find more everyday awe show evidence of living with wonder. They are more open to new ideas. To what is unknown. To what language can't describe. To the absurd. To seeking new knowledge. To experience itself, for example of sound, or color, or bodily sensation, or the directions thought might take during dreams or meditation. To the strengths and virtues of other people. It should not surprise that people who feel even five minutes a day of everyday awe are more curious about art, music, poetry, new scientific discoveries, philosophy, and questions about life and death. They feel more comfortable with mysteries, with that which cannot be explained.

A stereotype of awe is that it leaves us dumbfounded and dazed, ready to subordinate reason to dogma, disinformation, blind faith, a local guru or trendy influencer. The scientific evidence suggests otherwise. In the state of wonder that awe produces, our thought is more rigorous and energized. As one historical example, Isaac Newton and René Descartes were both awestruck by rainbows. In wonder, they asked: How is it that rainbows form when the sun's light refracts through water molecules? What is the precise angle that produces this effect? What does this say about light and our experience of color? This wonder over rainbows led these two scholars to some of their best work on mathematics, the physics of light, color theory, and sensation and perception.

Laboratory studies have captured how awe leads to more rigorous thought. In one such study, after being led to experience awe by recalling a time of looking out at an expansive view, college students were more discerning between what is a strong argument, grounded in robust scientific evidence, and a weak argument, based on a single individual's opinions.

With our thinking energized by awe, we place vast mysteries within more complex systems of understanding. We perceive natural phenomena like tide pools, pollinating bees, or ecosystems gathering around a "mother tree" as the result of intricate interacting *systems* of causal forces. We see human affairs as the result of complex webs of cause-and-effect relations in history that transcend an individual's intentions. When thinking about our own lives, we become more aware of how vast forces—our family, our neighborhood, a generous coach or teacher, a fateful encounter with a wise elder, the good health we may enjoy—shape the courses our lives take. In awe, our minds open in wonder to the systems of life and our small part in them.

Saintly Tendencies

In moments of awe, then, we shift from the sense that we are solely in charge of our own fate and striving against others to feeling we are part of a community, sharing essential qualities, interdependent and collaborating. Awe expands what philosopher Peter Singer calls the circle of care, the network of people we feel kindness toward. William James called the actions that give rise to the circle of care the "saintly tendencies" of mystical awe—to sacrifice, share, put aside self-interest in favor of the interests of others. Our studies find that these "saintly tendencies" arise in encounters with all eight wonders of life.

In one study on this theme, longtime collaborator and professor at UC Irvine Paul Piff and I led one group of participants to feel awe by watching BBC's *Planet Earth*. Other participants watched the hilarious antics of dogs, bears, cats, monkeys, and apes in their natural habitats in the British comedic nature show *Walk on the Wild Side*. When given points that would determine a chance to win money and asked to share with a stranger, people feeling awe gave more. In fact, they gave more than half their points to a stranger.

Awe empowers sacrifice, and inspires us to give that most precious of resources, time. Memphis University professor Jia Wei Zhang and I brought people to a lab where they were surrounded by either awe-inspiring plants or less-inspiring ones. As participants were leaving the lab, we asked if they would fold origami cranes to be sent to victims of the 2011 tsunami in Japan. Being surrounded with awe-inspiring plants led people to volunteer more time. The last pillar of the default self—striving for competitive advantage, registered in a stinginess toward giving away possessions and time—crumbles during awe.

Awe awakens the better angels of our nature.

The Sequel

Perhaps there will be a sequel to *Inside Out*. And who knows, perhaps Awe will be a character in Riley's mind, transforming her sense of self, opening her to wonder, and inclining her to saintly tendencies after encounters with the wonders of life. In the sequel, Riley could be older, perhaps a college student, and moved by Awe to youthful encounters with moral beauty, dancing at parties, outdoor concerts, and late-night conversations about the meaning of life, all so very fitting for a young adult.

And if I had my druthers, in this sequel Riley would be a budding neuroscientist. If so, there could be a scene in which she presents to her lab a video called "Waterfall Display," which is narrated by her hero, Jane Goodall. In the video, a solitary chimpanzee approaches a roaring waterfall. He piloerects (fluffs up his fur). He moves in swaying, rhythmic motions, swinging from one branch to another near the rushing river. He pushes large rocks into the river. At the end of this "dance" he sits quietly, absorbed in the flow of water. Jane Goodall observes that chimpanzees do the waterfall dance near waterfalls and roaring rivers, as well as during heavy rainstorms and sudden winds. She then speculates:

> I can't help feeling that this waterfall display, or dance, is perhaps triggered by feelings of awe, wonder, that we feel. . . . So why wouldn't they also have feelings of some kind of spirituality, which is really being amazed at things outside yourself?

At the short video's conclusion, Riley would pose questions to her lab. Is the chimpanzee's piloerection the same as our chills? What do those chills mean, anyway? Do chimpanzees have spiritual feelings? Why do we feel awe?

THREE

EVOLUTION OF THE SOUL

What Our Tears, Chills, and Whoas *Tell Us about the Why of Awe*

> *And if the body were not the soul, what is the soul?*
>
> · WALT WHITMAN

I only "cried" with the furrowed brow, closed mouth, and wince a few times while watching Rolf die and in the grief that followed. But I teared up all the time, when reminded of what brought us together in what was primary and good in our brotherhood.

In hearing music—the Beatles' *Sgt. Pepper's Lonely Hearts Club Band*, Fleetwood Mac's *Rumours*—that moved our young bodies during our formative family years, and songs—from Radiohead and Talking Heads—we sang driving up into the mountains. In seeing tennis and basketball courts and baseball diamonds in parks, fields of play during warm afternoons and dusks of our youth, and grassy golden-reddish California hills, the form and color of those dusks.

The summer after Rolf passed away, I drove into the eastern Sierras near Mammoth Lakes, California, to hike to Duck Lake, a thirteen-mile loop we had done the July before his colon cancer took hold of our lives. As I returned to that familiar place, the silhouetting line of mountain ridges surrounded me, backlit in the oranges, blues, fuchsias, and purples of sunset. Tears rose in my eyes, in thinking of the trails that held us as we wandered toward high granite passes. Chills rushed up my neck, in sensing him next to me in the car, as if we were leaning in together again, wondering about the mysteries of the Sierras. I heard the sound *whoa*. I felt overcome, and awestruck, by what was vanishing.

Why is awe accompanied by this constellation of tears, chills, and *whoa*s?

To answer this question, we will tour the new science of the emotional body. Our guides will be Charles Darwin and William James, two angst-ridden Victorians who treated the emotional body like the corpse in a murder mystery: a vessel of clues that reveal the origins of our body's present state. Both men grappled with the question of why we experience awe and related states, so close in meaning to our sense of a soul, that which is primary, good, and life-giving in human nature. And both would find answers in our bodies.

Darwin looked outward, tracing our emotional expressions back in evolutionary time to mammalian patterns of behavior, as Jane Goodall did in her observations about the chimpanzee waterfall dance. James looked inward, offering ideas about how emotions originate in our bodies. Their writings offer a radical thesis: transcendent emotions such as devotion, bliss, beauty, and awe—what you might think of as the subjective life of the soul—are grounded in bodily responses. Within the science of emotion that Darwin and James helped found, the tears, chills, and *whoa*s offer clues to the origins of awe in our mammalian evolution, revealing its primordial meaning, its elemental qualities, before language and symbolic acts of culture.

The emotional body has long been vilified as sinful, animalistic, base, and below matters of reason, and antithetical to what is primary and good in human nature, or what I have called the soul. The science we are soon to tour will lead to a different view, one best expressed by the poet Walt Whitman. Late in his life, Whitman observed that the soul follows "the beautiful laws of physiology." In seeking to understand the why of awe, and how it originates in mammalian tendencies that shaped its universal patterns in humans, we will go in search of those laws, encountering questions such as: Why do we tear up at others' acts of kindness and overcoming? What does it mean when we get the chills while listening to music or standing with others near a young couple at the altar? How might we think about the evolution of our soul?

Tears

Our current scientific understanding is that tears come in at least three varieties. There are no doubt many more. A first is the near-continuous watering of the surface of the eye produced by the lacrimal gland just above and behind the cornea. This kind of tearing smooths out the rough surface of the cornea so that you can see the world more clearly.

A second kind of tear arises in response to physical events— chopping onions, thick smoke, a gnat flying into your eye, a poke to the eye when roughhousing with kids. It is produced by the same anatomy as the first kind of tear but is a response to a physical event.

And then there are tears of emotion, when the lacrimal gland is activated by a region of your nervous system that includes the vagus nerve. The vagus nerve wanders from the top of your spinal cord through your facial and vocal muscles and then through your lungs, heart, and intestinal wall, communicating with the flora and fauna of your gut. It slows your heart rate, calms the body, and through enabling eye contact and vocalization can bring about a sense of connection and belonging. In tearing up at the sight of mountains I had hiked with Rolf, I was recognizing how those mountains gave us the feeling of stride-by-stride belonging one finds in hiking.

Some 2,500 years ago, scholars offered one taxonomy of the tears of emotion: we shed tears of sorrow, gladness, contrition, and—closest to awe—of our experience of grace, the feeling of Divine provenance of the kindness and goodness of life. Examples of this last kind of tear—sacred tears—appear throughout our history. For Saint Francis of Assisi, it was the divinity in all living beings that brought him such tears; legend has it he shed those tears so often that he went blind. For Odysseus, such tears arose frequently during his odyssey when he marshaled the courage to face overwhelming trials.

Translating these observations to contemporary science, anthropologically minded psychologist Alan Fiske has proposed that we tear up when witnessing acts of "communal sharing"—a way humans relate to one another grounded in the sense of interdependence, caring and sharing, and a sense of common humanity. So vital is this way of relating in our collective life that when we witness acts of communal sharing—a stranger's generosity, one person soothing another, or two athletic adversaries embracing—tears well up in our eyes. During political elections, Fiske finds, we are moved to tears by candidates who unite us: during the 2016 U.S. presidential election, campaign videos of Hillary Clinton moved her supporters to tears, and videos of Donald Trump did the same for his red-hatted supporters.

Tears, then, arise when we perceive vast things that unite us into community. The way this meaning of tears changes as we age adds texture to this thesis. Early in life, a child's tears are a lifeline to parents. Children cry to signal hunger, fatigue, physical pain, and separation, vocalizations that within a tenth of a second activate an ancient region of the brain (the periaqueductal gray) in people nearby, which prompts compassion and caregiving. Our early experiences of tears connect us to what may be our first encounters with what is vast and uniting, our caregivers, who pull us into skin-to-skin contact and calm with soothing touch, rhythmic movement, melodious vocalizations, and bodily warmth.

As children get older, they shift to tearing up when feeling small and lacking agency vis-à-vis forms of authority. This is true, for example, in being scolded by a teacher, pressured by a coach who takes her job too seriously, reprimanded by a parent having a bad day, or teased inappropriately by a popular peer. At this stage, our tears arrive when we feel small in relation to the vast forces of local culture—peers, parents, teachers, coaches, and other adults. The embrace we seek is in the acceptance of others within our culture, in particular our peers.

In adulthood, the vast things that elicit our tears become more symbolic and metaphorical, as is true of nearly every human experience. We tear up during cultural rituals and ceremonies; while appreciating certain kinds of music, movements in dance, films, and scenes in theater; when celebrating sports championships; and even when hearing about abstract ideas like justice, equality, rights, or freedom in speeches or portrayals of historical events. And we tear up when seeing meaningful places where we found awe with those who have departed. Tears of awe signal an awareness of vast things that unite us with others.

Chills

"My childhood was one of extreme awe." That is how Claire Tolan responds when I ask about her early experiences of awe. Her phrase makes me wonder, as do her fierce eyes and mussed-up hair.

Claire grew up in Ohio and found awe outside. She began writing at age twelve, producing volumes of poems and prose throughout her teens. She found early poetic sublimity in the words of William Carlos Williams, which led her to study poetry as a college student and then attain a PhD in information science.

Upon graduating, Claire moved to Berlin to work on an app that she described to me, in a café in that city, as "Airbnb for refugees." Her landing in the new city, though, was rough. She felt anxious and tense. The unsettling presence of that twenty-first-century malaise—loneliness—overtook her. Her sleep was disrupted. She often found herself wide awake before dawn, her mind whirring and worrying.

Claire found comfort in ASMR. What is ASMR? If you are younger than thirty you likely already know and may have bookmarked your own diet of its digital offerings. If you are over thirty, it sounds like another mysterious acronym of a younger generation mocking your dance moves and coming to take your job.

ASMR stands for *autonomous sensory meridian response*. This indecipherable mouthful of words refers to a constellation of sensations in your body, including tingles in your spine, shoulders, the back of your neck, and on the crown of your head. The poet Walt Whitman was perhaps thinking of this sensation in writing about the "body electric."

How people like Claire find ASMR is where the story gets strange. There are millions of ASMR videos online. These videos often feature a person, filmed up close, whispering and carrying out actions as if moving closer to you, the viewer. The person may make sounds of daily living—of chopping food, tapping countertops, rustling cellophane packaging, or intimate conversation. Or the tongue clicking in a moistened mouth, gentle lip smacking, the sounds of eating, and, from South Korea, a whole ASMR genre of slurping shellfish. Videos of caregiving acts in intimate spaces—dental procedures, chiropractic adjustments, or ear cleanings—can also trigger ASMR.

For Claire, experiencing ASMR soothed her anxiety; it gave her a strange sense of comfort. Of place. Even home. At the end of our conversation, I ask her what it all means. She reflects:

It is like being surrounded by the sounds from childhood. Hearing your parents talk at dinner. The clinking of silverware on plates and the wood table. It feels like when your mom comes close to say good night as you drift off to sleep. They are the sounds of being surrounded by intimacy. The first years of life. Of being embraced.

What are we to make of this possibility, that certain kinds of chills are registers of the idea of having someone you love approach you, of being surrounded by the sounds of home? The framework for an answer is found in William James's letters to his brother Henry, the great novelist. These letters include vivid descriptions of back pains, upset stomachs, tingly veins, and bodily fatigue. The dramas in the minds of these highly sensitive brothers played out in the sensations of their bodies, and would lead William to one of his most enduring ideas: Our mental life is *embodied*. Our conscious experience of emotions, and the lenses through which we perceive our lives—in the case of awe, that we are part of something larger than the self—originate in bodily sensations and their underlying neurophysiology. For James, "our mental life is knit up with our corporeal frame."

Today a new science of embodiment with roots in William James's thinking reveals that many of your most significant thoughts have correlates in bodily responses. Your perception of risk, for example, tracks shifts in your systolic blood pressure, when the heart's quarter-second contraction sends waves of blood through your arteries. How we hold our bodies shapes the reality we perceive. It is easier to recognize concepts (e.g., "vomit") when you move your facial muscles into the configuration of the related emotion (e.g., of disgust). Simply adopting the furrowed brow and tightened mouth of anger leads people to perceive life as more unfair (try glaring with clenched jaw while listening to a loved one and see what comes to mind). Your judgments about whether someone is trustworthy or not track sensations in your gut.

Claire Tolan's experiences with ASMR are a poetic example of embodiment: her chills were accompanied by ideas of feeling close to her parents and being surrounded by a sense of home. This theme—that some kind of chills accompany the sense of joining with others to face the unknown—appears across history in descriptions of moments of awe and the wonders of life.

Within the arts, certain qualities of music can produce the chills, such as crescendos, high-pitched solos, expansive guitar riffs, fast drumming, and dissonant chords. The chills also arise when music brings us closer to others in a sense of shared identity.

When reading a novel or a poem, a "literary frisson"—the sudden chills in recognizing the vast forces of a plot—may ripple through our bodies. Here is Vladimir Nabokov on reading Charles Dickens's novels: "Although we read with our minds, the seat of artistic delight is between the shoulder blades. That little shiver behind is quite certainly the highest form of emotion that humanity has attained when evolving pure art and pure science. Let us worship the spine and its tingle." As with music, the chills of literature unite us with others in grappling with the vast unknowns we face together.

We often experience the chills during epiphanies whose recognition joins us with others in common cause. At the coffee maker one day while reporting on the Watergate scandal that ended Richard Nixon's presidency, *Washington Post* reporter Carl Bernstein was overtaken by the chills. He turned to his colleague Bob Woodward and blurted out: "Oh my god, this president is going to be impeached." Chills signal to our default mind that yet-to-be-recognized forces of social change are nearby—in this particular case, that the discoveries Bernstein and Woodward were unearthing would unite a movement to bring down a president.

Different kinds of chills occur with regularity in encounters with the Divine, as in this example from the book of Job:

In thoughts from the visions of the night, when deep sleep falleth on men, fear came upon me, and trembling, which made all my bones to shake. Then a spirit passed before my face. The hair of my flesh stood up.

Within the Yogic tradition, the chills are a sign of devotional love, part of Kundalini, the feminine, ego-dissolving spiritual energy of mystical interconnectedness experienced during yoga. In the vein of Buddhist literature known as Abhidhamma, the bodily shiver is seen as a sign of ecstasy, of losing the self in relation to the Divine. If the soul is embodied, as Walt Whitman observed, the chills would seem to be one register of our recognition that we are connected to something primary, good, and larger than the self.

But what are we to make of the various meanings of "the chills"? That they accompany awe and terror? Bliss and dread? Ecstasy and horror? Union with the Divine and condemnation?

Inspired by questions like these, awe scientists have mapped the meanings of "the chills." In one illustrative study, people wrote about an experience of the chills and then reported on the degree to which they felt four sensations—cold shivers, shudders, tingling, and goose bumps—as well as various emotions. This study would reveal that "the chills" can refer to two distinct bodily responses with very different embodied social meanings.

The first is a cold shiver and shudder—what I will refer to as cold shivers—which accompany feelings of horror and dread. Human depravity and baseness can trigger cold shivers, for example when reading about genocide, torture, cannibalism, or pedophilia. Cold shivers are accompanied by the sense of being alienated, alone, and separate from others. In mystical experiences involving cold shivers, the individual feels condemned by an omnipotent god, fearing an afterlife of solitary torment and isolation, reminiscent of Dante's hell. Our more everyday experience of the eerie—

when we feel a strange and unexpected emptiness in a familiar place—can trigger cold shivers.

A second kind of chills is a tingling sensation in the arms, shoulders, back of the neck, and on the crown of the head—"goose bumps." ASMR resembles this form of the chills. This was the sensation that washed over me in returning to the eastern Sierras to hike to Duck Lake, as Rolf and I had done before he passed. Studies have found that goose bumps are associated with a heightened sense that you are joined with others in community. Our experiences of awe are accompanied by goose bumps but not cold shivers. Once again, more evidence of the distinctions between awe and fear and horror.

If we follow these two kinds of chills back in our evolutionary history, where does this journey take us? Here is the latest thinking on the mammalian beginnings of awe, or, if you feel a bit expansive, the evolution of the soul.

Alongside eating and keeping oxygen at the right level, maintaining the right body temperature is fundamental to survival. Complex brain and body mechanisms kick into gear when we are too hot or too cold. Highly social mammals, such as certain rodents, wolves, primates, and humans, have an additional tool in their tool kit for handling extreme cold: they huddle. This is in keeping with a broader evolutionary principle, that social mammals like rats, dogs, and humans lean in and coordinate with others when facing peril.

Social mammals' first response to extreme cold is piloerection, the bodily reaction underlying goose bumps. Piloerection causes the skin to bunch, rendering it less porous to the cold. Visible piloerection signals to others to huddle, initiating proximity and tactile contact, which in humans takes the form of supportive touch and even embrace. Proximity and tactile contact activate a neuro-chemistry of connection. This includes the release of oxytocin, a neurochemical that travels through the brain and body promoting openness to others, and activation of the vagus nerve. When our mammalian relatives encountered vast and perilous mysteries—numbing cold, roaring water, sudden gusts of wind, thunderous deluges, and lightning—they piloerected, and found warmth and strength in drawing closer to others.

Should huddling be unavailable, mammals facing perilous cold turned to shivering and shuddering, vigorous muscle contractions that warm the body's tissues. Today we humans shiver and shudder when facing imperiling mysteries and unknowns alone; when feeling rejected socially, ostracized, or acutely lonely; or when encountering the horrors others perpetrate. The cold shivers have a much different neurophysiological profile than goose bumps, involving activation in threat-related regions of the brain (the dorsal anterior cingulate cortex) and elevated blood pressure. In Jean-Paul Sartre's novel *Nausea*, the protagonist Roquentin experiences a "horrible ecstasy," trembling and becoming nauseated when he looks at a chestnut tree while sitting alone on a park bench. His trembling and shuddering embody the central idea of existentialism, and for some the individualistic twentieth century: that we are alone in making meaning out of the mysteries of life.

Awe indeed follows Whitman's "beautiful laws of physiology." Our tears register our awareness of vast things that unite us with others. Our goose bumps accompany notions of joining with others and facing mysteries and unknowns together. Today we may sense these laws of bodily awe when moved by a favorite musical group, or in calling out in protest with others in the streets, or in bowing our heads together in contemplation. And in such rushes of tears and chills, Whitman's body electric, we may glean a sense of what our souls might be.

As chills and tears wash over us, we often are left wordless and wondering, appreciating what is vast and mysterious about our place in it all. Being the hypersocial primate, we often reflexively communicate with others about the wonders of life. We do so in body movements and sounds that were our earliest language of awe.

Whoas

Rainbows stirred Newton and Descartes, we have learned, to some of their best mathematics and physics. For Paul "Bear" Vasquez, such harmonious colors in the sky led to a creation for our digital age. His three-minute video from 2010 of his encountering a double rainbow outside his home in Yosemite has been seen, as I write, nearly fifty million times. In the video you watch a double rainbow's appearance over grassy foothills near Yosemite. Over the course of the three minutes, Vasquez travels through the sounds of transcendent states. He exults with *whoa*s and ecstatic *aah*s. He howls. He cries and laughs the kind of existential laugh we emit when recognizing something vast and profound, beyond the narrow view of the default self. As the video nears its end, he observes, "Too much" and "Oh my god," and wonders several times, "What does this mean?" In awe, we utter sounds of transcendence.

For Charles Darwin, Vasquez's *whoa* illustrates how we alert others to the wonders of life and align ourselves in understanding and action. In *The Expression of the Emotions in Man and Animals* from 1872, Darwin detailed the evolution of our emotional expressions, like the chimpanzee waterfall dance or social mammals huddling when feeling perilous cold. Three of the emotional expressions he described are relatives of awe: admiration, astonishment, and devotion. *Admiration* involves a smile. *Astonishment*—when we are stunned by a vast, unexpected event—lacks the smile, but involves the hand placed over the mouth. And *devotion* involves behaviors that signal a recognition of the sacred. The face points upward. The body kneels humbly. The eyes close, as in Bernini's well-known sculpture *The Ecstasy of Saint Teresa*. Hands might be open and turned up, as in Giotto's painting of Saint Francis preaching to an audience of birds as he wondered "much at such a multitude of birds and at their beauty."

Is there a universal expression of awe, one that has united us throughout our evolution to recognize together the wonders of life? To answer this question, my Yale collaborator Daniel Cordaro gathered data in China, Japan, South Korea, India, and the United States in search of the body of awe. In a lab in each country, most often just an empty classroom, participants first heard short stories about emotional situations from a speaker of their native language, and then they expressed the emotion portrayed in the story with their bodies in whatever fashion they liked. It was an experiment in emotional charades. Eight months of coding the millisecond-by-millisecond unfolding of bodily movements revealed the following.

People from the five countries screamed with fear, snarled in anger, licked their lips and puckered during desire, and sometimes literally danced with joy. What about awe? Across the five cultures, people expressed awe with eyebrows and upper eyelids raised, a smile, jaw drop, and head tilting up. About half of the bodily movements of awe were universal or shared across cultures. A quarter of each expression was unique to the individual, shaped by that person's life story and genetics. And about 25 percent of the movements were specific to each culture, in the form of culturally specific "accents." In India, for example, the expression of awe included a seductive lip pucker; perhaps it's all those erotic sculptures and treatises on tantric sex that are embodied in the Indian expression of awe.

Vasquez's *whoa* is what is known as a vocal burst, a pattern of sound that lasts a quarter of a second or so, doesn't involve words, and is intended to convey emotion. Other examples of vocal bursts include sighs, laughs, shrieks, growls, *blech*s, *ooh*s, *aah*s, and *mmm*s. Vocal bursts are millions of years old and were a primary language of *Homo sapiens* prior to the emergence of words some 100,000 years ago. Many social mammals, including great apes, horses, goats, dogs, elephants, and bats, have repertoires of vocal bursts by which they communicate about threat, food, sex, affiliation, comfort, pain, and play.

To understand whether awe's *whoa*s are universal, we had people vocalize their feelings associated with different situations, such as: "You've stubbed your toe on a large rock and feel pain." *Ouch!* Or "You see someone who is physically attractive and want to have sex." *Mmm* (very similar to the sound we make when tasting delicious food). Or "You have just seen the largest waterfall in the world." The vocal bursts of awe sounded like *whoa* or *aaaah* or *wow*. When we played these sounds to people from ten countries, they correctly identified vocal bursts of awe nearly 90 percent of the time. This finding struck us: the vocal burst of awe is the most universal sound of emotion, and readily recognized by people in a remote village in the Himalayas of eastern Bhutan, whose residents had minimal contact with Western missionaries or expressive media from the West and from India. Before the emergence of language some 100,000 years ago, we were saying *whoa* to our kith and kin to join together in facing the vast mysteries of life.

Awe and Culture Evolving

In our tour of the why of awe, we have journeyed back in evolutionary time to imagine an early hominid profile of awe involving tears, piloerection, huddling, sounds like *whoa*, widened eyes, open arms and hands, and other social behaviors, such as touch. This was the awe, we can imagine, of perhaps ten thousand *Homo sapiens* a couple hundred thousand years ago, which brought them together to unite in food sharing, huddling when cold, scaring off predators, and hunting large mammals—tasks required for our hypersocial survival, and in relation to patterns in weather, ecosystems, life cycles of flora and fauna, and migrations of animals. These early forms of awe were about joining together to face peril and the unknown.

Some 80,000 to 100,000 years ago, the archaeological record reveals, language, symbols, music, and visual art emerged. *Homo sapiens* became a cultural primate and would quickly archive awe with our ever-evolving symbolic capacities. With the emergence of language-based *representation*, we began to describe the wonders of life to others, using words, metaphors, stories, legends, and myths, and with visual techniques in paintings, carvings, masks, and figurines. Through *symbolization*, we dramatized our bodily expressions of awe in singing, chanting, dance, dramatic performance, and music. And through *ritualization*, we formalized the patterns of awe-related bodily tendencies, for example bowing and touching, into rituals and ceremonies.

In archiving awe in myriad cultural forms, we joined with others in cultural and aesthetic experiences of awe to understand the mysteries of our very social living. This was the thesis offered by Robert Hass, the U.S. poet laureate from 1995 to 1997, in a twelve-minute tour of the role of awe in literature and poetry at a conference in Berkeley in 2016. As he detailed this idea, he embodied literary epiphanies with *whoa*s, our ancient sounds of recognizing the sublime.

Hass began with a riff on Aristotle's idea of *catharsis*. Twenty-five hundred years ago, *catharsis* was a purifying ritual: a person would wash themselves with oils prior to entering the home if they had encountered dangerous spirits. Drama, poetry, and literature, which allow us in the safe realm of the imagination to wonder and gain insight into human horrors, can serve as symbolic, ritualized acts of cleansing—transforming human harm and horror into aesthetic representations that stir awe.

Hass then moved on to Sophocles's *Oedipus Rex*: A king sleeps with his mother, kills his father, and then gouges out his own eyes. At the play's end the chorus sings of being cursed with such knowledge about the horrifying conflicts that can ruin families. Turning to the audience, Hass raised his eyebrows and leaned in:

WHOA.

Hass then fast-forwarded two thousand years to Shakespeare's *Hamlet* and *Antony and Cleopatra*, both ending in scenes of horrifying death. At the end of *Antony and Cleopatra*, "the earth cracks and shivers at its core." Cleopatra's death is so powerful it gives chills to the earth! Noting this, Hass lifted his gaze from his notes and looked out to the audience:

WHOA.

Audience members startled. Laughing and nudging friends, they wondered where Hass's tour would take them next, and then shifted their attention back to the podium.

There Hass turned to a lifelong source of awe for him: haiku. It is customary for haiku poets to write one poem about Mount Fuji, a sacred place of awe for more than two thousand spiritual communities in Japan. He quoted the legendary poet Bashō.

In the misty rain
Mount Fuji is veiled all day—
how intriguing!

WHOA.

And then this haiku about a neighbor the poet lives near:

Autumn deepens—
the man next door, what does he do
for a living?

WHOA.

We can find everyday awe in wondering about other people's minds and the patterns of their lives.

At about the eighth minute of this brief history of literary awe,

Hass landed in the words of Emily Dickinson—"one of the greatest writers in the language," he observed. Her poems come out of a state of low blood sugar, Hass joked. They reflect her efforts at grappling with the yearning to connect with infinity in the nineteenth century, as the "big daddy" God was fading. He notes her abiding interest in death and grief.

He read:

There's a certain Slant of light,
Winter Afternoons —
That oppresses, like the Heft
Of Cathedral Tunes —

Heavenly Hurt, it gives us —
We can find no scar,
But internal difference —
Where the Meanings, are —

None may teach it — Any —
'Tis the seal Despair —
An imperial affliction
Sent us of the Air —

When it comes, the Landscape listens —
Shadows — hold their breath —
When it goes, 'tis like the Distance
On the look of Death —

In hearing "certain slant of light" and "the Landscape listens" and "look of Death," my heart paused and my eyes teared up slightly, accompanied by a faint rush of chills up my spine. I understood in my body the vastness of loss, leaning in with other audience members in a shared awareness of this fundamental truth. And then heard Hass again:

WHOA.

And then to finish, a poem by Gary Snyder. Sitting near a small fire in the Sierras, Snyder draws connections between the fire warming his body, the volcanic fires that created the mountain he was near, and Buddhist fire rituals that purify the soul. Hass ends with a saying of the Buddha:

We are all burning.

WHOA.

Hass's *whoa*s and the poetic words he read stirred audience members to open their minds, to wonder about our moral failings, death, our connections to neighbors and the mysterious operations of their minds, the meanings of light and cathedral tunes, and how fire creates mountains and granite and, metaphorically, our souls. Literature, drama, essay, and poetry join us in the experience of awe and allow us to benefit from its transformations. In one test of this idea, students were first presented with this question: "Why are we alive?" They then wrote a poem to capture their thinking and reported upon the awe they felt while writing. The poems were then rated by PhD students of literature for how sublime they were according to these criteria that date back to ancient Greece:

Did the poem have boldness and grandeur of thoughts?

Did it raise passions to a violent or enthusiastic degree?

Did it show skillful use of language? Graceful expression?

Did it reveal elegant structure and composition?

Another group of participants then read the poems and reported on how much they were inspired by their words. The critical finding: the more student poets felt awe in writing their poems, the more those poems were judged as sublime by the PhD students; and the more sublime the poem, the more inspiration student readers felt. We can transform experiences of awe into shared aesthetic experiences that unite us into something larger than the self.

This archiving of awe, of translating the body of awe into a cultural form, was part of how Claire Tolan would make her way in Berlin. She transformed her sensations of ASMR into creative acts of twenty-first-century culture. She hosted a show on Berlin community radio featuring live ASMR collages. With a fellow artist, she hosted social events in Berlin nightclubs that involved ASMR karaoke, where participants whispered songs and audience members whispered for encores.

WHOA.

Awe and culture are always evolving. Several thousand years ago, it was a time of *everyday awe*. Indigenous peoples found awe in relation to nature, stories, ceremony, dance, chanting, song, visual design, and in states of consciousness beyond our ordinary ideas about space, time, and causality. Lao Tzu would orient a continent to the mysteries of a life force, *Tao*, in nature. Plato would declare that wonder is the source of philosophy, and the means by which we answer life's great questions, including those that have concerned us here: What is our soul? How do we find what is sacred to us?

Twenty-five hundred years ago, accounts of mystical experiences, like those of Julian of Norwich, begin to dominate the written history of awe, from the Buddha and Christ until the Age of Enlightenment. This archiving of mystical awe in legends, myths, teachings, ceremonies, iconography, and temples would become a fabric of religions. Awe was transforming, at least in the historical record, into a largely religious emotion, reflecting our efforts to make sense of the Divine and to build community in the face of violence, expanding trade, the breakdown of the family, and the privileging of self-interest over communal sharing.

As we emerged out of the Dark Ages, we would archive awe in an explosion of art, music, literature, rhetoric, drama, and urban and architectural design. Shakespeare's plays, for example, would stir audiences to wonder anew, as they do today. Several centuries later, Edmund Burke would detail how awe can be found in the mundane, a first philosophical championing in the West of everyday awe. The heroes of Romanticism—Rousseau, Shelley, Blake, Wordsworth— would exhort us to search for the sublime, especially in nature. They would inspire American transcendentalists, who would celebrate our roots in everyday awe found in walking in nature (Ralph Waldo Emerson), free intellectual exchange (Margaret Fuller), ordinary people in their daily lives (Walt Whitman), and mystical experiences found in religion, visions, and drugs (William James).

These ebbs and flows of awe's history offer another answer, alongside the evolutionary one, to the question "Why awe?" Because awe allows us to get outside of ourselves, and integrates us into larger patterns—of community, of nature, of ideas and cultural forms—that enable our very survival. Tears arise in our recognition of those larger patterns that unite. And the chills signal to us that we are seeking to make sense of such unknowns with others.

We are nearing an end to our first section, devoted to a science of awe. We have seen how awe arises in encounters with the wonders of life and leads to a vanishing of the self, to wonder, and to saintly tendencies. Our interrogation of tears, chills, and *whoa*s locates awe deeper in our mammalian evolution, finding its roots in the tendencies to recognize vast forces that require that we unite with others.

Guided by this mapping of awe, we are ready for more focused studies of how it works within our taxonomy of the eight wonders of life. Experiences with these wonders, for example with music or mystical encounter, so often transcend the reach of language and the tendencies of science to define, measure, and hypothesize within linear, cause-and-effect theorizing. Recognizing this, we will need to lean more heavily upon people's stories of awe, such as those I heard inside prisons and near symphony halls, from veterans speaking of what it is like to nearly die in combat and from an Indigenous scholar who nearly died in a community hospital in Mexico. These stories begin in experiences of vast mysteries and unfold in individual lives through the transformative power of awe.

Stories of Transformative Awe

FOUR

MORAL BEAUTY

How Others' Kindness, Courage, and Overcoming Inspire Awe

*Over time, these last forty years, I have become
more and more invested in making sure acts of
goodness (however casual or deliberate or
misapplied . . .) produce language. . . .
Allowing goodness its own speech does not
annihilate evil, but it does allow me to signify
my own understanding of goodness: the
acquisition of self-knowledge.*

· TONI MORRISON

San Quentin State Prison is a level-two prison located on San Francisco Bay. It houses 4,500 prisoners—the men in blue—including those sentenced to execution in California. In 2016, I first visited inside to give a talk as part of an inmate-led restorative justice (RJ) program, which served two hundred men.

On the night before my first visit, I looked over the instructions for visitors: Wear greens, beiges, browns, and grays—colors with no ties to gangs and which correctional officers can easily distinguish from the blues that prisoners wear, should things get out of hand. Don't touch the inmates. No drugs. And don't bring in weapons.

One reason for giving the talk that day was my interest in restorative justice. My deeper reason for going was being moved to awe in reading Michelle Alexander's *The New Jim Crow* and Bryan Stevenson's *Just Mercy*. Those two books archive the big idea of U.S. history: the subjugation of people of color by a succession of social systems, from the genocide of Indigenous people to slavery to mass incarceration. The awe I felt reading those books opened my mind to wonder about the everyday horrors of the U.S. caste system: about the chokehold a friend, now a professor at Stanford, had been subjected to as a teen when stopped by the police; about how an Indigenous friend was asked to leave a pharmacy when getting medicine for her parents; about how a Mexican American student of mine called his grandparents each night about the latest movements of ICE; about seeing a prizewinning honors student at Berkeley, who grew up unhoused, pick at his food suspiciously because of a lifetime of chronic hunger. Awestruck by these books, I was drawn inside San Quentin.

On the day of the visit, a handful of other RJ volunteers and I made our way to the dusty waiting room near the first security gate. Waiting amid wives and mothers and friends and children of the prisoners inside, we took in an art exhibit created by the prisoners—drawings, woodcuts, and paintings of flowers, sunsets, bay views, and faces of family members. It was my first encounter that day with how prisoners seek in so many ways to surface what is good in who they are—*allowing goodness its own speech*, as Toni Morrison put it. At the second security gate, we showed our IDs to guards standing in a plexiglass booth. Once approved, we passed through massive doors, the echoing clank of the locks astonishing in their sound of finality.

Inside San Quentin we were escorted into the prison chapel, where I grabbed a seat in the pews amid 180 men in blue. The chapel walls were bright, reflecting a pure white light glancing through the fog off the bay. The men in blue were almost all men of color, something rapper Tupac Shakur anticipated in his song "Changes" from 1998, as harshening drug laws filled U.S. prisons:

It ain't a secret, don't conceal the fact
The penitentiary is packed, and it's filled with blacks.

The morning began with ceremonies from different religions: Christian, Muslim, Buddhist, and Jewish. A prisoner named Grey Eagle performed on a wooden flute a sacred song from his Native American tribe, the reedy, rising notes taking our shared awareness out beyond the windows of the chapel. The morning culminated in a haka war dance led by a prisoner named Upu, 280 pounds of muscle and a force on his prison softball team. Polynesian haka dances symbolize the shimmering energy of Hine-raumati, the wife of the Polynesian sun god. She herself is an image seen in the vibrating heat that rises from the ground on hot days. This dance involves squatting with bulging biceps, fierce shouts, and threat faces of widened eyes, open mouths, and tongue displays. Upu led six enormous Polynesian islanders in the dance, shaking the room with their stomps and calls. The prisoners in the pews a few feet away watched with widened eyes and slightly open mouths.

When we mingled with the men in blue at break time, they shared pictures of their artwork. They unfolded and read carefully crafted letters to a grandmother or father. They spoke of victims and of mothers mourning lost lives. Those on the outside living privileged lives, like me, have stories that follow a coherent pattern, like the jacket copy for a novel. The stories the men in blue tell are elliptical and metaphorical, like poems—words reaching to translate chaotic, violent forces—and move with the punctate cadences of rap and the elongated tones of a sermon narrating redemption. The stories begin with youthful transgressions that I would have been locked up for were it not for the color of my skin—using drugs, selling them, shoplifting, trespassing, driving recklessly. And then fate-changing violence.

Here is my memory of one:

I grew up in a whorehouse. My dad was gone before I was born. My mom was hooked on crack cocaine. She was pimped out by my stepdad. My living room was always full of people partying. I started doing knuckleheaded things when I was ten—drugs, break-ins, carjackings. My stepdad gave me a gun when I was twelve. He tried to pimp out my sister. We got into a fight in our living room. I killed him.

And . . .

One day, two guys from a gang came to my cousin's house, looking for him. He wasn't there, so they shot his mom. She was sitting in her La-Z-Boy watching TV in front of her two-year-old son. My friends gave me a gun and said I had to get revenge. I tracked these guys down after school and shot two of them. But I got the wrong guys.

Social scientists now tally up ten early traumas known as adverse childhood experiences, or ACEs. Many of the men in blue are near a score of ten by the time they head to kindergarten, a vast fate that kicks the stress system into high gear, dampening prospects and shortening lives.

As the day progressed, I had the gnawing sense that awe—a focus of my talk that day—was irrelevant to the men in blue. It might even be an offense, the product of the myopia and tone-deafness of my white privilege. Of what matter is awe to people with life sentences, living twenty hours a day in a nine-by-twelve-foot cell?

Fifteen minutes into my talk, standing on a dais amid microphones and the amps of the church band, I asked:

What gives you guys awe?

And then I waited. After a second or two, here is what I heard:

My daughter
Visitors from the outside
Singing in the church band
The air
Jesus
My cellie
The light outside on the yard
Reading the Koran
Learning how to read
RJ at SQ
Today

The Wonders of Others

It is a myth that awe is rarefied, reserved for when we have enough wealth to enjoy lives of taste and "culture." The responses of the men in blue tell us this is so. So too does recent empirical work. One study found that people who have less wealth report feeling more frequent awe during the day, and more wonder about their everyday surroundings. It is tempting to think that greater wealth enables us to find more awe, in the fancy home, for example, or exclusive resort, or high-end consumer goods. In fact, the opposite appears to be true, that wealth undermines everyday awe and our capacity to see the moral beauty in others, the wonders of nature, or the sublime in music or art. Our experience of awe does not depend on wealth; everyday awe is a basic human need.

In our daily diary studies in different countries, it was *other people* who were most likely to bring our participants everyday awe—actions of strangers, roommates, teachers, colleagues at work, people in the news, characters on podcasts, and our neighbors and family members. On rare occasions, disturbing acts did so, as in this story from a Spaniard:

> It was in a metro station in Paris, France. It was about ten thirty p.m. We were alone at the station waiting for the train to arrive when a man arrived, swearing and screaming. He was saying something about God. I think he was sick, he took out a knife and he was punching everything he bumped into, and notching everything. We started running to get out of the metro, I don't think I will get to the metro alone again.

And from Singapore, a story about being dumbfounded by the rise of authoritarian leaders:

When the results of the Philippines presidential elections were announced two days ago, I felt a sense of awe. The winner was this guy Duterte, who was linked to killer squads, asked to be the first to rape an Australian lady missionary who was indeed raped and killed in a prison riot, and threatened war with China! Such a man could win a presidential election??? What a man!!! Now this means that someone like Trump could be president of the United States!!! That would be awesome too because they both speak the same language. Tough talk that appeals to the most basest of human emotions. And they win!!!

We can be astonished by the depravity of fellow humans, both strangers we encounter and leaders in the public sphere, but these were rare sources of awe around the world.

Instead, over 95 percent of the moral beauty that stirred awe worldwide was in actions people took on behalf of others. Acts of *courage* are one kind of moral beauty with sublime potential. People using CPR to revive victims of heart attacks, parents raising children with serious health conditions, bystanders interrupting crimes or defusing fights, and organizations like Doctors Without Borders all inspire awe. Here is a story of lifesaving, courageous awe from Chile:

I remember it was a nice day and we decided to go fishing with my older brother and his friend of the same age, back then I was seventeen years old and my brother was almost twenty. We got plastic string that our neighbor let us borrow but with high regard so we take care of it. We went to San Pedro de la Paz, I do not remember if it was the big or small lagoon, the line got stuck meters into the lagoon. Our friend jumped into the water to free the nylon and started sinking so started yelling for help, my brother despite not being a good swimmer he jumped in to save him. The moment my friend felt my brother's body, he clung to him by his waist so both of them started drowning by disappearing from the surface. I was freaking out yelling my brother's name, Mariooo, Mariooo, Mariooo, but my voice will choke because I felt like crying. Out of nowhere, a man in a bathing suit came running, jumped into the water and saved both of them. It was a miracle that the person was there, he was a God-sent angel that saved my brother and my friend. We all finally returned home.

God so often appears in extraordinary stories of awe; we invoke the Divine to explain the sublime.

Others' kindness was evocative of awe around the world: having car repairs paid for by a restaurant owner; being given money by friends when broke; seeing citizens assist strangers in the streets; reading about moral exemplars, most frequently the Dalai Lama. This story from the United States combines courage with compassion:

1973 at my cousin's restaurant. My father worked there as a bartender. I was there and my best friend from high school walked in. He is Black and I am white and I had not seen him in five years. I stood and embraced him and we began to talk. A guy at the bar said to my father, "How can you allow your son to have a N as his friend?" My father looked at this guy and loudly told him to get out of his bar and never come back. I have never been more proud of my father, who was fifty-nine years old at that time.

Overcoming obstacles was a universal as well: People thriving despite profound racism and poverty. Jews who had survived the concentration camps. People who transcend mental and physical challenges, as in this story from South Africa:

When watching my daughter, who was born with bilateral club foot, dance in a ballet recital for the first time I was filled with awe. I was in the audience with my mother and my little girl was dancing onstage. I had been backstage with her before and had been getting her ready for the performance. While watching I felt the beginning of tears in my eyes and my heart felt like it was going to burst with pride. I had flashbacks of the time when she was born with her feet upside down and I felt awestruck by how far she has come since that day years ago.

We often turn to literature, to poetry, to film, to art, and, on occasion, to the news for inspiring stories of overcoming, *allowing goodness its own speech*. Here is such an example from Norway:

When I read an article in the paper about an eight-year-old girl in Yemen who had run away from a forced marriage and taken up the fight against her parents in the judicial system. It hit me how much courage and fighting spirit that can live in a person, and that you can fight for your cause and actually make a change. I was an adult when I read this article. I was alone, but had to tell several people about it later. I didn't do anything special with my own life afterwards, but had an aha-experience.

Finally, others' rare *talents* brought people awe around the world. For a young man from Mexico, it was the trapeze artist and contortionist in the Cirque du Soleil. For a woman in Sweden, her husband's strength in moving large household objects around the home. For an Australian, watching swimmer Sun Yang's last 100 meters in a 1,500-meter world-record swim. For another Australian, watching surfers ride 50-foot waves. For a student in Japan, listening to a talk by a Fields Medal–winning mathematician. Here is a story about rare talents from Indonesia:

> There was an autistic boy named Andre. Andre's parents are poor, such that he doesn't go to school at all. Andre tends to leave home without saying goodbye, and once he left home only to be found two years later. Andre has a rare talent, he can know precisely on what day does a certain date fall whenever that is. Me along with five other friends who visited him, he could tell precisely our birth dates. He could also do addition, subtraction, multiplication, and division without any calculating tool whatsoever.

Parents' stories about their children were also common— listening to a fetus's heartbeat, hearing a one-year-old's first word, seeing a two-year-old gallop, being in the audience at a grammar school dance performance. Children are small, but their development is vast, and a source of awe for parents on their better days.

Everyday moral beauty can transform lives. Steven Czifra grew up in a home that was so violent that one night one parent threw boiling water on the other; he doesn't remember who it was. He dropped out of school at ten, got into drugs, shaved his head, and ran with a Mexican gang. One day he broke into a parked Mercedes to steal its stereo the very moment the owner, who happened to be an LAPD officer, arrived. His first night in jail, he told me, he was chained to a chair for eight hours alone in a cold room—some of the longest hours of his life.

It was everyday moral beauty that transformed him. In solitary confinement in prison, he encountered a knowing librarian who fed Steven's hunger for reading; Shakespeare's *Julius Caesar*, and its archiving of courage—"I love the name of honor more than I fear death"—was an epiphany for him. Upon his release from prison, at a halfway house, Steven tells me, a biker got him off drugs and a job clearing brush for seventy dollars a day. More moral beauty. Later, at a community college, a Shakespeare teacher named Larry taught Steven to read Milton like a literary critic, and that the self-loathing in his mind was just that, thoughts, fleeting notions from parents who could have done better. Steven, now in graduate school, would cofound the Underground Scholars Initiative (USI) at UC Berkeley. This is a network of formerly incarcerated students guiding people in prison and just out to make their way to college. USI allows these unlikely college students to find opportunities to allow their *goodness its own speech*.

Within the study of morality it has long been the view that we find our moral compass in the teaching of abstract principles, the study of great texts, or the leadership of charismatic gurus and great sages. In fact, we are just as likely to find our "moral law within" in the awe we feel for the wonders of others nearby.

Illumination

About 4,000 of the 700,000 unhoused people in the United States live on the streets of Oakland, California. Dr. Leif Hass devotes much of his day to caring for their health problems—mental illness, diabetes, hypertension, festering wounds, poor nutrition, drug addictions, and the deterioration of the brain that the cold nights and hard pavement of homelessness bring.

Many health professionals get burned out from this work. Leif Hass stays resilient and close to the Hippocratic oath—to reduce harm—through the moral beauty of the people he cares for. Here is a story of awe he sent me called "A Ray of Light," about a patient who was born with cerebral palsy and lost the use of his hands due to a surgery. The following exchange moved Hass to awe.

"Hey! How you been, Ray?"
He replied: "I just wake up every day and think about what I can do to make people happy."
The goose bumps rise on my arms . . .
"Wow, Ray, you are an amazing person, my friend. Now tell me about what brought you in to the hospital?"
Ray fills me in on the details in the slightly strained and slurred speech that sometimes comes with cerebral palsy. My mind goes to work trying to diagnose this mysterious case of happiness.
We chat for another ten minutes about God and love and looking out for one another.
Finally, I say, "Sorry Ray, I gotta go . . ."
Leaving the room, I feel enlivened, yet also strangely humbled.

Encounters with moral beauty can take us aback, as in Leif's story of awe—they have the power of an epiphany or unforgettable scene in a novel or movie. Philosophical analyses of spiritual epiphany, and novelists' portrayals of personal epiphany, find that the experience is imbued with a sense of light, clarity, truth, and the sharpened recognition of what really matters. Leif's story is titled accordingly—"A Ray of Light"—and follows the patterned unfolding of awe. Ray's overcoming cerebral palsy strikes Leif as vast and mysterious. Ray's generosity shifts Leif from his default self's doctor-patient checklist to appreciating Ray's kindness. Leif wonders why Ray is so happy. His body registers Ray's goodness in goose bumps, a bodily reminder of being part of something larger than the self. He feels "enlivened" and humbled.

Empirical studies have charted the power of witnessing others' courage, kindness, strength, and overcoming. In a study typical of this literature, people first view a brief video of an inspiring act—of Mother Teresa, for example, or Desmond Tutu—or a moving teacher. Or participants are asked to simply recall a personal encounter with everyday moral beauty. These encounters lead people to feel more inspired and optimistic. They feel more integrated in their community—that expanding circle of care. Their faith in their fellow humans and hope for the human prospect rises. They hear a voice akin to a calling to become a better person, and they often imitate others' acts of courage, kindness, strength, and overcoming. Or they share stories of moral beauty with others, like the Norwegian who read the news story about the courageous Yemeni girl. Witnessing acts of moral beauty prompts us more generally to be ready to share and lend a helping hand.

In a compelling study in this vein, participants watched one of three videos. The first was a short clip from the television show *60 Minutes* about Amy Biehl, a white American college student who was murdered by Black youths in South Africa. In their grief, her parents created the Amy Biehl Foundation (now called the Amy Foundation), funding youth programs that help underprivileged Black South Africans to better their lives. Or participants watched a feature about Joel Sonnenberg, who, at twenty-two months old, was badly burned when Reginald Dort slammed his truck into Sonnenberg's family car while trying to crash into a woman he knew. Joel needed forty-five surgeries to survive. At Dort's sentencing, which occurred years after the incident, Joel was the last to speak:

> This is my prayer for you—that you may know that grace has no limits. We will not consume our lives with hatred because hatred brings only misery. We will surround our lives with love.

After watching one of these videos or a control video, the participants—white college students in the United States—could give money to the United Negro College Fund. The twist was that some of these white students had reported high levels of "social dominance orientation," or SDO, an attitude that predicts increased prejudice toward Black people. Hearing the stories of Amy Biehl and Joel Sonnenberg, though, led participants to give more money to the United Negro College Fund, including white participants with strong SDO attitudes. The awe felt in encountering humanity's better angels can counter toxic tribal tendencies.

Witnessing others' acts of courage, kindness, strength, and overcoming activates different regions of the brain than those activated by physical beauty, namely cortical regions where our emotions translate to ethical action. These encounters lead to the release of oxytocin and activation of the vagus nerve. We often sense tears and goose bumps, our body's signals that we are part of a community appreciating what unites us. When moved by the wonders of others, the soul in our bodies is awakened, and acts of reverence often quickly follow.

Reverence

As a child in Xalapa, Mexico—the "City of Flowers"—Yuyi Morales passed the days wondering about extraterrestrials, sometimes hoping they would take her away. Years later, when her son was two months old, her partner learned that his grandfather in San Francisco was very ill. They worried that Grandpa Ernie wouldn't get to meet his only grandchild, so they left in a rush, saying good-bye only to Yuyi's mother.

Once in San Francisco, Yuyi was prevented by immigration law from returning to Mexico. Lonely and isolated, speaking only a few words of English, she struggled. Caring for the new baby exhausted her. She knew no one. Every day, she cried.

So she took to walking.

She wandered the streets of San Francisco with her son in a stroller. One day, she discovered a public library and ventured in. There, in the quiet of a public space, a librarian transformed Yuyi's life. She introduced Yuyi to books. Awestruck, Yuyi would learn to read English. She began sketching scenes from her imagination, which would become her own children's books, including two about people of moral beauty to her—Frida Kahlo and Cesar

Chavez—that have won international awards, most notably the Caldecott Medal. Yuyi's most recent book, *Dreamers*, has an unusual hero—a librarian, archiving the wonders of moral beauty, and *allowing goodness its own speech* for the people checking out books.

When I spoke with Yuyi, she shared a letter of gratitude she sent to the librarian who inspired the story, whose name is Nancy:

Hola Nancy,

Do you remember me? I could never forget you. True, at first I might have been scared of you, guardian at your desk, and too close to the basket of baby books that my son always walked towards when we entered this unbelievable place. The children's book section of the Western Addition public library.

At first I might have been afraid of you. What if I made a mistake? Or broke the library rules? Would you tell us to leave the library because we didn't belong? Instead one day, you talk to me, in English I didn't quite understand, and before we knew it, you were giving Kelly a library card. I was puzzled. Kelly was barely two years old. How could he have anything?

Today, Kelly is a 24-year-old lover of books. He also writes. And he often helps me review and correct my still imperfect English when I write the children's books I create. Books like the ones you put in my hands. Nancy, ever since the library became my home, and books became my path for growth, you have been an amazing guardian. Thank you.

Yuyi's letter of gratitude is one of many acts of reverence in which we appreciate moral beauty, and, more generally, mark the wonders of life as sacred. Subtle is everyday reverence—how we shift our speech with compliments, solicitous questions, and indirectness to show respect for others. Like many mammals, we momentarily shrink the size of our bodies in a subtle head bow or slouch of the shoulders to convey reverential deference. With a simple warm clasp of another person's arm, we can express gratitude and appreciation, activating oxytocin release and the vagus nerve in the recipient of our touch.

We ritualize these ancient and simple acts of reverence into cultural practices. We create symbolic gestures, like the Anjali Mudra greeting gesture in India of palms pressed together and the bowing of head and body, to express respect and shared humanity. We find sacred objects to touch as physical reminders of the wonders that have given us awe—a deceased father's tie, a rock from a backpacking trip, the menu from an engagement dinner, T-shirts from a favorite show. In many hunter-gatherer cultures, people carried around bones and skulls of deceased family members to appreciate their place in their lives. I still regularly touch a wristband Rolf gave me on one of my last visits to him and feel his presence somehow. Acts of everyday reverence, expressed in bowing and touch, for example, can be seen in religious ceremony, funerary rites, and christenings.

So powerful is our tendency to revere, to mark as sacred what brings us awe, that when we witness others expressing gratitude—the simplest act of reverence—we ourselves are moved to kindness. In one study on this, participants were tasked with editing a movie review that was authored by a writer. Before doing their own editing work, participants first looked at a past editor's efforts. In one condition, participants viewed the writer expressing appreciation to that editor with a "thank you." Witnessing this simple act of reverence led participants to be more willing to assist the writer they were responsible for editing. Others' acts of reverence stir us to likeminded actions. We find ourselves joined with others in interconnected webs of reverence.

Moral Beauty Inside and Out

If we are lucky, when we are children our lives are surrounded by everyday moral beauty.

This was not the childhood Louis Scott was born into. When he was six years old, he saw his father murder a man. His mother was a sex worker, and her business filled the days of his childhood, he says, more so than Little League baseball or playing with Tonka trucks. It was only a matter of time before Louis was pimping— and doing very well at it—which led to a host of pimping and pandering convictions and a prison sentence of 229 years. Here is a story of awe he shared with me:

> I was standing before the judge being sentenced to 229 years to life. I can remember being so angry, frustrated, feeling so hurt and ashamed. I felt as though I was being made a public spectacle. Everyone in the courtroom was white. I didn't know if someone was going to step out of the crowd and attempt to shoot me. I can remember my thoughts were everywhere at that time. It was as if I was having an out-of-body experience. I'm standing there watching myself argue with the judge during the sentencing phase of my trial, telling the judge that sentencing me to 229 years to life isn't going to do anything. I was so angry I told the judge that I haven't done anything that this country was not founded upon and I feel that I'm still paying for that statement to this day.

Institutions that embody moral beauty—universities, museums, cathedrals, courthouses, monuments, the criminal justice system—can inspire awe in those who live lives of privilege. For those who've been subjugated by such institutions, the feeling is often much closer to threat-based awe and its bodily expressions, shudders and cold shivers.

Once inside, Louis was transformed by an idea: a way he could bring peace to the confines of prison and stir an awareness in those on the outside about the kindness and courage of those on the inside, allowing a *goodness* so rarely considered *its own speech* within prison. Moved, he has produced award-winning shows for San Quentin Radio on the illusions and costs of gang loyalty inside, living and dying with hepatitis C, and the stigma of AIDS in prison. For the *San Quentin News*, he interviewed the Golden State Warriors and people like Susan Sarandon, Helen Hunt, and Van Jones when they visited SQ. He is the only prisoner to have been elected to the Society of Professional Journalists.

Louis was one of four restorative justice facilitators that first day I visited San Quentin. RJ is grounded in principles of nonviolence: it centers upon perpetrators recognizing the harm they have caused, taking responsibility for their acts, making amends, and expressing remorse. It is a radical and ritualized implementation of the idea that if we allow people, even those in the heat of conflict, the chance for *allowing goodness its own speech*, we can build more peaceful relations, often fragile ones. It is a cultural archive of moral beauty with a long past: RJ dates back to Gandhi and MLK, in our deeper history to Indigenous practices from around the world, and further back in our evolutionary history to mammalian peacemaking tendencies. It is grounded in the conviction of moral beauty, that all people, including those who have murdered and those who've lost loved ones and are overheated with thoughts of revenge, can find kindness and overcome.

A central practice of restorative justice is the talking circle, in which individuals sit in a circle and take turns sharing where they are that day while others simply listen. After my talk on awe, we broke into groups of ten, and Louis led the talking circle I happened to be part of. As we took turns speaking, the men in blue spoke of the following: their remorse, a cellie in his fifties dying in the infirmary, a son landing in prison, an upcoming appearance before the parole board, the latest thinking on sentencing laws, the school-to-prison pipeline, drug legalization, police brutality, and mass incarceration. The conversation often sounded like a graduate seminar in sociology. Louis provided a narrative thread to the disclosures with the slowly measured, grammatically pure clarity of someone used to narrating trauma and uniting warring sides.

On one of my last visits to San Quentin, I sat in a pew most of the day next to a white prisoner named Chris. He had been raised in a white neighborhood in Orange County, California, and fell into that region's street life of skinheads. They required him to go on missions, to "put violent intentions upon other people," namely, people of color. That led to many arrests, and a third-strike conviction for armed robbery, landing him in SQ. There he would join RJ. Here is what Chris said about what he was learning:

In order to make something grow, you gotta own a little dirt
My dirt, in order to grow myself

Chris was growing his hair long, to dissociate from the white supremacist skinheads inside. And he was getting the tattoos on his neck removed one by one. That day, he spoke to the audience of two hundred men in blue. He talked about being a Nazi skin-head. About assaulting people of color with baseball bats. From the pews, I could see the reddening of shame wash over his face. Darwin reasoned that the blush is a manifestation of our moral beauty, signaling that we care about the opinions of others; studies 130 years later would find that others' blushes trigger forgiveness and reconciliation in observers—a millisecond pattern of behavior joining perpetrator and victim in a transformative dynamic at the heart of restorative justice. At the end of Chris's talk, the men in blue shifted in their seats in an awkward silence. Louis strode to the dais and embraced Chris. He noted how much courage it took for Chris to do what he had done.

At break that day Louis introduced me to a prisoner who had done time in solitary. He stood off at an oblique angle, avoiding direct eye contact. People who have done solitary can be overwhelmed by others' faces, in particular, others' eyes. This prisoner, Louis explained, had been part of a hunger strike protesting solitary confinement. He had pressed small notes into the handle of the broom he used to clean parts of the prison. Those notes would make their way into the hands of other prisoners, who in turn passed them on to other prisoners. It was a vast, interconnected web of resistance.

Louis explained to the prisoner that I had written an amicus brief in the case *Ashker v. Governor of California*, which was inspired by the moral beauty of the hunger strike that took place at California's Pelican Bay State Prison. The Ashker in the case is white supremacist Todd Ashker, who had lived twenty-eight years in solitary at the Pelican Bay maximum-security prison in Northern California. In solitary, Ashker spent twenty-three hours a day by himself in a windowless cell about the size of a parking space.

He could see no other prisoners; nor could he hear them after correctional officers covered the front of his cell with plexiglass. Guards "messed with his mail" from his family. He was not allowed to hug visitors. In my brief I argued that depriving prisoners of touch, our most powerful language of reverence, harms them physically and mentally, and worsens their chances for reform. In one study of prisoners in solitary, 70 percent showed signs of impending nervous breakdown, 40 percent suffered from hallucinations, and 27 percent had suicidal ideation. Solitary confinement is the annihilation of everyday moral beauty. One inmate summed it up aptly: "I would rather have gotten the death penalty."

In his cell, Ashker began to call out to leaders of Mexican American and Black gangs in cells nearby and listen through a vent. Their conversations turned to stories of moral beauty: talk about parents and grandparents, fathers and uncles, sisters and brothers, and children. And how hard solitary was. Ashker and his neighbors called for a truce among the rival gangs. On July 8, 2013, Ashker led that hunger strike, which involved more than 29,000 prisoners protesting that solitary confinement is a violation of the Eighth Amendment, which prohibits the use of cruel and unusual punishment. It was the largest hunger protest in U.S. history. Now *that* is vast. In 2015, the case was settled in favor of the prisoners, and more than 2,000 prisoners statewide were moved out of solitary confinement.

When Louis introduced me to the SQ prisoner, we made glancing eye contact, a 250-millisecond act of recognition. I felt a rush of goose bumps at being part of something much bigger than any study I would ever do or talk I might give.

At the end of that day, the men in blue stood to recite the principles of restorative justice. After the shuffle and groaning of two hundred people rising to their feet, a silence fell over us, in that powerful, quiet moment of shared attention. And then we all recited together:

I believe that violence is not a solution to any problem.
I believe that every person is endowed with a sacred dignity.
I believe that every person is capable of changing, healing, and being restored.
I pledge to respect the dignity of every person.
I pledge to overcome violence with love and compassion.
I pledge to accompany and support anyone affected by crime on their healing journey.
I pledge to be an instrument of restoration, of reconciliation and forgiveness.

At the last word, "forgiveness," men turned to one another to shake hands, clasp arms, chuckle softly, and make eye contact in the aftermath of *allowing goodness its own speech*. The room seemed illuminated. Standing at the back of the chapel, Louis and I broke a rule: we embraced. We did so at that slightly oblique angle at which men are wont to hug, one leaning a shoulder into the chest of the other.

That kind of embrace was the last act of reverence between Rolf and me. A couple of weeks before his death, he had been reclining on his couch in the living room, drifting in and out toward a deep sleep; the opiates rendered it oceanic and dreamlike. He rose to a sitting position on the couch and called me, my wife, Mollie, and our daughters, Natalie and Serafina, over to come near him. We pulled in chairs, sitting in a semicircle around him. He gave each of us gifts, telling stories, so often humorous and quirky, about the place of our moral beauty in his life. My gifts were a red, white, and blue wristband, reminiscent of the headband of the same colors that I wore every day when I was thirteen, and a French Opinel knife. I touch its wooden handle every day. The sensations that arise through that tactile contact make me think of Rolf's hands.

Labored, deliberate, Rolf slowly stood up. Body angled by pain, he shuffled to his kitchen. I followed, my body's motion synced up with his since our first years of life. There we embraced. For only two or three seconds. But it felt longer. As we released, he looked to the ground and said:

We made our way.

Other than those words, I can't really remember what we all said that last day in conversation. There was no summing up of a life or speechmaking. What I remember is feeling his chest and shoulder leaning into mine, the top of his head touching near my temple, his large hands on my shoulder blades, and the feelings of awe that ensued. I feel this tactile impression of Rolf today when I embrace people, like Louis. It brings to my mind Rolf's face and eyes. I can almost hear his laugh, and how he answered the phone "Dachman!" It sends me down webs of memories of his courage, kindness, strength, and overcoming: how as a fifth grader he protected the least popular girl in my seventh-grade class from eighth-grade bullies; how he loved to barbecue for large crowds of friends; how he could throw a softball into the sky until it would disappear; or how in his everyday work as a speech therapist he taught the impoverished and most ignored children in our country, who have lived lives thrown off course by ACEs, to utter the sounds of speech. *Allowing goodness its own speech.*

My default self rightly observes that I will never feel that embrace again, or be inspired by new acts of his moral beauty. But my body tells me in this sense of being touched that he is still somehow nearby. That our life together is registered in some permanent, electrochemical awareness in the millions of cells in my skin that make sense of being embraced by my brother. That there is something beyond the corporal body of others' lives that remains in the cells of our bodies when they leave. And that there is so much moral beauty, and so much good work to do.

FIVE

COLLECTIVE EFFERVESCENCE

How Moving in Unison Stirs the Awe of Ritual, Sport, Dance, Religion, and Public Life

*Once the individuals are gathered together, a
sort of electricity is generated from their
closeness and that quickly launches them to an
extraordinary height of exaltation. . . .
Probably because a collective emotion cannot be
expressed collectively without some order that
permits harmony and unison of movement,
these gestures and cries tend to fall into rhythm
and regularity.*

· ÉMILE DURKHEIM

After graduating from college, Radha Agrawal led a hard-charging life in New York City as an investment banker, drinking cocktails she had no thirst for and having conversations that left her mind wandering. Things changed at Burning Man, the annual celebration in the Nevada desert.

Like festivals throughout history, Burning Man weaves together the wonders of life in an experiment in collective awe.

Money is not allowed (although the celebrants are usually well heeled!), so people give to meet mundane needs, enjoying rushes of oxytocin and vagus nerve activation in their acts of food sharing, trade, and grateful embrace. Desert sunrises and sunsets begin and end each day to the *whoa*s and *aah*s of appreciative observers. Music and dance move people into patterns of collaboration, openness, and curiosity throughout the day. Trippy, immersive art installations astonish throughout the pop-up city.

Radha was transformed in dance:

> I couldn't sleep and rode my bicycle out to deep playa (what they call the far ends of the grounds) by myself and found a giant art car (a converted bus that had the most epic sound system I had ever heard with the most incredible bass that I could feel deep into my bones) with a converted roof that was now the throne of a DJ and a hundred-plus people in the sexiest costumes dancing. I threw my bike on the ground and found a spot in the dusty dance floor and closed my eyes and felt the music and bass course through my body in a way that I had never fully allowed (I was sober too!) and let the beat move me the way my body was meant to move, probably for the very first time.

Wondering how to re-create this experience of *moving her body the way it was meant to move*, Radha later hosted a dance party in a basement of a New York City lounge. Bouncers at the door were replaced with huggers. Attendees drank wheat grass instead of alcohol. The celebration took place in the morning rather than at night. And then a couple hundred people danced, experiencing Durkheim's "collective effervescence," the electric exaltation of moving together. The new community called for more. So, Radha, along with her husband, Eli, and his friend from college Tim, created Daybreaker, which now hosts monthly dance parties for 500,000 people around the world. It is a sacred community of groove.

I first meet Radha in 2020 in a San Francisco hotel. Daybreaker is the opening act of Oprah's 2020 Vision tour. When Radha exits the hotel elevator, she shimmies up to me in a sparkling silver jacket that resembles a bird's feathers or fish scales (which she lets me know later she designed herself). Eli is right behind, carrying their daughter, Soleil. They all look weary, having been on the road for ten shows.

We hop into a black van and drive to the Chase Center in San Francisco. In transit, Radha tells me how the grind of working in finance disconnected her from a sense of deeper meaning and community, noting scientific findings as she speaks: Americans today enjoy half as many picnics as we did two decades ago. We have one fewer dear friend in our circle of care than thirty years ago. Thirty-five to 40 percent of people report suffering from loneliness. This dissolving of our sense of community gets our brain's social rejection center humming (in the dorsal anterior cingulate cortex, which tracks the sense of loneliness, rejection, and isolation), which kicks into gear our inflammation response, heating up our bodies in that agitation of being alone. In our twenty-first-century life, we have lost occasions for collective awe.

Daybreaker's act begins with a pulsating performance of three taiko drummers. Backed by dancers, Radha comes onstage and leads 14,500 people through an aerobics-style dance, directing our attention to chakra-like concepts: the forehead and the power of reason, the chest and the warmth of kindness, the stomach and intuition, the sexual regions and passion. Full-on embodiment.

William James would have smiled, and perhaps even swayed his hips. Four high school hip-hop artists bound onstage and electrify the audience.

Standing to the side of the stage, I look into the purple light of the arena. Nearly 15,000 people are dancing. Tightening their lips as they dredge up moves from their past, like the Bump, now shaking more wiggly and wobbly middle-aged bodies. Waves of laughter, clapping, clasped hands, and embraces ripple through rows of people in the arena.

In his 1912 work, *The Elementary Forms of the Religious Life*, Émile Durkheim proposed that this kind of "unison of movement" is the soul of religion. In moving in unison, he theorized, we shift to exalted feeling; we develop a shared awareness of what unites us; we represent this symbolically, often with supernatural and metaphorical ideation, and ritualize moving in unison into rites and ceremonies; and our sense of self transforms. Prior to the big God religions, people were finding the Divine in moving their bodies together *the way they were meant to move.*

Today, a new science of synchrony has figured out the methods and mathematics to chart the patterns in which people sync up their actions with others to reveal how Durkheim's thesis works. We are quick to move in unison with others. In doing so, we feel what others feel, through empathic processes in the brain we shall soon consider. As we become aware of folding into collective movement and feeling, we invoke symbols, images, and ideas to explain what unites us—vast experiences require vast explanations. We explain the pulsating feelings of dancing at a rave in terms of a spiritual principle, for example, or the waves of cheers of a hundred thousand fans at a game by invoking a kind of character, or spirit, that defines our team. We feel awe as our default self gives way to a sense of being part of an interdependent collective. We lose track of time, our goals, and, often, our social inhibitions. Free from the burdens of the self, we feel part of something larger, and inclined toward the "saintly tendencies" of awe.

This wonder of life can overtake us almost anytime we move in unison: In more obvious contexts honed by thousands of years of cultural evolution—rituals, ceremonies, pilgrimages, weddings, folk dances, and funerals. In more spontaneous waves of movement at political protests, sports celebrations, concerts, and festivals. And in more subtle, barely perceptible ways in our mundane lives, such as when we're simply out walking with others as part of the rhythm of our day.

Human Waves of Awe

As Daybreaker's dance unfolds, the emcee, Elliot, pointed to the right side of the arena and announced it was time to do a wave. The waves of sound that were his words stirred a wave of human movement. Like ocean waves far out from shore, this human wave of arms rising began slowly. It picked up momentum as it circled the four curving sides of the arena. Coming into its homestretch, individual bodies became one undulating movement, exulting with *woos*, *woo-hoo*s, and, for those caught off guard by the effervescence of it all, *WHOA*s.

Human waves now ritualistically arise at football games, political rallies, concerts, and graduations. They tend to move clockwise and travel at a speed of twenty seats per second. They occur when nothing meaningful is happening; waves initiated during a keynote speech or the penalty kick will dissipate quickly in half-hearted movements. And they can be started by as few as 20 people in a stadium of 100,000. It takes just a handful of people to stir collective awe.

Moving in unison can also emerge in chaotic contexts. One group of scientists analyzed the movements of concertgoers at a heavy metal show. At the center of such a show is the mosh pit, a maelstrom of colliding bodies. This vortex of bodily chaos, the study found, is surrounded by a slow, undulating wave of tightly packed concertgoers protecting the crowd surfers on top of the mosh pit from truly dangerous falls. Mosh pits, a very symbol of social disorder, have an order that "permits harmony and some unison." Little did those metalheads and punks know.

Our readiness to become part of human waves of different kinds speaks to how wired we are to move in unison. Studies find that four-month-olds mirror the tongue protrusions and smiles of adults, and older children imitate the postures and gestures of teachers, parents, coaches, hip-hop artists, and sports stars. As adults, we mirror others' postures and hand movements; their tones of voice and grammatical tendencies; and their smiles, frowns, blushes, and furrowed brows, often without consciously realizing it. Through such mirroring, the boundaries between self and other dissolve, opening us up to the awe we feel in being part of a collective. Poet Ross Gay observes in his wonderful *The Book of Delights* how striking this "porosity" of human bodies is, "how so often, and mostly unbeknownst, our bodies are the bodies of others." *Moving the way our bodies were meant to move.*

As our bodies become the bodies of others, our biological rhythms synchronize with those of others. Sports fans' heart rhythms synchronize when they watch games together, their collective pulse tracking the agonies and ecstasies of the game. The same proved to be true of villagers in San Pedro Manrique, Spain, who gathered at night to watch a fire-walking ritual. Sources of collective effervescence—ceremonies, musical performances, sports, dances, rituals within churches—shift the rhythms of our bodies to a shared biological rhythm, breaking down that most basic barrier between self and other, the idea that we are physically separated by the boundaries of our skin.

As our bodies and physiologies align with those of others, so too do our feelings. The study of emotional contagion finds that as individuals share spaces and daily living as roommates, neighbors, romantic partners, and work colleagues, their feelings come to resemble one another's. The default self assumes our feelings are unique; the more likely truth is that we are nearly always feeling together.

Through moving in unison and convergence in feeling, a transformation in consciousness occurs: we shift from an egocentric view, seeing the world through our eyes only, to a shared attention to what is transpiring. In elegant and important work, psychologist Michael Tomasello has documented how synchronized social behaviors during childhood—play, pointing, exploring, working on tasks together—enable this capacity for shared attention. In these moments, we combine separate perspectives into a shared perspective, what you might call shared awareness, a collective consciousness, or extended mind.

This is the beginning, quite early in development, of how as adults we gravitate to shared representations of reality. For example, studies find that after traumatic events like terrorist attacks, people initially express unique perspectives, such as the fear of another attack or outrage at the innocent being killed. Over time, individuals' emotions converge; people develop a shared and collective understanding of what has transpired. This convergence in mind leads to goodwill, cooperation, and a transformed sense of self as part of a community.

This process of moving in unison, contagious feeling, shared attention, collective representation, and transcendent self brings us awe in cultural practices when we realize our actions are part of a movement, a community, a culture. These feelings can arise during the rites of funerals, which our twenty-six-culture study found to be a human universal. Here is an experience of awe at a funeral in Sweden, during a moment in which the mourners gathered to collectively say goodbye:

> It was at a funeral where my best friend was buried. I was very sad and it was time to go around the coffin to say the last goodbye. When I laid down my rose on the coffin and said some words to my friend, what she had meant to me for many years, I felt awe. After the ceremony I gave my friend's daughter a hug and went down to the sea because that is the place where I feel calm.

Graduations are also organized around shared attention and moving in unison, as well as exalted feeling, collective representation, and ushering in new identities. Psychologist Belinda Campos experienced this at her graduation recognizing her PhD, at a time when only a handful of Mexican Americans received such an honor—all the more unlikely in her case given that her parents had to stop their educations in fifth grade to go to work. As Campos was leaving the ceremony, a Mexican grandmother told her how much it meant to see someone like her up onstage receiving a doctoral degree. Here is Campos's story of awe:

> The woman's words jerked me out of myself. There were so many sacrifices, individual and collective, that made it possible for someone like me to be up on the stage that day. The chain of life, and sacrifice, suddenly seemed to stretch for generations and span countless people. . . . But the thought of the collective struggle, the people trying to rise, and the urgency of the need for a better, more equal, world fills me with fear-ish wonder and reminds me that anything anyone does is part of the grander human experience.

Ceremonies like graduations locate our individual selves within larger narratives, often occasioning awe and "fear-ish wonder" for historically marginalized people entering mainstream society.

The instinct to move in unison is deep, the transformative power of collective effervescence widespread.

Walking

Perhaps the simplest form of moving in unison is walking with others. Our evolutionary shift from arboreal life to bipedal walking paved the way for awe. As we began to walk upright, our perception of the world changed; we encountered vast vistas and mysteries of what lies beyond. We became a wandering species, timing our migrations and settlements to the cycles and patterns of the sun, weather, seasons, life cycles of flora and fauna, and migratory patterns of other mammals. The ways in which we defended ourselves from predators shifted from scampering individually into trees to fending off peril in synchronized movements together. Through the hunting of large mammals (and also with the emergence of agriculture), food sharing arose, enabled by ritualized ceremonies tied to seasons and harvests. We would eventually walk in small groups (perhaps as small as ten to thirty) to all the continents in the world, beginning in our second out-of-Africa meandering some fifty or sixty thousand years ago.

Today, in walking we routinely shift to moving in unison in ways as principled and predictable as our actions within a human wave. Consider the flow of pedestrians in cities. When sidewalks are exceptionally crowded, studies find, we fall into streams of pedestrians to cross streets, navigating tight spaces and time constraints with greater efficiency. At times this may feel alienating, when we sense we are simply a cog in a city's machine; at other times, it's awe-inspiring, when we feel part of a collective or cultural moment.

In one study of walking in unison, participants were brought to an unusual lab indeed: an enclosed stadium in New Zealand. There, for five minutes, in large groups, participants either walked around the stadium in sync with an experimenter, or they walked freely in their individual gaits and rhythms. Those people who walked together in synchrony, in particular, in arousing, fast movements, stayed closer to one another when asked to disperse, and worked harder on a subsequent task of picking up washers together. Walking in unison gives rise to goodwill and collaboration.

The transcendent feeling of moving in unison is at the heart of rituals and ceremonies. In a study of the narratives of Irish celebrants after St. Patrick's Day parades and Hindu pilgrims to the Magh Mela festival in India (who engage in purification rituals in rivers), experiences of awe were an organizing theme. Celebrants spoke of being part of something much larger than themselves, of a spiritual community, and of being moved by a heightened sense of purpose. In *Keeping Together in Time: Dance and Drill in Human History*, historian William McNeill observes the same, that walking in unison—military units marching, university bands at football games, protesters moving through the streets—activates our sense that we are serving a purpose larger than the self.

In her cultural history of walking, *Wanderlust*, Rebecca Solnit details the revolution in walking that overtook Europe in the seventeenth century, when roads became safe and the outdoors more open to travel, wandering, and exploration. This opening of Europe to walking would give rise to forms of collective walking, from postprandial strolls in town and city squares to wandering with friends in the wild. These different kinds of walking, ranging from the more collective to the solitary, produce, in Solnit's theorizing, an awe-like form of consciousness in which we extend the self into the environment. In walking, we may make connections, for example, between our actions and those of others with whom we are walking, between our thoughts and those of fellow human beings moving through their day, and between the contents of our minds and patterns in nature—the movements of wind through trees or the shifting clouds in the sky. In walking among others you may notice how your bodily actions are part of larger patterns that hold together human societies: schoolkids crossing a street in the early morning, office workers streaming out of buildings to get lunch, shoppers moving through a farmers market at the day's end, young people playing pickup basketball.

Grounded in this idea that walking engages an awe-like form of consciousness, UC San Francisco neuroscientist Virginia Sturm and I developed an awe practice called the awe walk. We were simply naming what has been a universal tradition to seek awe in walking meditations, pilgrimages, hiking, backpacking, and after-dinner strolls. Here were our instructions:

1. Tap into your childlike sense of wonder. Young children are in an almost constant state of awe since everything is so new to them. During your walk, try to approach what you see with fresh eyes, imagining that you're seeing it for the first time. Take a moment in each walk to take in the vast-ness of things, for example in looking at a panoramic view or up close at the detail of a leaf or flower.

2. Go somewhere new. Each week, try to choose a new loca-tion. You're more likely to feel awe in a novel environment where the sights and sounds are unexpected and unfamiliar to you. That said, some places never seem to get old, so there's nothing wrong with revisiting your favorite spots if you find that they consistently fill you with awe. The key is to recognize new features of the same old place.

We suggested that participants take their regular awe walk near trees or bodies of water, under the night sky, or in a place where they could view a sunrise or sunset, and if in urban areas, near large buildings, a historic monument, a neighborhood they had never been to, a stadium, or in a museum or botanical garden. Or, we concluded, they could just wander the streets.

We assembled two groups of participants, all over the age of seventy-five. Why this age? Because starting in our midfifties, until about the age of seventy-five, people get happier. As we get older, we realize that what matters most in life is not money, status, title, or success, but meaningful social connections. At age seventy-five, though, things change. We become increasingly aware of our own mortality, and we see people we love die. After seventy-five, happiness drops a bit and depression and anxiety rise. It's a great age to test the powers of the awe walk.

In our study, in the control condition participants were randomly assigned to engage in a vigorous walk once a week for eight weeks, with no mention of awe. In the awe walk condition, once a week our elderly participants followed the instructions to go on mini awe journeys. All participants reported on their happiness, anxiety, and depression and took selfies out on their walks.

Three findings are of note. First, as our elderly participants did their regular awe walk, with each passing week they felt more awe. You might have thought that when we more often experience awe in the wonders of life, those wonders lose their power. This is known as the law of hedonic adaptation, that certain pleasures—consumer purchases, drinking a savory beer, or eating chocolate, for example—diminish with their increased occurrence. Not so with awe. The more we practice awe, the richer it gets.

Second, we found evidence of Solnit's notion of the self extending into the environment. Namely, compared to participants in the vigorous walk control condition, in the awe walk condition, people's selfies increasingly included less of the self, which over time drifted off to the side, and more of the outside environment—the neighborhood they were strolling in, the street corner in San Francisco, the trees, the sunset, the cavorting children on a climbing structure. The two photos in the top row on the following page come from a woman in our control condition who was gracious enough to share them, with the photo on the left coming from the start of the study and the one on the right taken when out for a

walk; the two photos in the bottom row are from a woman in our awe walk condition (I can see in her second photo a slight laugh of real joy). Pictorial evidence of the vanishing self, and an awareness of being part of something larger.

And finally, over time the positive emotions generated by the awe walk led our elderly participants to feel less anxiety and depression, and to smile with greater joy.

The dour Danish philosopher Søren Kierkegaard, known for his writings on anxiety and dread, found great peace in walking in public spaces. Walking gave him "chance contacts on the streets and alleys," leading him to observe that "it is wonderful, it is the accidental and insignificant things in life which are significant." More everyday awe. And very likely, an awareness of everyday moral beauty in walking among others. Jane Jacobs's thesis in *The Death and Life of Great American Cities* is much the same, that coming into regular contact on foot with neighbors reduces crime and increases well-being. We find community in syncing up our daily wanderings with others, and in the wonders such walking can bring.

Games

I guess I'm the Forrest Gump of basketball.

That's how Steve Kerr sums up his life in basketball on the phone to me, with the 2020 NBA season halted by COVID-19. What he means is that for a skinny, six-foot-three professor's kid, Kerr has had a wonder-filled career playing with Michael Jordan, playing for "Zen master" Phil Jackson and legend Gregg Popovich, and now coaching the Golden State Warriors, who have won three championships under his guidance with some of the most awe-inspiring scoring in the game's history.

I'm on the phone with Steve thanks to Nick U'Ren, director of basketball operations for the Warriors and a former special assistant to Kerr. Hearing of our science of awe, Nick invited me to drop by Warriors practices from time to time. Amid their championship seasons, he landed me tickets for games, where I watched

15,000 fans dance in sync, moved by waves of Warriors scoring. Over a beer one night I asked Nick what the team's secret is. After some thought, his reply: *Movement.*

Seeking to unpack this mystery of movement, I first ask Steve about his early experiences of awe. He quickly recalls watching UCLA basketball as a kid. His dad—a professor of political science at UCLA—had three season tickets, hot items for Steve, his brother, and, on occasion, to their youthful consternation, their mom, who liked to attend but couldn't really tell you who won or lost the game. Steve tells me about a UCLA game from 1973, which he recalls with the precision of a historian. It was UCLA, ranked number one, against Maryland, ranked number two. Coached by John Wooden, UCLA was in an eighty-eight-game win streak, considered the greatest winning streak in sports history (sports analytics awe!). That night UCLA won by one point.

Steve recalls the visceral awe he felt at the game. The pulsing sound of the brass band. The cheerleaders moving in unison leading throngs of fans in waves of cheers. The astonishing size and grace of the UCLA players. The students and fans singing the school song, chanting, clapping, and roaring in harmony with the game. And amid this moving in unison, collective feeling, and shared attention, Steve saw a golden wave of light that moved across the tubas, trumpets, and trombones of the UCLA band.

I ask Steve about his philosophy of movement, expecting to hear about some basketball strategy, new sports analytic, or philosophy of coaching. Instead, he remembers his grandparents Elsa and Stanley Kerr, who built an orphanage for child survivors of the Armenian genocide while living in the Middle East. As Steve travels the world for basketball, Armenians make their way through waves of fans to express their appreciation.

Telling this to you gives me the chills . . . Steve reflects.

He continues: *It's so humbling to think how over one hundred years ago my ancestors and those of the Armenians I meet intersected in ways that changed their lives.*

Steve Kerr's philosophy of movement, of how to coordinate five big, fast bodies into patterns of synchronized collaboration, is found in the forms of moral beauty that moved him from his past, and the idea that different individuals, with their varying cultures and unique tendencies, can be brought together to produce something good. And that games unite people in the appreciation of this moving in unison.

Sports and games, like religion, ritualize our everyday moving in unison, and unite community in the effervescence of playing, watching, cheering, and celebrating (or consoling), as well as reflecting on human capacities, courage, and character. Historical studies find that the Olympics began in 776 BCE in Olympia, Greece, when women and men regularly ran races to settle, playfully, who was fastest. The myth of the games' origins holds that five brothers, gods of fertility, decided to have a running race in honor of the goddess Hera. These races brought communities together in the delights of playful competition and spectatorship, and over time combined with elements of funeral rituals, hymns, prayers, dance, and other physical contests to become the Olympics that inspire awe today.

Some one thousand years before the Olympics began, the Olmecs, Mayans, and Aztecs of Mesoamerica were playing the oldest ball game known—ullamaliztli—on courts throughout Mexico, Guatemala, Belize, and Nicaragua. On the day of the game, priests would consecrate the field with prayers, songs, chanting, and rituals. In the competition, teams of two or three players from neighboring villages tried to push a ball with their hips and elbows through rings on a narrow court surrounded by paintings of Nahua warriors, monkey gods, and Quetzalcoatl, the feathered serpent god. At the game's conclusion, the villagers would gather for dance, music, song, laughter, and revelry. Cultural forms that ritualize moving in unison weave together many wonders of life.

Such movement matters. Flocks of flying birds, schools of fish, and herds of wildebeests fare better against predators when moving in harmony. This is true for humans as well. Cricket teammates whose laughter and joy spread to one another bat better in ensuing innings on the pitch. In one study, it was the *shared feeling* of success, above and beyond players' skills, that predicted the likelihood of victory for teammates playing cricket, football, baseball, and a popular video game. And outside of sports, when musicians in string quartets sway their bodies more in unison, their performances are of higher quality.

As Steve Kerr's Warriors won games thanks to waves of scoring rarely seen before, experts offered explanations. It was the result of certain kinds of passes, or trick plays that Steve had learned like a comedian picks up jokes on the road, such as "the cyclone play" of the Iowa State Cyclones basketball team. When I mention these possibilities, Kerr laughs.

> Basketball is like music. . . . In a band, you don't need five drummers or guitarists. . . . The question is how five players all fit together.

This is a deeper principle of our hypersocial evolution: successful groups move in unison and integrate different talents into a smoothly functioning, synchronized whole. One of the most successful species on the planet, the leafcutter ant, puts the varying skills of its different members to use in a coordinated whole: there are leaf cutters, haulers, builders—all cutting leaves, transporting them, building their home, tending to the queen. Evolution favors species that *move their bodies in the ways they were meant to move.* Our feelings of awe signal to us when we are integrated into these patterns of coordinated movement with others.

I ask Steve about the secret of collective movement. It is the fans, he tells me. *When we are playing our best, they are joyful. They get up off their feet, cheer, and dance.*

Indeed, watching beloved teams brings us awe. Inspired by Durkheim, one sociologist immersed herself in the lives of Pittsburgh Steelers fans. At games on Sundays, fans fall into moving in unison in walking to the stadium and parking lot to enjoy pregame rituals, often involving beer and barbecued food. The collective feelings are effervescent, evident in embraces, crying, howling, arms thrust in the air, and, for some, devotional acts, "saintly tendencies" of physical sacrifice:

A man with a stern face in front of me, probably in his late twenties to early thirties, began to remove layers of clothing. Finally, he pulled his final shirt up over his head and stood cheering and screaming without a shirt in temperatures around 15 degrees Fahrenheit. After a second stellar play on behalf of the Steelers, the man beside him also took off his many layers of coats and shirts and the two clutched hands and screamed.

Steelers fans focus their attention on sacred objects representing their shared identity: Steelers-themed jerseys, coats, lawn chairs, and, during the game, the Terrible Towel, a black-and-gold towel that seventy thousand fans wave in unison to appreciate great plays. Devoted fans describe themselves as "family" and "Steeler Nation"—the default self giving way to something larger.

As we near the end of our conversation, Kerr's former teammate Michael Jordan is on his mind. He recalls how Jordan would remind his teammates that "there are young fans in the stands, there perhaps for their only NBA game, who came to watch us play."

When I ask Steve what his life in sports means to him, he ends our call with this:

It is a civic duty to give people joy.

Grooving

When European colonialists first traveled to Africa, they were awestruck, and more often horrified, by the dances of the people they encountered. Dance's pervasiveness, effervescence, and power unnerved these Westerners seeking fortunes and to "save souls." In Africa, communities danced to appreciate childbirth, puberty, weddings, and death, moving people into a shared understanding of the cycle of life. Groups fell into rousing song with martial sounds and empowering dance when nearing war or when heading out for a hunt, whose success would lead to celebratory dance that paved the way for food sharing. Even forms of labor were symbolized in dances representing agricultural work, planting, digging and harvesting. *Moving their bodies in the way they were meant to move.*

And in Africa, and many Indigenous cultures worldwide, dance was and often still is a physical, symbolic language of awe. Dance symbolized experiences of being in the presence of the Divine. Specific dances told stories about gods and goddesses. The origins of life and the afterlife. Battles between good and evil. People danced to symbolize feelings of awe for thunder, lightning, heavy rains, and overpowering winds, a tradition which, apparently, traces back to a distant predecessor of the chimpanzee waterfall dance.

The idea that dance symbolized the themes of our social living, including the wonders of life, may seem foreign nowadays. That is because in the West, religious powers and the upper classes of European societies extricated dance from our social lives. They did so to constrain and tame its symbolic power, aware of how dance could express passion, freedom, and desire, and not infrequently lead to waves of protest against the ruling classes. Today dance revolutionaries like Radha Agrawal are bringing back this wonder of life, enabling us to *move our bodies the way they were meant to move.*

How might dance allow us to express awe? A sophisticated answer to this question is found in the Natyashastra, a 2,300-year-old text thought to have been written by Hindu sage Bharata Muni in the second century BCE. With the precision you might find in a manual for putting together an IKEA shelving unit, the Natyashastra details how we are to move our feet, hands, fingers, arms, torsos, heads, facial muscles, knees, and hips to express rasas, or emotions, in dance.

Thus, the Natyashastra details that we express anger and rage in dance with a crouch, poised body, clenched hands and arms, tightened mouth and jaw, and fixed gaze (like the haka dance led by Upu of the men in blue).

For love, the Natyashastra recommends that we are to relax our bodies, tilt our heads, open our arms and hands, smile, and mirror the gaze of the beloved (think Gene Kelly in his iconic "Singin' in the Rain" dance.)

For awe, we are to widen our eyes and mouth, look up, and open our arms, shoulders, chest, and hands, the very behaviors we found that express awe in different cultures from around the world. One can see such awe-filled dance today when Pentecostal Christians are moved by the holy spirit or revelers are rolling at a rave.

Dance transforms us in the ways of awe. In a study from Brazil, high school students engaged in dance-like movements, either in sync with others to the beat of a metronome or out of sync with those nearby. Those who "danced" with others, in particular when making more vigorous movements, felt more interconnected. They could also tolerate more pain, a sign of elevated natural opioids, which accompany feelings of merging. Even twelve-month-old babies will help an experimenter pick up dropped pens if the babies have bounced in synchronized rhythm to music with the experimenter.

Over the thousands of years of its evolution, dance, like sports, music, art, and religion, became a way to document awe. In dance, we recognize in a symbolic language what is wonderful (and horrifying) about life. In one relevant study, a classically trained dancer in the Hindu tradition made four- to ten-second videos of her Natyashastra-inspired performances of ten emotions, or rasas. Western Europeans had no trouble discerning the emotions expressed in these brief performances, including those of wonder. When moving in unison through dance, we communicate with others about the sublime.

When we watch the expression of rasas in dance, the Natyashastra continues, we as spectators feel aesthetic emotions known as bhavas. These aesthetic emotions are different from the emotions of our mundane lives, or rasas; we feel bhavas in the realm of the imagination, where we are momentarily and delightfully free of the concerns of our quotidian lives.

How does this work? Current thinking holds that when we see others dance, we instinctively start to mimic their actions, which you may sense in your foot tapping or body swaying. These bodily movements then lead our embodied minds to bring to consciousness ideas, images, or memories related to the actions expressed in the dance. A dancer's portrayal of awe, for example, might lead you to open your body ever so slightly and shift your gaze upward. You may recall past encounters with a wonder of life or imagine possible wonders you might enjoy. All of this, it merits noting, takes place in the realm of the imagination, where we are free to consider what is possible.

When dancing together, we share the delights of moving our bodies. And we experience flights of our imagination in seeing others dance. This all can bring about a porous intermingling of bodies and minds we experience as collective effervescence. No wonder dance is so transporting, and so often borders, like the collective effervescence of sports, on the spiritual.

SIX

WILD AWE

How Nature Becomes Spiritual and Heals Bodies and Minds

*Those who dwell, as scientists or laymen,
among the beauties and mysteries of the earth
are never alone or weary of life.*

· RACHEL CARSON

My collaborators Jennifer Stellar and Neha John-Henderson and I had a hunch about how awe may be an antidote to our overheated and overstressed times. We suspected that awe may reduce the inflammation produced by our immune system, in particular that which arises in response to chronic threat, rejection, and loneliness. How? Why might the wonders of life shift this problematic inflammation? Because in many ways, awe is the antithesis to the social threats that cause the release of proinflammatory cytokines.

Proinflammatory cytokines are released in immune cells throughout your body to kill invading bacteria and viruses. In the short run, cytokines heat up your body to kill the pathogen, leaving you feeling sluggish, vague, achy, and disoriented as the body marshals resources to fend off the attack and recuperate. The trouble, though, is that the human mind treats social threats like an invading pathogen: studies find that social rejection, shame, being the target of prejudice, chronic stress, loneliness, and threats to loved ones elevate cytokine levels in your body.

Awe, by contrast, heightens our awareness of being part of a community, of feeling embraced and supported by others. Feeling awe, we place the stresses of life within larger contexts. Perhaps everyday awe, we wondered, would be associated with lower inflammation.

To test this hypothesis, we gathered measures of inflammation (as assessed in the biomarker Interleukin 6, or IL 6). Participants also reported on their everyday awe by offering responses on a seven-point scale (1 = not true, 7 = very true) to questions like:

I often feel wonder about what is around me.
I feel awe outside regularly.

We also measured the tendency to feel other positive emotions, such as pride and amusement. In this study, it was *only awe* that predicted lower levels of inflammation. Everyday awe, then, can be a pathway for avoiding chronic inflammation and the diseases of the twenty-first century such inflammation is associated with, including depression, chronic anxiety, heart disease, autoimmune problems, and despair. This finding caught the attention of a very large human being who knew the inflammation of trauma well.

Stacy Bare stands six feet, eight inches tall. He has a giant beard and a massive head that stretches the biggest beanies. His voice has the tree-shaking pitch of a moose call. When thoughts of his deployments in Iraq and Afghanistan move through his mind, his gaze shifts to the side and his lips retract—traces of a cry of distress, perhaps, for brothers in combat or innocent Iraqis lying dead by the side of the road. When he talks about the need to do more for veterans than numb their minds with pharmaceutical cocktails, or when he recalls a veteran friend who just took his own life, his prose and prosody slow, moved by a conviction found in getting very close to human suffering.

During his childhood in South Dakota, Stacy was inspired by his grandparents' stories of awe from serving in the U.S. Navy in World War II. At age nineteen he tried to enlist but was rejected; he was too tall. Instead, he joined the army, serving in Iraq and Afghanistan. During these engagements, he suffered from chronic inflammation. This didn't prevent him from finding awe:

During my year in Iraq I was in a near-constant state of low-grade to high-grade funk. I was being forced into a horrific policy decision and a poorly run war every day. I'd lost friends, watched Iraqis being killed, endured blasts and rifle shots and mortar fire and food that made me crap my pants once a month. I worked mostly for a string of ever-changing leadership, each one intent on "making a difference" in their own way.

The light shifted dramatically.

I turned around and saw a huge, pulsing orange wall charging down the road and obliterating everything in its path. Less than a second and the buildings and cars that stretched on either side of the road were gone. I ran, laughing and smiling, to duck into a concrete structure, a little bunker, on the side of the road. I kept my back against the wind but all around me the bunker filled up with fine misted sand. It caught in my mouth and in my throat, but I couldn't stop smiling or laughing.

The world was a huge place and I was just a tiny speck in it. My challenges and concerns and worries of life all were erased in an instant as I just tried to breathe. It was a remarkably freeing feeling amidst an otherwise incredibly imprisoning year. In its total obliteration, I also found the dust storm magnificently beautiful.

Even after the dust storm raged past, the orange sky stuck around for a while. There would be other orange skies that I'd stare up into that year in Iraq but never had I been stuck inside the storm as it scoured past me. We can do whatever we want on this planet, I remember thinking, but the world will always win—so we might as well build as much joy, real joy for all people while we're here.

So often, vast circumstances confine us, like a life sentence in prison or tending to people who are dying, or racist immigration law, or combat, circumstances that seem to "always win." But in recognizing the vastness of such fates, that we are "a tiny speck" in a "huge place," we can find a "freeing feeling" and even an urge to build "real joy for all people." We so often experience transformative awe in the hardest of circumstances.

After returning to the United States, Stacy fell into an over-heated abyss. He had lost good friends on tour. His girlfriend broke up with him while he was away. Images of the dead invaded his mind: a young girl killed by U.S. bullets; a dog eating the neck of a bloated dead man in a pile of trash. About one in five Gulf War veterans falls into major depression. The suicide rate for younger veterans, like Stacy, is among the highest of any group in the United States. About a quarter of veterans binge-drink regularly. Stacy turned to hard alcohol, cocaine, and speed. And edgy, compulsive partying. A suicidal voice was making loud suggestions in his mind.

As he was spiraling downward, a friend insisted that before Stacy blow his brains out, he go climbing with him on the Flatirons near Boulder, Colorado, a series of five sandstone slabs that jut upward to heights of over seven thousand feet. Stacy had rappelled down tall vertical walls dozens of times. On this day, though, tied to a wall of rock, looking down hundreds of feet, he froze. His body trembled. He sobbed. What was the point of his service? A career in the military? The lives of the people he saw die? His life? A single phrase arose in his mind.

GET OUTDOORS.

Strange Sympathies

Every experience of awe you enjoy today links you to the past, to others' experiences of the sublime and how they made sense of them within the ever-evolving cultural forms that archive the wonders of life. Stacy Bare's experience of wild awe traces back to an epiphany experienced by Jean-Jacques Rousseau.

In 1749, Rousseau was on his way to visit his friend, the philosopher Denis Diderot, who was serving time in a prison in the outskirts of Paris. As he walked through rolling hills, Rousseau mulled over this question: "Has the progress of the sciences and arts done more to corrupt morals or improve them?" Today we might ask: "Have globalization and capitalism lifted up our quality of life, or paved the way for our demise?"

Contemplating that question knocked Rousseau to the ground. In a trance state, he saw the brightness of a thousand lights. He sobbed uncontrollably. He was shaken by an epiphany: The much-hyped promise of the Age of Enlightenment, of science, industrialization, formal education, and expanding markets, was a lie. It was destroying the soul of humanity. It was a companion of the systems of slavery and colonization, and a cause and rationalization of economic inequality. It was decimating the forests of Europe, polluting its skies, and filling its streets with filth. And smothering the wisdom of emotion.

Rousseau's epiphany was that in our natural state, we are endowed with passions that guide us to truth, equality, justice, and the reduction of suffering—our moral compass. We sense these intuitions in music, art, and, above all, being in nature. It is institutions like the church and formal education that disconnect us from our nobler tendencies. In that experience outdoors in the hills outside of Paris, Romanticism was born.

Within the philosophy of Romanticism, the purpose of life is to free yourself from the confines of civilization. Find yourself in freedom and exploration. Passion, intuition, direct perception, and experience are privileged over reductionistic reason. Life is about the search for awe, or what the Romantics called the sublime. Music is a sacred realm. Natural processes—thunder, storms, winds, mountains, clouds, skies, life cycles of flora and fauna—have spiritual meaning and are where, above all else, we find the sublime. Rousseau was urging Europeans to get outdoors.

The spirit of Romanticism would inspire Mary Shelley to write *Frankenstein* during a stormy holiday in the Alps. It would stir the poetry of Coleridge, Percy Bysshe Shelley, and Wordsworth, which my mom taught in her English courses at California State University, Sacramento. This spirit gave rise to a holistic kind of science that sought truth in images, metaphors, art, and unifying ideas alongside the necessary, reductionist breaking down of phenomena into parts. It led to the epic voyages of James Cook, Alexander von Humboldt, and eventually Darwin, and their poetic portrayals of the natural world. Romanticism transformed our relationship to nature, once viewed with terror and superstition.

Ralph Waldo Emerson was moved by this spirit of Romanticism. Grief-stricken at the death of his wife, Ellen, at age twenty-two, Emerson traveled to Europe, making his way to Paris. There, in July 1833, Emerson experienced an epiphany in the Jardin des Plantes.

In 2018, I felt impelled to visit the Jardin des Plantes, and went inside its Gallery of Paleontology and Comparative Anatomy, which is the size of a basketball gym at a small college. Its insides look like a train station that might have been painted by impressionist Claude Monet: cast-iron frames surround an off-white, diaphanous ceiling illuminated from outside. Upon entering, the visitor is greeted by a sculpture from 1758 of a skinless man with

Here is our leader of the awe walk of comparative anatomy. This sculpture is from 1758 and was used at the Académie des Beaux-Arts in drawing classes.

123

taut red muscles. He stands in front of a procession of a hundred or so skeletons of every imaginable species, from gorillas to narwhals to hyenas to chimpanzees. It is a day-of-the-dead awe walk of comparative anatomy. His head and eyes are oriented upward to a far-away horizon, or perhaps the skies, his mouth open, his eyes alive. He is awe in the flesh.

Touring the perimeter of this march of skeletons, I encountered jars containing the brains of pigs, dogs, elephants, and humans. One held a white kitten floating in blue fluid, frozen as if falling from deep space to the ground. Crude papier-mâché sculptures of bisections of various animals stood in cabinets. In one area, jars contained genetic anomalies—a headless puppy, a two-headed pig, human twin fetuses joined at the jaws. Visiting children stood unusually close to their parents, leaning in, their mouths agape. The parents fumbled for words to explain.

For Emerson, the riches of nature, of organized flora and fauna, that he encountered in the Jardin des Plantes stirred wild awe:

Here we are impressed with the inexhaustible riches of nature. The universe is a more amazing puzzle than ever, as you glance along this bewildering series of animated forms. . . . Not a form so grotesque, so savage, nor so beautiful but is an expression of some property inherent in man the observer,—an occult relation between the very scorpions and man. I feel the centipede in me,—cayman, carp, eagle, and fox. I am moved by strange sympathies. I say continually "I will be a naturalist."

In Emerson's being moved by "strange sympathies," we find the pattern of awe—vastness ("inexhaustible"), mystery ("the universe is a more amazing puzzle"), and the dissolving of boundaries between the self and other sentient beings ("occult relation"; "I feel the centipede in me"). Amid the profusion of forms of different species, even the lowly centipede, there is an intuited life force that unites us all. Emerson's epiphany was about the big idea in the air at the time: that all living systems, from the skeletons, organs, muscles, and tissues of different species to the sense of beauty and design in our minds, have been shaped by natural selection. He was sensing a sacred geometry underlying what Darwin would call "endless forms most beautiful," and decided that day to "be a naturalist," finding his spiritual life in wild awe.

A Need for Wild Awe

In 1984, Harvard biologist E. O. Wilson called the "strange sympathies" Emerson felt in the Gallery of Comparative Anatomy *biophilia*, the love of life and living systems. Biophilia encompasses a rich palette of passions we feel in relation to nature. The most widely studied of these is the feeling of beauty, which we experience in viewing familiar and pleasing landscapes, such as those with rolling hills, trees, a stream or other source of water, thriving flora and fauna, and a place of elevation. Those feelings of beauty signal to our minds the resource abundance (or scarcity) and safety of a locale and orient us and those we are moving in unison with (in the context of our evolution) to set up camp in what we would call home.

We experience biophilia in almost any kind of nature, from viewing the changing colors of leaves to the phases of the moon. More everyday awe. There are robust communities that have grown out of the awe we feel for clouds, the ocean, waves, trees, and birds, to name just a few. And gardens. Should you encounter flowers in a garden, fragrant pollinating forms of colorful geometry, you are likely to feel sensory delight, a sense of beauty, and perhaps awe, and be more inclined to cooperate. The scents in the garden—of basil, rosemary, camellia, peach, pine—send neurochemical signals from your olfactory system through emotion- and memory-related regions of the brain to the frontal lobes, including the orbitofrontal cortex, where our tendencies toward ethical actions are moved by our emotions. Scents in gardens take us on an awe-inspiring journey, often back in time to other moments of significant fragrance. Those scents signal to us what is pure, life-generating, rewarding, good.

How might we make the case that we have a biological need for wild awe, a need that is on par with our needs for protein-rich food, thermoregulation, sleep, oxygen, and water?

Or the more social needs, like being loved, cared for, touched, esteemed, and respected?

Basic, evolved needs unfold reliably during our development, are supported by specific neurophysiological processes, and if unmet, lead to poor health and social dysfunction. Within this framework, our biological need to belong is clear: it emerges reliably early in a child's life, is supported by broad networks of neurochemicals (dopamine, oxytocin) and regions of the body (the vagus nerve), and if unmet—think solitary confinement or being an orphan from a civil war—leads to the deepest kinds of dysfunction, such as the stunting of the growth of the brain, chronic illness, depression, and premature death.

Do we have a biological need for wild awe? Let's begin with the question of development. When given the chance, children find abundant awe exploring the outdoors; pouring liquids and filling buckets of sand; collecting bugs, twigs, and leaves; climbing trees and digging holes; splashing water; and marveling at the rain and clouds. Our remarkably long childhood emerged in our evolution to allow for the exploration and play necessary for learning about the natural and social environments. Less controlled by the prefrontal cortex (and the default self), children's brains form more synaptic connections between neurons than adults' brains and are more oriented toward novel explanation and discovery. The child's awe-filled relationship to the natural world is a laboratory for deep learning about the systems of life, essential to our survival.

With respect to the neurophysiology of wild awe, the sights, sounds, scents, and tastes of nature lead to awe-related vagus nerve activation and reduce fight-or-flight cardiovascular response, blood pressure, cortisol, and inflammation. Here are but a few empirical examples of how our bodies are like an antenna when outdoors in nature. The sounds of water activate the vagus nerve. Certain scents in nature calm our stress-related physiology. Many plants give off phytoncides, chemical compounds that reduce blood pressure and boost immune function. Encounters with images of nature lead to the activation of dopamine networks in the brain, which animate, you will recall, exploration and wonder.

And as with any biological need, when our need for wild awe is satisfied, we fare better, and when it is thwarted, we suffer in mind and body. In testing this thesis, controlled studies have had people go on walks in nature, or had them view images or videos of awesome nature or see how people living near accessible green spaces fare. Scientists in South Korea and Japan have studied the effects of forest bathing, where people are led through immersive awe experiences in forests—for example, walking, taking in scents, feeling leaves and bark on the skin and with the hands, contemplating for a moment a tree and its remarkable design. When we satisfy our need for wild awe, it is good for our minds; we concentrate better, handle stresses with more resilience, and perform better on cognitive tests of different kinds.

Frances Kuo, a pioneer in the science of wild awe, had children diagnosed with attention-deficit/hyperactivity disorder go for a walk of comparable length and physical exertion in a green park, a quiet neighborhood, or noisy downtown Chicago. Children scored better on a measure of concentration only after the walk in the park. Getting outdoors in nature empowers our attention, what William James called "the very root of judgment, character, and will," and our ability to discern what is urgent from what is not and how to place the hectic moments of our days into a broader narrative. In geographical regions where the population has greater access to beautiful green spaces, people report greater happiness and goodwill toward others.

In fact, it is hard to imagine a single thing you can do that is better for your body and mind than finding awe outdoors. Doing so leads to the reduced likelihood of cardiovascular disease, respiratory disease, diabetes, depression, anxiety, and cancer. It reduces asthma in children. It leads to reductions in everyday aches and pains, allergies, vertigo, and eczema. These benefits of being in nature have been observed across the life span, ranging from newborns (who enjoy higher birth weight when born near green spaces) to the very elderly. Our bodies respond to healthy doses of awe-inspiring nature like we respond to a delicious and nutritious meal, a good sleep, a quenching drink of water, or an uplifting gathering with friends or family: we feel nourished, strengthened, empowered, and alive.

Our need for wild awe is strong.

Wild Awe on a River

When Stacy Bare finished climbing the Flatirons and was back on his feet, he would get outdoors with force, rock climbing, hiking, backpacking, skiing, and rafting. He was struck by an idea about the inflaming traumas of combat. When deployed, people in the armed services find awe in the places where they serve and people they meet, in their sense of family, in the transcendent intensity of being on tour, and in the frequent courage seen in combat. It is often a dark, threat-filled awe that can quickly shift to horror at carnage, chaos, violence, perpetrating harm, and watching young people die. But there is awe there. And the transition to civilian life leaves veterans hungering for awe.

Moved by this idea, Stacy dedicated his life to giving wild awe away. In his work with the Sierra Club, he created programs for hundreds of thousands of people each year to find wild awe on walks, hikes, backpacking, rafting, and rock climbing. He took veterans who had lost limbs in combat and climbed with them up sheer rock faces. He has returned with veterans to places of combat but for purposes of recreation, skiing with locals in the beautiful mountains of Iraq and Afghanistan. For this giving away of wild awe he was named a National Geographic Adventurer of the Year.

When Stacy heard about our study showing how awe reduces inflammation, he suggested we collaborate on a study of wild awe. Our lab was a collection of rafts on the American River, a 120-mile-long watercourse that begins in the Sierra Nevada mountains and winds its way through the foothills to Sacramento, passing through the hills that Rolf and I wandered throughout our brotherhood. Rafting the river alternates between lazy, daydreaming meandering and exhilarating, at times frightful, moments navigating class II rapids with names like Meat Grinder, Satan's Cesspool, Dead Man's Drop, and Hospital Bar, which if navigated poorly lands you on Catcher's Mitt, a big rock that has a penchant for trapping rafts. After the Hospital Bar, though, rafters can heal their banged-up bodies in the Recovery Room. Some of my fondest memories from my childhood are navigating that river in rafts and inner tubes with Rolf and our parents and their friends, drifting in the sun, looking for hours at light on the water, seeing the shadowy brown outlines of rainbow trout below, and feeling the flow and character of the river currents move our bodies and laughter and conversation into a sun-saturated, sparkling unison.

We had two groups of participants. The first included students from underresourced high schools in Oakland and Richmond, California, schools lacking the green spaces and organic gardens often present in private schools and well-to-do suburban public schools. Many of the teens had never been camping. Growing up in poverty, like these teens did, leads to elevated stress, a greater likelihood of anxiety and depression, and chronic inflammation. Veterans comprised our other group. Veterans can show the same trauma-shaped stress profile as kids raised in poverty: disrupted sleep, intrusive thoughts, difficulties concentrating, and the vigilant sense that peril hovers nearby.

Prior to the rafting trip and one week after, I and my collaborators at UC Berkeley, Craig Anderson and Maria Monroy, gathered measures of stress, well-being, and post-traumatic stress disorder (PTSD), the latter based on reports of sleep disruption, intrusive memories, flashbacks, and feeling on edge. Before and after the rafting trip, participants spat into little vials so that we could assay changes in stress-related cortisol over the course of the excursion.

We mounted GoPros on the fronts of the rafts, allowing us to film, up close, coordinated rowing, synchronized hoots and hollers, collective laughter, oar touching and celebratory calls after navigating dangerous rapids, shrieks of fear, and vocal bursts of awe—*wow, ooooooh, aah, whoa*. After lunch on the day of the rafting trip, we asked our teenagers and veterans to write about their experiences on the river, to tell their stories of wild awe.

As in walking, playing and watching sports, dance, ritual, and ceremony, over the course of the day raft mates' emotions and physiologies synchronized. At the start, raft mates' cortisol levels were all different; by the end of a day of moving in unison, their cortisol levels converged. The raft mates also synchronized in their emotional expressions: some rafters emoted together on their rafts in shrieks and howls; others vocalized together in symphonies of *oooh*s and *whoa*s. The porous bodies of raft mates were merging.

A week after the trip, both teens and veterans felt less stress. They reported greater well-being. The teens reported better relations with friends and family. Veterans showed a 32 percent drop in the feelings and symptoms associated with PTSD.

The reasons why rafting might benefit us are many: the endorphin high of physical exertion, recreating with others, enjoying a breather from life's hardships, the sights and scents of trees and sounds of the river. In more fine-grained analyses we found that it was awe that brought about the mind-body benefits of being outdoors. Here is a story of awe from a teenage participant:

> There was a point today where I noticed . . . everything. There was smoke rolling over the hills, I felt in awe. There was water cresting and breaking over the boat, I felt wonder. I felt peaceful.

And one from a veteran speaks to how awe can heal trauma by putting things in perspective:

> Looking up at the star-spattered sky, I thought about the universe and how infinite it is. It makes what I do feel less important; but the opportunity of what I could do more powerful and lightweight. I never see how many stars are in the sky like I did tonight.

Awe can make us feel that our life's work is both less important than our default self makes it out to be and yet promising in purpose and possibility. Teens' and veterans' reports of feeling awe during the middle of the trip, rather than pride or joy, accounted for why they felt less stressed, more socially connected, more loving toward their families, and happier one week later.

Teenagers in our study of wild awe

Mean Egotism's Demise

One clear, frigid day, while crossing a common in Concord, Massachusetts, Ralph Waldo Emerson was overcome by wild awe, which he described in a well-known essay from *Nature* from 1836:

> In the woods, we return to reason and faith. There I feel that nothing can befall me in life—no disgrace, no calamity (leaving me my eyes), which nature cannot repair. Standing on the bare ground,—my head bathed by the blithe air and uplifted into infinite space,—all mean egotism vanishes. I become a transparent eyeball; I am nothing; I see all; the currents of the Universal Being circulate through me; I am part or particle of God. The name of the nearest friend sounds then foreign and accidental; to be brothers, to be acquaintances, master or servant, is then a trifle and a disturbance. I am the lover of uncontained and immortal beauty.

In many ways, "mean egotism" has become a defining social ill of our times. For various reasons, our world has become more narcissistic, defined by self-focus, arrogance, a sense of superiority, and entitlement (although since 2009, narcissism, encouragingly, has dropped slightly). Narcissism can trigger a myopia to others' concerns, as well as aggression, racism, bullying, and everyday incivility. Not to mention hostility toward the self: narcissism fuels depression, anxiety, body image problems, self-harm, drug abuse, and eating disorders.

To test Emerson's mean egotism hypothesis, UC Irvine

professor Paul Piff and I took students to an awe-inspiring stand of blue gum eucalyptus trees on the UC Berkeley campus. The Eucalyptus Grove is very near the museum that houses the replica of the *T. rex* skeleton where students did the I AM study of how awe reveals our collective selves. Out in the trees, in one condition, participants looked up into the bark, branches, leaves, and light on the eucalyptus for two minutes, and took in the wonders of what trees are and give. In the other, they stood in the same place, but looked up at a science building (see images below).

After briefly looking up into the trees, our participants reported, in response to questions asked of them by the experimenter, that they were feeling less entitled and narcissistic. When told of the compensation for being in the study, they asked for less

The awe condition   The control condition

money, citing reasons such as "I no longer believe in capitalism, man." And as all participants were answering these questions, a person—actually in cahoots with us—walked by and dropped a bunch of books and pens. Our participants feeling wild awe picked up more pens than those who looked up at the building.

As mean egotism fades during wild awe, do we "return to reason"? Do brief doses of wild awe enable us to see our lives and worlds more clearly? In the most general sense, this is true: experiences of awe lead us to a greater awareness of the gaps in our knowledge and to consider more rigorously arguments and evidence. Consider the following study focused on wild awe and reasoning in backpackers out in the backcountry. Some backpackers completed a reasoning task prior to hitting the trails in the wilds of Alaska, Colorado, Washington, and Maine; others did the same reasoning task on the fourth day of the trip. The measure of reasoning was ten items from the Remote Associates Test, in which participants are given sets of three words—e.g., "age," "mile," and "sand"—and asked to generate one word that relates to all three. The answer in the example is "stone." This requires that people find solutions based on diverse kinds of reasoning—noting synonyms, creating compounds of words, and tracking semantic associations. Backpackers on their fourth day out in the backcountry performed 50 percent better on this reasoning task than those hikers just setting out.

Perhaps the most perilous flight from reason today, outside of the denial of human-caused climate crises, is the trend toward polarization in politics. It's a kind of collective mean egotism. Polarization—viewing ideological and moral issues as matters of a culture war between good and evil people—has risen in the past twenty years as the result of biases in reasoning. We assume that we are reasonable judges of the world, and when we encounter people who have different views than our own, we attribute their views to ideological bias, concluding that they are nothing but wild-eyed, fanatical extremists.

My Berkeley collaborator Daniel Stancato and I wondered whether experiences of wild awe might defuse such polarization. In our study, participants watched either BBC's *Planet Earth* or a control video. They then were asked to indicate their own views on one of the most polarizing issues of the times—police brutality. Following this, they placed other U.S. citizens into different camps on the issue and offered estimates of those partisans' views. Awe led participants to perceive the issue in a less-polarized fashion, meaning that they believed that the gap between their views and those of their opponents to be less vast.

Natural Divine

As we have returned to the outdoors in the spirit of Romanticism, many have found more than the quieting of the default self, healthy body and mind, and sound reason. In-depth interviews reveal that Americans often sense the Divine in nature, and feel that they are near that which is primary, all-encompassing, and good. When looking at the movement of a river, or hearing birdsong, or watching clouds, or sitting quietly amid a stand of trees, people feel as though a benevolent force is animating the life around them, which they are part of. In other research, people reported spiritual experiences in backpacking, birding, rock climbing, and surfing.

Still other evidence suggests that nature may be its own kind of temple, offering innumerable spaces where we might experience what we perceive to be the Divine. In one study, sociologists assessed the natural beauty of each of the 3,100 counties in the United States, in terms of the sun, weather, water, and topographical diversity that the county offered. As a county's natural wonders rose in abundance, its denizens were less likely to attend church or adhere to a religion's dogmas. Getting outdoors is its own form of religion, though one that takes people away from the buildings, gatherings, ceremonies, and dogmas of a formalized church.

Getting outdoors is returning us to what Indigenous scholars call traditional ecological knowledge, or TEK. TEK is an Indigenous science of our relationship to the natural world, taking varying and local forms in the five thousand or so Indigenous cultures around the world. It has evolved into a cultural belief system, or way of knowing, or science, through tens of thousands of hours of observing flora and fauna, weather systems, the powers of plants, migration patterns of animals, and life cycles; compiling the data; testing hypotheses with empirical evidence and cultural input from elders; and the transmission of knowledge through oral, religious, and pictorial traditions.

Within TEK, species are recognized as *interdependent*; they are interconnected and collaborating within ecosystems.

All things are animated by a vital life force, spirit, or *shared substance*. During experiences of wild awe, we may sense that we share a form of consciousness with other species, a thesis tested in studies showing how plants, fungi, flowers, and trees communicate with one another, and even show forms of intentionality, awareness, and, dare one say, kindness toward others.

Within TEK, *impermanence* is assumed: all living forms are in flux, always changing, being born and dying, from the first moment of life to its end. We sense this principle in the cycles around us, of the light of the day and night, seasons, the growth and decay of plant life, and life and death itself.

Finally, *the natural world is to be revered*. And indeed, awe promotes the reverential treatment of nature. In one study, after brief experiences of awe, people in China reported being more committed to using less, recycling more, buying fewer things, and eating less meat (former U.S. secretary of energy Steven Chu observed that the carbon emissions of the world's cows alone, if considered a country, would rank right behind China and the United States).

Wild awe awakens us to this ancient way of relating to the natural environment. And in this awakening, we find solutions to the inflaming crises of the times, from overstressed children to overheated rhetoric to our burning of fossil fuels. Wild awe returns us to a big idea: that we are part of something much larger than the self, one member of many species in an interdependent, collaborating natural world. These benefits of wild awe will help us meet the climate crises of today should our flight from reason not destroy this most pervasive wonder of life.

In the summer after my brother's passing, I planned a number of high-altitude hikes, hoping in some way that Rolf would be by my side. The first was a one-hundred-mile route around Mont Blanc, which Jacques Balmat first summited in 1786 after fifteen tries. Mountaineer Horace Bénédict de Saussure, who summited Mont Blanc shortly after, heard the voice of the natural Divine there:

The soul ascends, the vision of the spirit tends to expand, and in the midst of this majestic silence one seems to hear the voice of nature and to become certain of its most secret operations.

Moved by this ascent, poet William Wordsworth walked seven hundred miles from Cambridge, England, to see the mountain with his sister, Dorothy. Book 6 of his epic poem, *The Prelude*, is devoted to that journey. In wandering the valleys, villages, ridges, and passes toward Mont Blanc in search of "Supreme Existence," Wordsworth found "life's morning radiance" on the hills and "benevolence and blessedness." And the vanishing self in leaving behind "life's treacherous vanities."

The poem's first line would return to me many times in my search for awe:

O there is a blessing in this gentle breeze.

In grief, I felt my brother to be touching me, speaking to me, in breezes.

A few lines later, Wordsworth observes:

Or shall a twig or any floating thing
Upon the river point me out my course?

This sentence oriented me to everyday awe: look to the ordinary, like the twig floating in the currents of the river, to find new wonders of life and, for me in grief, new directions my life will take now lacking my younger brother.

After I landed in Geneva and located my hiking group, we took a bus to Chamonix, France. *The Prelude* was in my backpack, a gift from my mom from her decades of teaching this archive of awe. On our ascent into the Alps, I saw a wind move through a stand of aspen trees, flickering leaves into alternating patterns of light and dark in the midday sun. I heard Rolf's sigh moving the leaves.

A previous summer—on our last annual mountain hike together—he and I had stood amid a group of aspens in the eastern Sierras that flickered in the same way, laughing at this arboreal show of interdependence and impermanence.

After the orientation that first night, I was approached by a woman in our group of twelve, tall and reserved, with clear, simple phrasing. She would have been very much at home in California's Gold Rush era in the Sierras where Rolf had lived. Upon meeting me, she asked, "Are you Rolf Keltner's brother?"

I would learn on the trails that she was his colleague at the school where he taught as a speech therapist, her office right across from his. She told stories of awe about his work. How he could calm the boys down with bear hugs when they were out of control. The spring following Rolf's death, a vine she had planted blossomed for the first time in years. She sensed him in that flowering.

Hiking each day, we would catch glimpses of Mont Blanc at ever-changing angles, through always-shifting cloud cover and fast-moving mists, while wandering through green valleys and up rocky passes, seeing Wordsworth's "morning radiance" and being awe-struck by the Alps' "succession without end." Mont Blanc is never the same. Cloud-shrouded one day. Luminous and creamy the next. Often barely discernible. Other times vast and transfixing. I came to feel transparent to "the all." I felt the green seep into my body, porous to the mountains. The blithe air indeed lifted my sense of self into an infinite, clear space. I sensed Rolf spread out through the Alps' valleys and in the air surrounding their peaks.

On the last day of the tour, I took the gondola up to the top of Mont Blanc, packed in with rock climbers, tourists, Swiss families, and excited children, all hooting when we were carried up the face of the mountain. On the return we dropped down near the face of

Mont Blanc in that gondola, all feeling grateful for Swiss engineering. Small, dense rainbows shimmered on the imposing ice of the mountain. They shifted, pulsing, from green to blue to purple to red. The last color was a reminder, for me, of Rolf's red hair. And that at certain angles white light reveals a spectrum of color that astonishes. And that there are still wonders and mysteries that lie ahead. And that, somehow, he is still part of them.

Cultural Archives of Awe

SEVEN

MUSICAL AWE

How Musical Awe Embraces Us
in Community

I listen with my body and it is my body that
aches in response to the passion and pathos
embodied in this music.

· SUSAN SONTAG

Yumi Kendall senses the world in musical forms. When she hears the horn of a Honda, she tells me, it is a G-sharp, and B-natural in a minor third. At a Philadelphia Phillies baseball game, a foul ball hits the rafters nearby—to her ears and mind, it is a pure B. C major is her home base, where she feels open to the world.

Yumi's mother was raised in a traditional rice-farming village in Japan. Upon learning of her parents' plans for her marriage, she said "no" with youthful gusto, Yumi tells me, and moved to St. Louis, Missouri. There she began a new life as a babysitter, taking care of children who studied violin with Yumi's grandfather, John

Kendall, who brought the Suzuki method to the United States. In the context of those lessons, Yumi's mother met John Kendall's son; they married and created a very musical family.

Yumi was breastfed listening to her older brother learning the violin. At five, Yumi chose the cello. Playdates were chances to play music with childhood friends. She fell asleep to a lullaby her dad sang nightly. When Yumi recounts this to me, she begins to sing ever so faintly:

Come over the sea in my boat with me
The waves are breaking high
It's up and down we wander
Beneath the summer sky . . .

Lullabies are a sonic medium in which parents create somnolent awe, ushering in the wonders of sleep and dreams. Those lilting songs, mixed in with the rituals of gentle touch and soothing words, shift the child's physiology to a high-vagal, oxytocin-rich profile associated with a sense of belonging and connection. This is true for infants, one study found, even when listening to lullabies from other cultures. Lullabies integrate parent and child into the high-touch, synchronized patterns of community, and occasion early embodied ideas about locating ourselves within them.

Today, Yumi is an award-winning cellist for the Philadelphia Orchestra, a position that was not easy to attain. Since the 1970s, performers have auditioned behind screens, but that didn't always prevent conductors from rejecting Yumi upon discovering her gender—even after judging her the best. Seeing Yo-Yo Ma play Bach's Cello Suites, though, was an experience of musical awe and moral beauty: it taught her that a human being can play these complex pieces in one sitting, no matter the gender and racial biases of the times.

For Yumi, music is a symbolic medium of awe. It is where we express and understand together what is vast and mysterious, and how we make sense of the wonders of life. This notion found full expression in the writings of the Romantics, who viewed music as the artistic realm of the sublime. Beethoven, a hero of Romanticism, created music that, in the words of E. T. A. Hoffmann, "sets in motion the machinery of awe, of fear, of terror, of pain, and awakens that infinite yearning which is the essence of romanticism."

Fifty years after the era of Romanticism, Charles Darwin timed his daily walks near gardens to listen to the music in King's College Chapel in Cambridge. The local flora and fauna and music fed his thinking as he wandered and wondered about evolution. These encounters opened his mind to questions:

> I acquired a strong taste for music, and used very often to time my walks so as to hear on week days the anthem in King's College Chapel. This gave me intense pleasure, so that my backbone would sometimes shiver. I am sure that there was no affectation or mere imitation in this taste. . . . Nevertheless I am so utterly destitute of an ear, that I cannot perceive a discord, or keep time and hum a tune correctly; and it is a mystery how I could possibly have derived pleasure from music.

Mysteries of musical pleasure indeed.

Scholars of music have long believed that we create and appreciate music to understand emotions like awe. Here we ask: How? And why?

Darwin's reflections hint at three answers. A first is found in Darwin's musical "shivers," that bodily sign of merging with others to face mystery and the unknown. It is a human universal to get the chills and tear up when moved by music. That is because we listen to music, philosopher Susan Sontag rightly observed, with our bodies. Or as Miles Davis put it upon first hearing jazz greats Dizzy Gillespie and Charlie Parker:

"What? What is this?" Man, that shit was so terrible it was scary. . . . Man, that shit was all up in my body.

Music stirs awe by opening our bodies to its neurophysiological profile.

Music also opens our minds to the sublime beyond "affectation" and "imitation." In our twenty-six-culture study, people often wrote that music brought them moments of clarity, of epiphany, of truth, of really knowing their place in the great scheme of life. The writer Rachel Carson often listened to Beethoven to open her mind in this way:

Listening to Beethoven, the mood became, I suppose, more creative, and rather suddenly I understood what the anthology should be—the story it should tell—the deep significance it might have. I suppose I can never explain it in words, but I think you understand without words. It was a mood of tremendous exaltation, I wept.

Music has "deep significance"; it illuminates "patterns of life," in the words of philosopher Susanne Langer, whom you will soon meet. Music teaches us about love, and suffering, and justice, and power, and with whom and where we find our community. How does this work, though, that a pattern of sounds might lead us to understand, in the case of awe, the vast mysteries of life? By listening carefully to the symbolic meaning of sound we shall discover how.

Finally, we should not forget how social music is, that for 100,000 years, and most likely longer, we have been listening to and performing music with others. In music, as a community woven together in sound, we find a shared identity—Darwin's "taste for music."

Cashmere Blanket of Sound

In the autumn of 2019, I visited Yumi to hear her play music conducted by John Adams, a Pulitzer Prize–winning American composer. Fifteen minutes before the performance, I found my seat with 2,000 other symphonygoers, all buzzing in sounds of collective effervescence rising above curving waves of red velvet seats. Yumi strode onstage and waved, then sat down with the 100 members of the orchestra, all playing different notes. It was a cacophony. An acoustic assault. In one instant, though, an oboist played an A, and all musicians joined. Music. An orchestra exists.

During the performance, Yumi sat upright, her body erect and arms at disciplined angles, as if listening to her cello breathe. Her face moved through expressions of concentration, determination, ferocity, absorption, and bliss, when her eyebrows lifted and her eyes closed. Yumi seemed to drift into an invisible space surrounding her. I had seen that face earlier that day at the Rodin Museum, in Rodin's *Gates of Hell*, his Dante-derived, awe-inspiring sculpture of swirling bodies hovering near the doors to the afterlife.

The next day Yumi and I enjoyed a cup of tea at an outdoor café near Rittenhouse Square in Philadelphia. It was a fresh, sparkling fall day of changing maple leaves and urbanites walking with newspapers tucked under their arms and city-friendly dogs on leashes. I asked Yumi what it was like to play as part of an orchestra for two thousand people. She told me of how challenging Adams's composition was technically, and recalled her daily practice of exercising her forearms, biceps, wrists, and fingers.

Her tone then shifted. She talked about what it feels like in her body to play. She feels the vibrations of her cello. The wood touching her arms. When she is playing, her thoughts travel to new spaces, soaring and floating, not knowing where she is going. As she spoke, her hands rotated outward with fireworks-like twinkling movements of the fingers. She continued:

> When I receive the score of a piece to play, I see my part, one of many dozens of parts that make up the piece of music. I have the sense that I am connected to the past of our species, of our history of making music that is tens of thousands of years old. And to our present and future. It's so humbling. When we perform we put something out there in the space . . . some pattern of notes of our instruments. . . . I think all the notes that have ever been played in the hall are still there. I mean, if the roof was taken off of the symphony hall, where would the notes go? When I play, I feel the vibration in my heart. Those patterns go out into space. They envelop people.

Surround them in texture. It is beyond language. Beyond thought. Beyond religion. It is like a cashmere blanket of sound.

We find awe in playing music with others, as part of a history of music making that is tens of thousands of years old. The awe that music moves us to does seem beyond speech, a new kind of thought, and, for many, more powerful than religion (and for many who are religious, a pathway to the Divine). But what are we to make of Yumi's metaphor that the notes she plays surround listeners in a "cashmere blanket of sound"?

When Yumi moves her bow across her cello's strings, or when Beyoncé's vocal cords vibrate as air moves through them, or when Gambian griot superstar Sona Jobarteh plucks the strings of her kora, those collisions move air particles, producing sound waves—vibrations—that move out into space. Those sound waves hit your eardrums, whose rhythmic vibrations move hairs on the cochlear membrane just on the other side of the eardrum, triggering neurochemical signals beginning in the auditory cortex on the side of your brain.

Sound waves are transformed into a pattern of neurochemical activation that moves from the auditory cortex to the anterior insular cortex, which directly influences and receives input from your heart, lungs, vagus nerve, sexual organs, and gut. It is in this moment of musical-meaning making in the brain that we do indeed listen to music with our bodies, and where musical feeling begins.

This neural representation of music, now synced up with essential rhythms of the body, moves through a region of the brain known as the hippocampus, which adds layers of memories to the ever-accreting meaning of the sounds. Music so readily transports us from the present to the past, or from what is actual to what is possible, spatiotemporal journeys that can be awe-inspiring.

And finally, this symphony of neurochemical signals makes its way to our prefrontal cortex, where, via language, we endow this web of sound with personal and cultural meaning. Music allows us to understand the great themes of social living, our identities, the fabric of our communities, and often how our worlds should change.

Recent studies reveal how music shifts our bodies to the neurophysiology of awe. Melodious, slow music reduces our heart rate, a sign of vagus nerve activation, and lowers our blood pressure. Faster, louder music—in one study, music by the Swedish pop group ABBA—increases our blood pressure and heart rate, but lowers levels of cortisol. Even more energetic, edgy music, then, will arouse us, but without the sense of peril that accompanies elevated levels of cortisol. When we listen to music that moves us, the dopaminergic circuitry of the brain is activated, which opens the mind to wonder and exploration. In this bodily state of musical awe, we often tear up and get the chills, those embodied signs of merging with others to face mysteries and the unknown.

In our history, music has most often been enjoyed with others, and when people listen to the same music together, their brains synchronize in regions involved in ascribing emotional meaning to the music (the amygdala), delight (caudate nucleus), and language and cultural meaning (prefrontal cortex). In one imaginative study in this vein, participants, all wearing brain-recording caps, listened to a live band together in a club rented out for the study. As they did, their brains synced up in the delta band, a brain wave frequency associated with bodily movement, inclining us toward moving in unison. Importantly, the degree of this shared brain activation predicted how much the individual was moved by the music and felt close to other people listening. Music breaks down the boundaries between self and other and can unite us in feelings of awe.

In his book *How Music Works*, David Byrne charts the history of this idea, that the sounds of music shift our bodies to a shared experience of awe. Some 2,500 years ago, the Greek philosopher Pythagoras proposed that the solar system emitted perfectly harmonious sounds that are the origins of the rhythms of life—of weather, seasons, cycles in nature, waking and sleep cycles, love and family life, our breathing, the beating of our hearts, and life and death. When we play and listen to sacred music, Pythagoras reasoned, these celestial sounds synchronize the rhythms of our lives, which fold us into what the Greeks called communitas, or social harmony. When we listen to music with others, the great rhythms of our bodies—heartbeat, breathing, hormonal fluctuations, sexual cycles, bodily motion—once separate, merge into a synchronized pattern. We sense that we are part of something larger, a community, a pattern of energy, an idea of the times—or what we might call the sacred.

Music surrounds us in a cashmere blanket of sound.

Sound and Feeling

After the performance in Philadelphia that night, Yumi emailed me a story of musical awe she experienced while playing Mozart's *Requiem* the week that her grandfather died:

This was Grandfather's piece. Mozart's Requiem, which we coincidentally played the week he died, January 2011. . . .

When we started playing Confutatis, all the tears I never shed when he died came out . . . the angry, aggressive 32nd notes, from all the 40 of us strings in unison playing with sharp accents . . . each one like punches. And suddenly, the heavens opened up with Voca me, and all the light shone through, bright white almost blinding light. Like sun rays beaming through in sound. Angels singing. Grandfather, and Grammy, were there with me . . . shining on us. And then the memory floodgates opened to when we sang this in high school chorus, with Mr. Gibson and my friends, in the music room . . . back in time. And then suddenly back to now, the re-entrance of the fortissimo accents and missed opportunities and grief and anger. I could feel tears streaming down my face because my eyes couldn't contain them anymore. Became momentarily aware that I was in performance . . . and let it go, it's a safe place on stage. I felt the surge of anger subside, and, by the time we finished the Requiem and ended the concert with Ave Verum . . . even with my tears, I felt glowing, calm, deep sadness, and peacefulness. I felt like Grandfather heard me.

Yumi's story follows awe's familiar unfolding. It begins with encounters with the vastness of her grandfather's death. Mystery strikes her in sensing her deceased grandparents' presence. Yumi's self transforms, moving through webs of associations—memories of singing in high school, a blending of sensory experiences known as synesthesia. She feels touched by bright light—an epiphany—bursting through sound. Her body gets into the act, glowing, overtaken with tears in recognition of the vastness of it all. Through the experience, she feels she is speaking with her grandfather.

Yumi's observations about the meaning of music find a home

in an influential philosophical study of the arts, that of Susanne Langer. In her books *Feeling and Form* and *Mind: An Essay on Human Feeling*, Langer advances her central thesis, that the arts' purpose is to objectify feeling. Each art, Langer details, is a unique kind of representation of emotion. In making music or visual art within a culture and moment of history, we archive our beliefs about what Langer called "the pattern of life," or what I will call life patterns. Life patterns are the great themes of social living and are central to our experience of emotion, such as what it means to suffer. To experience loss. To love. To protest unfairness. To be subordinated by forces more powerful than the self. To be in relation to the Divine. To encounter mystery. To live and die.

The arts, Langer continues, represent our experience of life patterns in a realm of symbolic meaning that differs from that of our spoken language. Our spoken word is typically held to standards of truth, or veracity. The syntax of language and its arrangement of subjects, objects, and verbs seeks to represent events in the three-dimensional space of our usual, waking experience. Events unfold forward in a linear sense of time. Cause-and-effect relations are unidirectional.

Music, Langer posits, is freed of the constraints of veridicality that structure so much of our spoken language. As a result, our experience of aesthetic emotion—through music or visual art, for example—follows different laws of space, time, and causality. In this realm of experience, fast, holistic intuitions arise about life patterns, or possible truths about our lives. The realm of meaning in the arts, Langer concludes, has "no counterpart in any vocabulary." Music "is a tonal analogue of emotive life."

Yumi's account of musical awe aligns with this thinking. For Yumi, 32nd notes are "angry" and "aggressive." Fortissimo accents express grief. Sounds "punch," tears "stream," anger "surges," like metaphorical descriptions in poems. She hurtles backward in time and is transported to a space where she is together with her deceased grandparents. Yumi's experience of awe in playing Mozart's *Requiem* allowed her to understand life's most reliable pattern—that it ends, even for those we love most, in death.

How does music relate life patterns to us? How does it allow our minds to grapple, in the case of awe, with how we relate to the vast mysteries of life? The easy answer is through lyrics. And indeed, in our twenty-six-culture study, people around the world wrote about how specific lyrics transformed their minds. You probably could quote right now lyrics from songs that brought you awe and an understanding of life patterns.

The more complex possibility is that the sounds of music, independent of the words that make up the lyrics, stir specific emotions. It has taken Swiss emotion scientist Klaus Scherer forty years to figure out how.

Scherer's theorizing goes as follows. When we are in an emotional state, like anger, compassion, terror, or awe, our neurophysiology changes: our breathing, heart rate, blood pressure, vagus nerve activation, and movements of muscles throughout the body all shift to support adaptive behaviors like fleeing, recoiling, soothing, embracing, exulting, or exploring. These bodily changes alter the mechanics of the vocal apparatus and, by implication, the acoustics of our voice. For example, when in an anxious state, the muscles around the lungs are tense, our tightened vocal cords produce less variability in pitch, and with less saliva in our mouths our lips tighten, resulting in high-pitched, unvarying, up-tempo sounds that convey anxiety.

Musicians express emotions, Scherer continues, by producing

sounds that resemble the acoustics of our vocal expression of emotion. In empirical tests of this idea, musicians are asked to use their voices, or an instrument, or even just a drum, to communicate different emotions. They do so, research finds, by producing music whose sounds resemble emotion-specific profiles of pitch, rhythm, contour, loudness, and timbre. Anger, for example, is conveyed in slow sounds with lower pitches and rising contours, like a roar of protest. The musical expression of joy is done with higher-pitched, quickly shifting sounds with rising contours, like the sounds of good friends tittering or a stream flowing during spring. When these samples of music are played to ordinary listeners, we have no trouble discerning ten different emotions, even from the beat of a drum.

To document how music expresses awe, Alan Cowen and I had participants from China and the United States first provide minute-long nonlyrical music samples that they personally felt expressed various emotions, including awe. We also had Chinese participants do the same with traditional Chinese music, which our U.S. participants had never heard. When we played these brief musical selections to new participants in the two countries, these new listeners could reliably detect thirteen emotions in the musical selections, including those provided by people from the other culture, and including our U.S. participants when listening to selections of traditional Chinese music. The feelings we perceive in music include the following: amusing, energizing, calm, erotic, triumphant, angry or defiant, fearful, tense, annoying, dreamy, sad, serene, and awe-inspiring. Aligning with Scherer's theorizing, the music that expressed awe had acoustics resembling the *whoa*s and *wow*s and *aah*s we vocalize when feeling awe.

Recent neuroscience suggests that when we hear music, we

perceive more than just a category of emotion, our focus thus far. We imagine emotion-specific actions, inferring from the musicians' sounds their bodily state and likely action. Those images of action trigger our mimetic tendencies, leading us to initiate similar movements in our bodies. Embodied images and memories from our lives, in turn, arise in our minds. What this suggests is that when we hear music that expresses awe, our own bodies and minds shift, even ever so slightly, to the wonder and saintly tendencies of awe.

This analysis dovetails with old ideas about the power of sacred music, which so often shares the acoustic features of vocalizations of awe. When we hear sacred music or we chant, sing, or play it, we are moved toward awe. We sense in such embodied experience that we are related to the provenance of the music, or part of it, most typically a spiritual figure or force. In Hinduism, uttering the sacred sound *om* is thought to connect those who chant it directly to Brahman, the universal soul. Reciting the Qur'an in the Islamic tradition transports the individual to a state akin to that of the prophet Muhammad in his moment of Divine revelation. As is true in many Indigenous cultures, the Kalapalo of central Brazil ritualistically chant, sing, and engage in a particular kind of dance, the experience of which transports them to a state in which they are in relation to the Divine.

If you listen carefully enough today, you might hear traces of *whoa*s and *aah*s of awe in a choir's performance during the holidays, a transfixing moment in a raga, monks chanting in Japan, or the exalted singing of Aretha Franklin or Bono. And the movements of your body and mind, chills, and sense of communitas signal to you that you are encountering an enduring life pattern, that we are connected to something vast, if only for the duration of a song.

Come Together

As humans walked out of Africa some fifty to sixty thousand years ago, we did so as a musical species moving in unison in small, wandering groups. Our most basic social interactions—those between parent and child, friends, flirting teens, and group members laboring together—were often structured within the patterns of music. We made flutes from bones, rattles from gourds, shakers from seeds, and early drums from tightened animal skins. Music would interweave with dance and storytelling. Music became a medium of being together.

Music moves us to synchronize our movements. From the age of one or two, children will move their bodies, bobbing the head, tapping feet, clapping hands, and swaying hips, in tight synchronization with the beat of a song. In one illustrative study, West and East Africans were better able to tap to their own culture's music than to a song from another part of Africa, a sign of who they will find it easier to sync up with.

And when strangers tap to the same beat, as opposed to different beats, they experience greater compassion and willingness to assist. Listening to music that brings us the chills, or awe, inclines us to trust and to share more with a stranger.

Around the world, music does have deep universals, as we have seen—how the temporal structure of notes gives music a beat; the use of pitch to convey meaning; the singing of words; descending sound contours; the use of percussion, repetition, and nonequidistant scales (such as C major). At the same time, cultures develop specific rhythms, beats, pitches, tones, contours, and timbres in their music—their own archive of life patterns, of what love is, for example, or power, or the Divine. In being moved by our culture's music, we are moved to its ways of perceiving, of feeling, of being, which can strike us with the awe of epiphany—of recognizing who we are. For example, adolescents gravitate to music that expresses themes that speak to their emerging identities: in one study, working-class students were found to prefer music that centers upon the struggles of life—rap and country; upper-class students found their identities, and no doubt some musical awe, in music that expresses individualism and freedom—alternative rock and jazz.

Music locates individuals within broader cultural identities to such an extent that the acoustics of one culture's music will resemble those of another culture to the extent that those two cultures resemble one another genetically. This has been observed in analyses of the music of thirty-nine African cultures, choral songs of nine Indigenous tribes in Taiwan, and the melody and pitch in folk songs from thirty-one Eurasian cultures, ranging from the Mongols to the Irish to the Navajo.

Musicians create music to express their feelings about life patterns in ways that unite them with other members of their culture. This certainly is true of Diana Gameros.

Diana grew up in Juárez, Mexico, one of five children in a boisterous family. Sensitive to sight and sound, she began playing music on a little toy organ that her mom gave her, which transported her to a quiet space of the imagination. She would learn the piano, and then the guitar, but rarely sing. In her family it was her two uncles who sang, with the full-chested, deep timbres of Mexican folk songs.

Today, Diana's award-winning music follows the forms of the

Mexican troubadour and ranchera songs of her childhood, mixing in sounds of the cello and her classical guitar playing, which she learned while finding her voice as a student in the United States. Her songs symbolize the concerns of immigrants from Mexico and the life patterns of exploitation and being away from home.

Upon getting a green card, Diana was allowed to return to Mexico after sixteen years and tour her home country (captured in the documentary *Dear Homeland*). Below are her musically rich impressions of that return while in the central zócalo, or square, of Mexico City. There she found awe in many of its sources: in walking with people; in the faces, voices, and colors of a place; and in music and a song her grandmother used to sing:

> I can feel it now. Estoy aquí. I am here. I am finally here in Mexico. All I had to do was turn them off—my phone, my thoughts—and deeply breathe. Deeply feel and listen. Really listen. And see, truly see. I recognize these voices, they speak my mother tongue. I recognize these colors, I was brought up by them. I recognize that song, it's the one my grandmother used to sing in Torreoncitos, Chihuahua. I recognize myself in this place and these sounds, on those walls, and those faces, on that flag. Y ahora soy una con ellos. And now I am one with them. It has finally sunk in. I am here in my dear, dear homeland. Mexico. Y me siento inmensamente feliz.
>
> And I feel immensely happy.

In musical awe we hear the voices and feel the sounds of our culture. We recognize, we understand, our individual identity within something larger, a collective identity, a place, and a people.

We find what is often seemingly far away—home. In this, we can find an immense happiness. This can be true in hearing music that has deep cultural roots, and in music we might not immediately understand.

Laughter in the Rain

The night I heard Yumi on the cello in Philadelphia, the orchestra played a piece John Adams composed, *Scheherazade.2*. Scheherazade, you may recall, told the thousand stories that make up *Arabian Nights*, a collection of folklore, legends, and myths about local gods—archives of awe at the heart of Middle Eastern culture, and inspiration of films and books throughout the world.

The tale begins with the king Shahryar, who has discovered that he and his brother have been cuckolded by their wives. Dishonored and enraged, Shahryar marries a virgin each day, ravishes her at night, and beheads her the next morning. Scheherazade intervenes (in Old Persian, "Scheherazade" translates to "world freer"). Well read and knowledgeable of myths and folklore, she volunteers to be the king's next wife.

On her first night, she regales the king until dawn with a story (one of the thousand myths of *Arabian Nights*). The king is moved to awe and begs for an ending to the story. And then another the next night. Scheherazade is saved by telling stories of awe. She repeats this pattern for one thousand nights, and the king and Scheherazade fall in love. He marries her and makes her his queen, and they have three children. For Adams, the story is about oppression, the violence women face at the hands of men, and the power of the female voice.

That night of the performance, Adams arrived onstage, followed shortly thereafter by the violinist Leila Josefowicz, whom Adams had in mind when he composed the piece. She played standing close to Adams, in a flowing, diaphanous outfit (with biceps bulging). The symphony has four movements, charting how Scheherazade tells her first story, falls in love, fights back against the threats of men, and flees and finds sanctuary.

For most of *Scheherazade.2*, I struggled to find my feeling. Like many, I love specific veins of music but can't explain why. Listening to many contemporary composers leaves me in a wordless state, lacking concepts and language to discern what life patterns may be symbolized in their sounds.

As the symphony begins, the voice of my default self is loud: it nags me about why I never wear the right clothes, how I'm a fish out of water at highbrow events like these, what time my flight departs tomorrow, or how in seeking to feel awe in music I undermine the very possibility.

The piece starts with loud drums. They hit me like the sudden strike of a breaking wave or roar of thunder. My heart slows—the orienting reflex to the new. I am still, transfixed, silent, motionless, and aligned with the people next to me. Our porous bodies have shifted, our shared attention fixed on the stage.

In the movement "Scheherazade and the Men with Beards," written to capture how women fight patriarchal oppression, Josefowicz's high-pitched, rising notes of protest are countered by deeper, louder, domineering sounds from the strings—the voices of men condemning her alleged adultery, threatening honor-killing. These are the sounds of a universal life pattern, the struggle between the powerful who subjugate and the powerless trying to survive and find forms of resistance.

I feel agitated and on edge, made uneasy by the violence of power. Images move through my mind. An unexpected trip to the ER in the Sierra foothills—Rolf's cancer had put him into a near coma. He was rushed to a small hospital, where he recovered, regaining blurry consciousness. During my stay, we walked the fluorescent-lit halls, passing two parents whose son was reeling from a psychotic break. Rolf weighing 148 pounds, walking with blue gown on, stooped, slowly moving in a sterile beige hall. Uncertain footsteps, scuffing thin white hospital-issued slippers. Light-hearted comments: "I guess I'm not what I used to be, am I? . . . I almost left that time."

As the symphony arrives at its end, Scheherazade flees and finds sanctuary. Josefowicz's playing is soft. It soars in places, and then ends in gentle, elongating notes of serenity. The struggle of a single outspoken, brilliant woman speaking truth to power with a gift for stories of awe is over. At the end of struggle and subjugation is peace, felt in Adams's composition in slowing, appreciative sounds whose notes drift off into space. Out of the quiet of the performance's end, the crowd roars. I sense tears and a fast rush of goose bumps.

After the show, I give Yumi a big hug in the lobby and head into a torrential downpour. Headlights stuck in traffic project beams of light that illuminate millions of drops of rain, all making their way from the sky to the ground and then vanishing in ricochets off the asphalt, dissipating in radiating rings of water molecules. People run to Ubers and cabs with programs and coats draped over their heads. Clad in slacks and dresses and high heels, they shout familiar sounds—*aah*, *wow*, *whoa*, and *woo-hoo*. And laugh as they drive away.

I don't know a soul around me. I go the wrong way trying to

locate my hotel. I get drenched, embraced in torrents of rain, creating such luminous light filled with droplets on the streets. But I feel located in the world, surrounded by the blanket of the evening's sound and the movements and shared rhythm of the people around me.

EIGHT

SACRED GEOMETRIES

How Our Awe for Visual Design Helps Us Understand the Wonders and Horrors of Life

> *A great deal of art, perhaps most art, actually is self-consoling fantasy. . . . Art, and by "art" from now on I mean good art, not fantasy art, affords us a pure delight in the independent existence of what is excellent. Both in its genesis and its enjoyment it is a thing totally opposed to selfish obsession. It invigorates our best faculties and, to use Platonic language, inspires love in the highest part of the soul. It is able to do this partly by virtue of something which it shares with nature: a perfection of form which invites unpossessive contemplation and resists absorption into the selfish dream life of the consciousness.*
>
> · IRIS MURDOCH

Jurassic Park is a visual paean to the wonders of life. Its high-spirited narrative careers through encounters with overpowering nature—the waves of a tropical storm—big ideas—gene editing, chaos theory—dinosaurs, and, like so many of

Steven Spielberg's films, the moral beauty of children. In the movie these wonders are imperiled by capitalists seeking to commodify awe.

When eleven-year-old Michael Frederickson first saw the brontosaurus in that film, he was awestruck. For those in the world of CGI (computer-generated imagery), that slow-moving, tree-trimming dinosaur is an act of Iris Murdoch's "good art," allowing "pure delight in . . . what is excellent." It is, for CGI artists, like the Lascaux cave paintings, Giotto's frescoes, the Dutch masters' portrayal of domesticity and light, Hokusai's paintings, and Cézanne's cubism-inspiring apples: a new way of seeing the world. With the magic special effects, Spielberg and his team created tyrannosaurs, triceratops, stegosauruses, and brontosauruses that we, as viewers, feel are real.

To explain to his parents how *Jurassic Park* moved him so, Michael bought the film's soundtrack and played it one night during dinner. As they sat listening, Michael burst into tears. His parents thought he was depressed. A year later, in sixth grade, Michael was given this essay prompt: *What is the best day you could ever have?* Michael's answer: "After lunch, do computer animation for Pixar." After studying computer science, where he often found digital awe in the patterns and systems of code, he would in fact make his way to Pixar and begin a career in visual awe.

Today, Michael is a "set artist" at Pixar. He uses the latest advances in computer graphics, big data, and machine learning to create the visual worlds of Pixar films—the streets of Paris in *Ratatouille*, the reef life in *Finding Dory*, and the interiors of Riley's mind in *Inside Out*.

For Michael, *Inside Out* allows its viewers to reflect upon loss and the search for identity. Working on it led him to insights about his own life, but once it was released in theaters, he felt adrift. As he tells me this, he quotes from Herman Melville's *Moby-Dick*: "in landlessness alone resides highest truth." Awe does leave us in a "landless" place, unmoored and unconstrained by the default self and society's status quo. He began giving a talk around Pixar, which he shares with me over a cup of coffee. After some pleasantries Michael opens his laptop to his first slide, "The Sixth Emotion." That emotion is awe.

For Michael and so many others, a point of visual art is to evoke awe. Art allows us to transcend, in Murdoch's words, the "selfish dream life of the consciousness." Or within the framework we have been developing here, art can quiet the oppressive excesses of the default self and lead us to "love in the highest part of the soul," feelings of joining with others in an appreciation of what is meaningful and life-giving. The slides in his talk offer one kind of proof of the centrality of awe to visual art. He shows a slide with dozens of awe expressions from films. Steven Spielberg cast Drew Barrymore in *E.T.: The Extra-Terrestrial*, he notes, because of her awe face. He then produces a convincing Keanu Reeves imitation from *The Matrix*—"Holy shit, this shit is amazing"—and then exults that *The Matrix* "is all IT." Luke Skywalker is "the galactic purveyor of awe," and here Michael covers Joseph Campbell's treatment of awe-guided heroic journeys in myth, an inspiration of *Star Wars*. It is a dizzying tour of how film documents awe.

The archaeological record suggests that we started creating visual art about 100,000 years ago, when we began beautifying our bodies with ocher paint, decorating shells for necklaces, burying people with sacred objects, and eventually—60,000 years ago—painting and engraving on rocks and rock walls, often in caves.

Today, the passions we feel from visual art are many, and range from feelings of beauty, to astonishment, to comic absurdity, to the sense of being mocked. And let's not forget boredom as you slog through a museum wondering what the point of art is. The question we take on here is: How is it that a painting, or the design of a building, or a textile, or a film, can move us to feel awe?

Life Patterns in Room 837

In 1977, my family made a pilgrimage to the Louvre before crossing the channel to Nottingham, England, for a sabbatical year. Rolf and I, then fourteen and fifteen, sprinted through the museum, snapping photos—with Kodak Instamatics—of *Mona Lisa*. Security guards told us to calm down—*Tranquille!* Not a lot of awe, I must say.

In room 837, things changed. My dad suggested we stand for a minute in front of the Dutch masters, in particular Johannes Vermeer, Pieter de Hooch, and Jan Steen. Visitors crowded around Vermeer, and softly *ooh*ed and *aah*ed in tones of reverence. His work, as luminous as it is, struck me as too staged and controlled; too much "perfection of form" for my teenage eye hungering to redeem the wild. I was moved by Vermeer's predecessor, de Hooch, a painter of "quietly revolutionary" paintings, in the words of art historian Peter Sutton.

De Hooch's paintings of seventeenth-century Dutch citizens of Delft, usually women, cooking, doing laundry, petting dogs, sweeping, holding infants, picking lice out of children's hair, breast-feeding, or admiring a glass of ale, changed how I see the world.

Susanne Langer, our guide to aesthetic awe, offered a hypothesis for how:

> It may be through manipulation of his created elements that he discovers new possibilities of feeling, strange moods, perhaps greater concentrations of passion than his own temperament could ever produce, or than his fortunes have yet called forth.

Seeing de Hooch allowed me to discover "new possibilities of feeling." I sensed a mathematics of moral beauty in a mother's glance at a child. I could feel from his painting the vast forces that unite us when moving in unison while doing laundry or being touched by morning light. Though I felt alienated most of the time at age fifteen, I too would experience sublime community over a beer with friends someday. De Hooch opened my eyes to the idea of everyday awe.

In 2019, I returned to Paris. I visited the Louvre and made my way past the endless line of selfie-taking *Mona Lisa* viewers and found myself in room 837. Once again, awe overtook me, this time in front of de Hooch's *La Buveuse* from 1658. In this painting, a man standing near a table pours a young woman a drink. She receives it with relaxed asymmetry, extending her legs in repose. Her face is awash in a coy smile, her eyes looking out toward what is possible. A man across the table looks off into the distance while smoking a pipe. An elderly woman standing nearby touches her chest.

How might I describe how this painting made me feel awe? And why? The concepts and language I might use fail to fully capture the intuitive, holistic processes visual art engages to move us to awe.

Our language-based theories of how our minds work don't often succeed in explaining how our minds actually work, for so many layers of the mind's operations occur prior to the stories and explanations we offer with language. Neuroscience is helpful in capturing more subconscious processes. Within the study of the brain, neuroaesthetics—which attempts to explain how our brain responds to art—highlights four ways that visual art moves us to feel awe.

Think about the last time you encountered a piece of visual art that made you feel awe, perhaps a painting, or a photograph, or a temple's patterned carvings or cathedral's vaulted apses and stained-glass windows, or a climactic scene in a movie. As you look at the source of visual awe, neurochemical signals move from your retinas to the visual cortex in the back of the brain, which begins to construct the rudiments of images out of the angles of lines, patterns of light and dark, early signs of shape, texture, and color. In this first stage of perception, art reveals *visual patterns* we may not be aware of in the moment, and this can initiate feelings of awe—the human geometry of the eyes and mouth of the face of a homeless drifter, patterns of light and shadow on the facade of a building in a city, or, in de Hooch's paintings, villagers moving in unison, going humbly about their daily affairs.

These neurochemical signals will next activate regions of the brain that store your *ideas* about objects. Through visual techniques, the artist can prompt us to ponder notions and concepts; for example, our relation to the wonders of life. The embracing light that touches the four figures in *La Buveuse* might trigger thoughts about the power of the warmth of the sun or how time endlessly passes as the light shifts across the day.

This neurochemical representation of visual art next activates networks of neurons, for example in the anterior cingulate cortex and anterior insula, which stir your body (e.g., heart, lungs, muscle groups, and immune system). In this moment, visual art can evoke the *direct embodied experience* of awe, all from standing in front of a two-dimensional painting or photo, often hundreds of years old.

Finally, the neurochemical signals arrive in the prefrontal cortex, where we ascribe *meaning* to the piece of art, with our words, concepts, learned interpretations, stories, and cultural theories about social living. Visual art can provoke us to reimagine reality. It can open us up to new ideas about who we can be and what our collective lives might be, in terms of our sexual identities, for example, and forms of social organization. My experience of awe in viewing de Hooch's painting when I was fifteen years old gave rise to an idea in my mind, a radical one for me at that time in my life: the possibility of experiencing everyday awe.

In *good art*, there are so many opportunities to reach *the highest part of the soul*.

Sacred Geometries

When I give talks on awe, I begin with the definition that began this book: we feel awe in encountering vast mysteries that transcend our understanding of the world. Over the years, often a hand has risen, and this astute question soon followed: What about the awe we feel from the minuscule? When looking at a cell under a microscope? Or the sixty-eight Thorne miniature rooms in the Art Institute of Chicago, which portray domestic interiors from the fourteenth to twentieth centuries in astonishing detail, down to the light filling the rooms from outside, each within a two-by-two-foot space? Or the near microscopic brushstrokes of Jan van Eyck? These champions of small awe might then cite William Blake's "world in a grain of sand" or Walt Whitman's spiritual homage to a blade of grass and cross their arms and raise their chins in defiance. They are onto something—microscopic awe.

Photographer Rose-Lynn Fisher archives microscopic awe. She has devoted many years to photographing the structure of bees' eyes, their honeycomb constructions, blood cells, and the tissue of bone. It was her photos of her tears that moved me to reach out.

As a child in Minnesota, Rose-Lynn found awe in patterns of snowflakes, in the profusion of soft hairs on pussy willows, on school visits to a museum of science and industry, and in classes on quilts and mosaics. She sensed patterns. Relations. Deep, unifying structures. "Sacred geometries," Rose-Lynn would repeatedly say, invoking the idea that there is transcendent, even spiritual, feeling found in seeing the deep geometric structures of the world. There are geometries of life patterns that we hear in the symbolic sounds of music and see in visual art.

When I visit Rose-Lynn in her home and studio in Sherman Oaks, California, her reverence for sacred geometries is on full display. On a table is a scattering of rocks of varied shapes and sizes; she grabs several and points out timeless patterns, visual stories of awe about the Earth's geological evolution. On a dresser in the hallway sits a construction from her art school days, interconnected parallelograms creating a pyramid. From simple geometric forms emerges awe-inspiring complexity.

Rose-Lynn's paintings from her thirties on her bedroom walls center upon "deconstructing the vanishing point" so notable in Renaissance painting, when the converging lines of a checkered floor in a cathedral or palace, for example, disappear. For

Rose-Lynn, the vanishing point in her painting speaks to that which has no end, no content, even no existence. In hearing her say this, I appreciate how a visual technique in art can enable us to understand a big idea of awe: that beyond the dissolving self is expansion and infinity.

One day while setting up to work, Rose-Lynn found a dead bee on a windowsill. She placed it under a microscope and took photographs with a lens that captures the microscopic. This first series of photos is in her book *Bee*. She shows me a photo from this series, that of a bee's eye. She then points to a photo of the luminous profusion of hexagons that comprise the honeycomb structure.

AWE!

She tells me: "There are patterns in nature beyond their physical form, and their deeper resonances make me sense a Golden Mean within us." Rose-Lynn then riffs on the sacred geometry of the hexagon—it is in the Star of David, the shape of a cloud on Saturn, the Hagal rune from Nordic traditions, and our DNA. Art allows us to find awe in seeing the unifying geometries of life.

One day, Rose-Lynn received a call from the son of a man she had come to know when she was a student wandering Europe in the late 1970s. While in Paris, she had an acute flare-up of Gaucher disease, an inherited genetic disorder that caused deterioration in her hip bones, among other issues. (In Gaucher, an enzyme deficiency prevents the complete breakdown of certain cells, and instead causes them to accumulate in the spleen, liver, and bone, with serious consequences.) She caught a night train to Florence; by the time she arrived she could hardly walk. She dialed a phone number a friend had given her, and met Patrick, who fed her soup, hoisted her across a piazza so she could at least see Giotto's frescoes and Michelangelo's tomb, and got her into a hospital, thus beginning a lifelong friendship. When Patrick's son called to say that he had died, she couldn't stop the flow of tears.

So she placed her tears on slides and began photographing them. From more than one thousand photos, one hundred experiences are represented in her book *The Topography of Tears*. The first two are *Tears of timeless reunion (in an expanding field)* and *Grief and gratitude*. They look like aerial maps (for her, of her emotional terrain), abstract forms made up of systems of the body—veins, capillaries, nuclei. Other photos have captions like *The irrefutable, In the end it didn't matter, The brevity of time (out of order) losing you*, and *Tears of elation at a liminal moment*.

Rose-Lynn explains: The lines, shapes, patterns, and movement of tears reveal the sacred geometry of her feeling. The images visualize what pain looks like. And gratitude. And grief. And awe. With more than thirty measures of our body's physiology, scientists can vaguely point out profiles of twenty or so emotions. With her photography, Rose-Lynn enables us to see that hundreds of complex feelings have distinct neurochemical profiles revealed in the shape of tears. William James would have said *Whoa*.

In looking at Rose-Lynn's photographs of tears of human emotion, I am transfixed by *The pull between attachment and release*, which is reproduced here. The lighter shape seems to be floating away, to my eye, from the first. Grief comes in fleeting waves of attachment and release.

Visual art also documents the geometries of our social lives: the symmetries of love between parent and child in depictions of Madonna and child by Raphael or da Vinci, or waves of collective

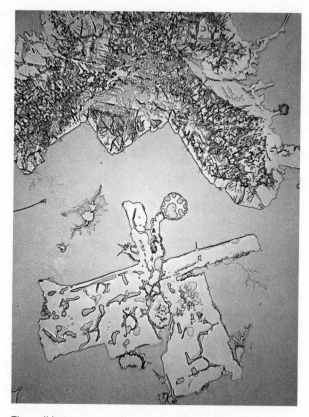

The pull between attachment and release. *Rose-Lynn Fisher*

effervescence in the drunken dinner scenes of the Dutch master Jan Steen, also found in room 837 of the Louvre. Sebastião Salgado's photos of masses of wet, muscular bodies working in unison in Brazil's Serra Pelada gold mine, which at its peak employed fifty thousand men, capture the sublime, hellish horrors of extraction-based capitalism, and how it reduces individual minds and bodies to means of production.

Visual art also allows us to see the deep structures, or sacred geometries, of the natural world. In the mid-nineteenth century, Ernst Haeckel described scientifically more than four thousand kinds of single-cell protozoa. Haeckel also believed that he could reveal scientific truths by drawing the species he studied, producing one hundred illustrations he would publish in a series of ten installments in *Art Forms in Nature* in 1904. This book has more than one hundred arresting renderings of jellyfish, sea anemones, clams, sand dollars, fish, and the occasional insect. Viewing his drawings is a strange and beautiful epiphany: the drawings reveal the signature qualities of each species in exaggerated artistic detail, allowing us to imagine how it adapted and survived in highly specific ways. In marveling at the symmetry and geometries shared by the species he drew, Haeckel enables the viewer to see the relatedness of different species, that the diverse forms that life takes are unified by a life force, or "artistic drive," in Haeckel's phrasing. His drawings allow us to see Darwin's idea about the evolution of species from earlier, primordial forms.

Rose-Lynn shows me photographs from a more recent series, of ghostlike cells originally from a fragment of her own bone. They look like the sign for infinity—drifting and, to my eye, unaware of how they, the product of a simple genetic variation in one group of cells, can introduce complex pains, horrors, insights, and wonders into a human's life. The geometries of all our lives, the traumas we have encountered, or the beauty, the curse you may feel running through your family's history, and its blessings, are found in the shape of cells we cannot see and in random mutations of our DNA.

Toward the end of our conversation, I sit in the living room near the small table with rocks strewn across its surface. Rose-Lynn calls out as she is making a cup of tea in her kitchen: "Awesome and awful. It's so striking that they go together."

We discuss the ninth-century etymology of "awe," and how the meaning of the word has changed.

She continues.

"Awesome and awful . . . they are mine to reconcile."

For Rose-Lynn, "art is a language, which through flashes of insight reveals the answer that exists within a question." In art we see life patterns, for both living and dying. In that moment of reconciliation, we might consider what to make of this cycle of life and death.

Hints of Vast Mysteries

Our default minds, so focused on independence and competitive advantage, are not well suited to making sense of the vast. So guided are we by prior knowledge and our need for certainty that we avoid or explain away the mysteries of life. Visual art, though, offers us hints at understanding the vast and mysterious.

There is no better guide to this idea than philosopher Edmund Burke, born in Dublin in 1729. His thin book from 1757, *A Philosophical Enquiry into the Origin of Our Ideas of the Sublime and Beautiful*, should be mandatory reading in art, architecture, film, and design schools.

Burke's thin volume opened eighteenth-century eyes to everyday awe. In those pages, he details how we can experience awe in all manner of perceptual experiences—thunder, shadows, patterns of light on a road, and even the sight of bulls (but not the more beautiful, affectionate cow!). The book has oddities, no doubt: Burke prioritizes the visual and auditory; according to him, scent cannot make us feel awe. (This notion offended, rightfully so, a Frenchwoman I met hiking who worked in the perfume industry.) Most critically, Burke offers ideas about how our experiences of the beautiful and the sublime differ.

For Burke, feelings of beauty arise out of a sense of familiarity and affection; awe, by contrast, arises in our recognition of what is powerful, obscure, and dreadful. Current studies in the science of aesthetics align with this distinction. Our default expectations about size, space, time, objects, other people, and causality streamline our efforts to make sense of the world. When what we encounter readily aligns with our mind's default expectations, we feel comfort and pleasure. This has been found in studies of faces, scents, images of furniture, and everyday scenes.

In visual art, we like and prefer scenes that reflect familiar, statistical regularities of the world—the visual expectations of our default self. We like placements that seem familiar, such as putting objects in the center of a scene. We find it pleasing when things that belong in the sky, such as birds, are high up as opposed to close to the ground. We prefer horizon lines that are typical of how we look at the world, and we find horizon lines that are unusually high or low unpleasant. Visual art that captures how we typically perceive the world brings us comfort, and its companion in the realm of aesthetic emotion, the feeling of beauty.

For visual art to stir awe, Burke continues, it must suggest vast mystery. One pathway is to hint at expansive causal forces. Perceived profusion—carvings on the facade of a church, a long line of trees in a garden, gravestones in a military cemetery—hints at the deep forces that organize our social and natural lives. As one example, Camille Pissarro's Boulevard Montmartre buzzes with a profusion of pedestrians, streetlights, and cafés, hinting at the transformative cultural energy of Paris in the late nineteenth century.

Simple repetition, Burke observes, is suggestive of vast causal forces that manifest in repeating forms. Images of waves, or mountains, for example, hint at large, unifying forces—the tides of the ocean or the geological evolution of the Earth. Swedish filmmaker Mikel Cee Karlsson relies on extended repetitions of everyday acts—brushing teeth, stroking a partner's hair, leg jiggles, nervous tics—to emphasize the conventions that organize the patterns of our social lives.

For Burke, patterns of light and movement can focus our minds. When scenes in art are unified by light (as in Rembrandt's paintings), sensed motion (Monet's flags in *Rue Montorgueil with Flags*), or a pervasive hue (Picasso's Blue Period), we infer that there is something vast that joins together the objects in the image.

And visual art can stir awe through subverting our default expectations about time, as in the use of slow motion in film (think Martin Scorsese's *Raging Bull*). And space: Vincent van Gogh's *Almond Blossoms* has no horizon or perspective; the thin branches seem to extend beyond the edge of the painting, producing a vertiginous, disorienting effect. He painted it for his nephew, newly arrived to the world. The painting seemed "to enthrall" the younger Vincent, as reported by his mother, Van Gogh's sister-in-law, Joanna.

As Iris Murdoch suggested, visual art helps us transcend the status quo expectations and ordinary way of perceiving our lives through the lens of the default self. Instead, through hints at vastness and mystery, art enables us to see the deeper structures to life around us, and grounds us within these interconnected patterns.

Direct Perception

It has long been thought that visual art enables new "possibilities of feeling," allowing us to perceive the world directly through the lenses of emotions. Seeing twentieth-century German artist Käthe

Kollwitz's portrayals of grief—she lost two of her children at young ages—opens our eyes to what the world looks like during experiences of loss. Jim Goldberg's photographs in *Rich and Poor* make us see the life-is-on-the-line, raw tenderness of living in poverty. Rothko's paintings can evoke the thought patterns of deep depression that led him to suicide at age sixty-six.

For Russian painter Wassily Kandinsky, a point of visual art is to evoke mystical feeling and "preserve the soul" through such "Stimmung," or mood:

> [In great art] the spectator does feel a corresponding thrill in himself. . . . Indeed the Stimmung of a picture can deepen and purify that of the spectator. Such works of art at least preserve the soul from coarseness; they "key it up," so to speak, to a certain height, as a tuning-key the strings of a musical instrument.

Visual art fine-tunes our experience of awe. Rest your eyes on a Huichol string painting from Mexico and you may sense you are hallucinating. South African artist Ernest Mancoba's paintings of spiritual experience are suffused with the bright, otherworldly light of mystical awe and interconnectedness of forms. Berlin's omnipresent street art—portrayals of ecstatic dancers or odd, dreamlike beings—may lead you to see the city through the lens of awe. Psychedelic artists like Alex Grey have sought to capture what it is like to see the world in a mystical moment on psychedelics. Art is a door of perception and can function as a lens of awe.

How visual art leads to the direct perception of awe inspired Rebecca Stone to forty years of study of Mesoamerican art. She has published papers on Andean textiles, Mexican tomb sculptures,

*Street art seen on an awe
walk I took in Berlin*

carvings on Incan agricultural devices, Ecuadorian petroglyphs, and the architecture of the Wari Empire (from 600 to 1100 AD in central Peru). She synthesizes these discoveries in her book *The Jaguar Within* (in Mesoamerican traditions, the jaguar is a sacred animal).

Within many Mesoamerican cultures, visual art preserves experiences of awe cultivated in what some call shamanism. Through the use of medicinal plants, dance, dreams, and ceremony, a shaman enables experiences of mystical awe for community members in which boundaries between self and others vanish, a sense of interdependence and proximity to a universal life force is felt, and a shared consciousness with other species and supernatural beings is sensed.

These experiences are archived in chants and songs, ceremonies, systems of knowledge about the powers of plants and other species, and visual art and design. Carvings, paintings, masks, woven baskets, and figurines decorate public and private spaces, their patterns stirring us to see the world through awe-inspiring undulating movement, spirals, iridescent color, and unusual illumination. Human and nonhuman hybrid figures—the merging of categories—are a common visual motif, challenging default expectations.

Viewing art activates the dopamine network in the brain. When paintings decorate the walls in public buildings and offices, people's minds open to wonder: they demonstrate greater creativity, inspiration, problem-solving abilities, and openness to others' perspectives. Art empowers our saintly tendencies. One impressive study, which involved more than thirty thousand people in the United Kingdom, found that people who practiced more art, like painting and dance, and viewed more art, for example by going to museums or musical performances, volunteered more in their community and gave more money away two years after the study's completion.

Visual design that encourages more everyday awe also promotes collective health and well-being. One recent study from Denmark found that hanging paintings on hospital walls led patients to feel more secure, to get out of their beds and socialize more, and to come to understand their illnesses within a broader narrative about the cycle of life. In cities judged from photos to be more evocative of visual awe, people report more robust health, even after controlling for income and local levels of pollution. In cities with pathways for walking, orienting landmarks, squares, and public buildings like libraries—elements of urban design that locate us within geometries of urban social living—people feel more open and report greater health and well-being. Simply being near cathedrals and in chapels inclines people to greater cooperation. Awe-based visual design enables us to see the world through awe, locating our individual selves within larger life patterns of interdependence.

Shock and Awe

During her childhood in Ohio, Susan Crile's family liked to go deep-sea diving. In the otherworldly, liquid ether of underwater, she found the sublime floating in vast quiet. Time dilated. She saw blurry outlines of life forms. She sensed mystery and felt peace.

This memory brings to mind another story of awe she tells me, about when her family dined with a Bedouin community camped out in tents in the Syrian desert. The stars, the pulsating music, the rocking, swaying bodies, the aromatic flavors—all left a lasting impression that brings tears to her today as she recounts this to me in her apartment in New York City.

When President George H. W. Bush launched Operation

Desert Storm in 1991, Susan felt riled up. The images of the "smart bombs" upset her. "Those are kids and moms being killed," she tells me. Historic buildings obliterated. The default language of the news—"collateral damage," "precision strike"—left Susan pacing her studio.

When Saddam Hussein set Kuwaiti oil fields on fire, it stirred Susan to action. She reached out to Boots & Coots, the company that extinguished those fires, and made her way to Kuwait. There, she traveled roads that had recently been combat sites, seeing children's toys strewn about, burned-out tanks, charred outposts, spent shells. The heat of the sizzling lakes of oil nearly knocked her down. The skies were enveloped by black smoke. The jetlike roar of the fires sounded like death. Later, working from the photos she took, she painted apocalyptic scenes of brilliant flames, vast black smoke, disorienting reflections in pools of oil. Awe mixing with horror.

Walking through Central Park to teach art at Hunter College on September 11, 2001, she passed people covered in ash, walking slowly in astonished horror, a pilgrimage of ghosts. This time she worked from videos. Her paintings capture the time dilation; the slow-motion building collapse; the profusion of ash; the repetition of Manhattan buildings with people climbing out of windows, which many recall today as a moment of awe.

When the photographs of prisoners tortured at Abu Ghraib were released, she reproduced them in a series of drawings that mix horror, brutality, awe, and compassion, an emotional blend that was what first led me to visit her. In her apartment on the Upper West Side of Manhattan, art books cover surfaces. Stacks of drawings lie under large tables. Pencils and pastels and chalks are arrayed on trays like crudités. The dust and scents of art are in the air, reminding me of moments from my childhood in my dad's studio.

As one enters the apartment, in the center of one's field of vision is a black box three feet tall by two feet wide—the size of a large Christmas present. It is the size of the box we put prisoners in solitary confinement in at Guantánamo Bay for weeks on end. Susan's black box makes you feel a life pattern: being subjugated and trapped by vast powers. It causes me to shudder. My mind opens to wonder about human horrors. *How long would it take for me to die in that space? And if I didn't die, what would my thoughts be like?*

Susan's series *Abu Ghraib: Abuse of Power* includes portrayals of dogs lunging at genitals, unconscious swollen faces, prisoners gasping for air in a tank of water, piles of nude bodies. The bodies are simple outlines, diaphanous and covered in sheens of light. One is tied up within the black box but looks resigned, even serene. *I want to move people to know in their bodies this suffering,* Susan explains to me. *To feel compassion.* She flips through an archive of awe and horror that inspired her: Goya's Disasters of War series, eighty-two prints depicting torture, killings, rapes, and the famine and inquisition during the war between Napoleon's Empire and Spain. As she flips through these prints, she points out moments of compassion amid horror.

Art creates an aesthetic distance, a safe space, from which we can consider the horrors humans perpetrate. In relevant studies, when people encounter images of genital mutilation or sexual harassment and are told they are pieces of art, the stress-related regions of their brains and bodies are less reactive. Within this safe space of the imagination, we are free to wonder, to think in broader, more open ways about how the act fits within moral frameworks that define our communities. How can we place a human being in a box the size of a Christmas present? We are back to Robert Hass's tour of how poetry, drama, and literature archive awe and horror. We are within the logic of the Natyashastra. Art allows us to contemplate horrors together and imagine social change fueled by awe and wonder.

This is what Leda Ramos teaches her working-class Latinx and immigrant students: art allows you to archive the patterns of life and wonder about social change. Leda's parents immigrated to Los Angeles from El Salvador in 1957 and landed in Echo Park, where she grew up with Brazilians, Mexicans, Nicaraguans, an elderly woman who had ridden in a Conestoga wagon from Oklahoma, and a hippie family whose mom didn't wear bras. As a child, Leda was awestruck by the magic of the carrom board, a game from India, so she made her own and put it in a grassy, overgrown space in her backyard. It would become a community center of laughter, flirting, roughhousing, and playful competition—a sacred social geometry of the play of neighborhood kids.

After stints at highbrow museums, Leda chose the path of the underpaid adjunct professor at California State University, Los Angeles. As I tour her studio in the Silver Lake neighborhood of Los Angeles, she points to a piece of graphic art outlining her immigrant story—it includes an image of her dad—"El Hijo"—in El Salvador, a web of cacti, and a plane in the upper right corner. Next to this piece is a digital painting Leda made with her students of the CARECEN mural *Migration of the Golden People*, by the artist Judy Baca, which includes scenes of activist Rigoberta Menchú, farmworkers marching with faces wizened from working in the fields, police beating nonviolent protesters on the dirt road of a small village, the lush Central American landscape.

Leda is working in the tradition of Central American and Mexican American political art, in which public art—murals, paintings, posters, and today T-shirts and stickers one puts on a laptop cover or a street sign—documents and awakens us to moral harm. Most famous in this tradition is Diego Rivera, but Leda was moved to awe by David Alfaro Siqueiros, who was brought to Los Angeles from Mexico to teach muralism and paint *Tropical America: Oppressed and Destroyed by Imperialism*, which depicted the brutality of capitalism toward immigrants. It was whitewashed, literally, by the Los Angeles City Council before eventually being recovered and restored by the J. Paul Getty Museum.

Leda dwells on an artwork she created for the exhibition, Central American Families: Networks and Cultural Resistance, at the Cal State LA University Library as part of the fiftieth anniversary of the Department of Chicana(o) and Latina(o) Studies at Cal State LA. Her piece has images of a Latina in cap and gown, people in ghostlike sheets protesting the dictator Efraín Ríos Montt in Guatemala, her family's immigration to the United States, and a Radio Sumpul radio tower, which broadcasted music and stories warning Salvadorians of U.S.-trained military death squads nearby. Dolores Huerta, who founded the United Farm Workers of America in 1962 with Cesar Chavez, gave the keynote speech that day. Leda's artwork was on walls nearby. Huerta closed her talk as follows:

> When we talk about our history, we are talking about the history of the United States of America. . . . It's our turn and this is our moment. So let's celebrate Chicano studies by making more history.

Of her work for that day, Leda tells me: "When I honor Dolores Huerta, I am honoring my Salvadoran mother and my Indigenous ancestors."

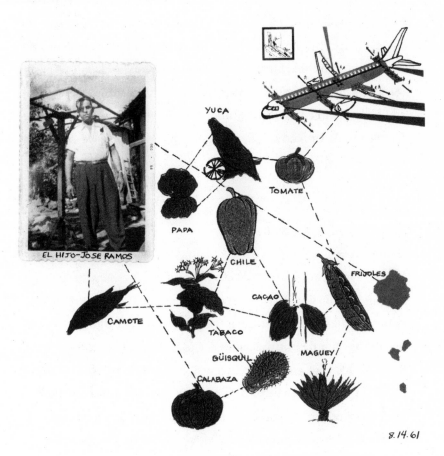

"Transmigración del moderno Maya-Pipil" (1997) mix media on blueprint paper. Artist Leda Ramos. Leda Ramos Collection, Central American Memoria Histórica Archive, Special Collections and Archives, Cal State LA University Library.

When visual art moves us to awe, it can change history. Studies report that we find art that progresses from one tradition, say realism, to another, and art that deviates from artistic conventions of the time and shocks us with the new, to be more powerful. More surprising and awe-inspiring cultural forms—whether they be visual art, *New York Times* stories, music, or urban legends—are more likely to be shared digitally and to transform how we perceive the world. Susan Crile's art archives the horrors of torture. In Leda Ramos's art and teaching, she and her students archive the place of the immigrant within a political narrative of a history of colonialism and violence, protest, and change. We feel shock and awe at this life pattern of subjugation, and wonder what we might do to end such oppression.

A Life of Visual Awe

In our evolution as a most cultural primate, humans have been finding awe in visual art for tens of thousands of years. Our aesthetic capacities for creation and appreciation have allowed us to see the geometries of the natural and social worlds and navigate those worlds with greater intelligence. Across history, awe-inspiring visual art has allowed us to find hints of what we make together of the ever-changing mysteries of life. Visual art allows us to directly experience awe and enjoy its individual and collective benefits. In the service of promoting cultural evolution through changing minds and history, visual art has shocked and awed people into new ways of seeing the world. These themes ran through a series of stories Steven Spielberg shared from his life of visual awe.

Spielberg and his wife, Kate Capshaw, hosted a small gathering in Los Angeles on technology and social progress, which I was lucky enough to attend. When it was my turn to present, I spoke of how to measure awe in the chills, in tears, in the vagus nerve, in the voice and face, and in the DMN, and how awe moves us to wonder and saintly tendencies. As I was talking about the chills, Steven raised his hand. I paused my presentation and, in a slightly absurd act, called on him. He told the story of being awestruck at seeing his new grandchild being born, Kate leaning into his leg while sitting on the floor.

Later that night I happened to sit next to Steven and Kate when out for dinner. They spoke of their careers in film and painting. Of *West Side Story*, the 2021 remake that Steven had just wrapped up. Of the funeral for Kirk Douglas, who used to frequent Steven's mom's restaurant in LA to flirt with her. Stories about how the crying was so intense on the set of *Schindler's List* that one actress needed three days of therapeutic intervention to recover from re-creating this awesome archive of the horrors of the Holocaust.

I had to ask:

Steven, what was awe like for you as a child?

Without missing a beat, he recalled seeing his first film when he was five. His dad, an engineer involved in the invention of the computer, took him from their home in Camden, New Jersey, to a theater in Philadelphia. As they inched forward in a long line near the brick walls of the theater, young Steven, holding tightly to his dad's large hand above, thought they were going to the circus. Instead, it was to see Cecil B. DeMille's *The Greatest Show on Earth* from 1952. After a wave of disappointment, Steven started to attend to the film's grainy images. Two trains career down the tracks. A character in a car drives alongside, trying to warn them. To no avail. The trains collide and cars fly everywhere, bodies hurtling into space. Young Steven felt suspended in time, wonderstruck. Awed.

At home, Steven began crashing the cars of his model train set. His dad had to repair the trains repeatedly, so he let Steven borrow the family video camera instead, which he used to stage and film more than one hundred toy train wrecks. No damage was done in this realm of the imagination, just the sacred geometry of make-believe destruction.

One night his dad gathered him up and hustled him into the car. They went to a field and lay on their backs on blankets. A meteor shower washed over the sky. Steven recalls the light, the profusion of stars, how vast the night sky was, and his experiments with seeing—directly, or out of the corner of the eye—fleeting patterns of stellar awe.

It was this wonder of life he hoped to give to others in *E.T.* and *Close Encounters of the Third Kind*.

As Steven asked for the check, he summed up why he still goes to movies and makes movies for others:

We are all equal in awe.

NINE

THE FUNDAMENTAL IT

How Spiritual Life Grows out of Awe

> *As I lay there thinking of my vision, I could see*
> *it all again and feel the meaning with a part of*
> *me like a strange power glowing in my body;*
> *but when the part of me that talks would try to*
> *make words for the meaning, it would be like*
> *fog and get away from me.*
>
> > • BLACK ELK

> *Twant me, 'twas the Lord. I always told him,*
> *"I trust to you. I don't know where to go or*
> *what to do, but I expect you to lead me," and*
> *he always did.*
>
> > • HARRIET TUBMAN

Growing up in a white town in Ohio, Jennifer Bailey—Reverend Jen, as she is known today—first felt the heat of racism when she was five. As she was jumping off a slide in a park, a classmate asked: *Why is your face dirty?* She ran into Bethel African Methodist Episcopal Church and felt embraced in the quiet of that space. Years later in the same church, she would hear Sister Oliver play on the organ and feel that cashmere blanket of sacred sound. In these experiences, she awakened to a big idea:

I am beloved in the eyes of God.

In her teens, Bailey served the impoverished and unhoused. At divinity school she found inspiration in scholars such as Reinhold Niebuhr, but felt agitated to transform Christianity into a more inclusive and diverse faith. Today her organization, Faith Matters Network, engages thousands on questions of spirit, faith, the soul, and the Divine. She ministers in skinny jeans, quoting Beyoncé alongside the Bible and other sacred texts.

We speak on the phone during a fraught time: she is pregnant as COVID-19 is just overwhelming New York, proving particularly deadly to people of color. At the beginning of our conversation, Reverend Jen takes stock of spiritual tendencies today. The numbers of the religiously unaffiliated are rising, in particular among people in their thirties, like her. They don't attend church regularly, follow a single dogma, or identify with one religion or another. It is an era of rising religious homelessness. At the same time, people today are deeply spiritual. This has been the case since humans began being humans, for relating to the Divine is a deep human universal. Two-thirds of young people in the United States, and 90 percent of all Americans, believe in the Divine, that some kind of spirit, or vast force, animates the course of their lives, and that there is a soul that persists beyond the life of the body.

When I ask Reverend Jen where she finds mystical awe, her answer comes easily: the strength and courage of African American women. Her grandmothers fled the terrorism, lynchings, and segregated spaces of the Jim Crow South of the 1950s. Her mother, raised in Chicago, was a student in the first integrated high school class of the 1960s. In thinking about these women, Reverend Jen slows. She cites how the trauma of racism is passed from one generation to the next in the damage it inflicts upon the cells of our bodies. She expresses reverence for how African American women from the past and present overcome. They do so, she says, in spirit. Spirit they find in the kitchen. In telling stories, laughing, singing, and dancing. And in church. There, in soulful community, they "make a way out of no way," as one of her grandmothers liked to say.

It was faith that sustained these women. Faith in God. In love. In justice. In hope. She feels this spirit today at spoken word events, in coffeeshops, at improv shows, in music, and at the dinner table. And most recently, at the "die-ins" she has led to call attention to police brutality. She feels guided by spirit, as Harriet Tubman did leading slaves to their freedom.

As Reverend Jen's story of awe makes its way to the present, she pauses. After a brief silence, she reflects: "I guess I am *composting religion*."

For thousands of years we have relied on nature metaphors to describe mystical awe, the feelings of encountering what we call the Divine, what we feel to be primary, true, good, and omnipresent. In some Indigenous traditions, Hinduism, and Taoism, for example, images and metaphors of the sun, sky, light, fire, rivers, oceans, mountains, and valleys are invoked to explain the Divine. Here is Lao Tzu describing Tao, the vital life force, or "way":

> Highest good is like water. Because water excels in benefitting the myriad creatures without contending with them and settles where none would like to be, it comes close to the way.

Reverend Jen's metaphor of "composting religion" may feel particular to our twenty-first century of organic farms, urban gardens, plant-based diets, and farmers markets. Composting, though, is thousands of years old. When we compost, we gather raw materials—food scraps, grasses, leaves, animal manure—and let them decay in a place of storage. Over time, microorganisms, bacteria, fungi, and worms break down the raw materials, consuming what is toxic and distilling a humus, an amorphous, sweet-smelling, jellylike black mixture of plant, animal, and microbial origin. The nitrogen of humus is absorbed by the roots of plants, nourishing life.

Reverend Jen's composting metaphor suggests that mystical awe follows a pattern of decay, distilling, and growth. This would seem to fit her own life story, of breaking down the sexist and colonialist strains of Christianity, distilling a spirit she found in the faith of African American women, and growing mystical feeling with others in her ministry. Perhaps our own experiences of mystical awe, or spiritual experience, if you like, follow this pattern of the decay of the default self's preconceptions about the world, which results in the distilling of some essential feeling that gives rise to the growth of our own spiritual beliefs and practices. Perhaps the 4,200 religions active today are doing much the same, transforming in a process of decaying, distilling, and growing as cultures and humans evolve.

Spiritual Humus

When Malcolm Clemens Young was in sixth grade, he and his classmates traveled to Ashland, Oregon, to attend a few Shakespeare plays. At night, they camped. At four o'clock one morning, Malcolm awoke and wandered outside his tent. In the quiet of this moment, he was awestruck by the patterns of moonlight on a nearby lake. In recalling this event, Malcolm told me what he wondered about in that moment of natural awe: "What could create such beauty?" A beauty that he could "feel at any time." It felt like an "extraordinary gift from God."

In his teens, Malcolm read the Bhagavad Gita, the Sutras of Buddhism, Thoreau and Emerson, and the Bible many times. After graduating from college, he had an unfulfilling stint as a financial consultant, so he enrolled at Harvard Divinity School. There, in Cambridge, Massachusetts, he tells me, he lived a few houses away from where Ralph Waldo Emerson gave his historic Harvard Divinity School address on July 15, 1838. To only a handful of faculty members assembled, Emerson exhorted people to let religious dogma decay and go in search of their own distilled experiences of mystical awe:

> The perception of this law of laws [for Emerson, that a benev-
> olent life force unifies all living forms] awakens in the mind a
> sentiment which we call the religious sentiment, and which
> makes our highest happiness. Wonderful is its power to charm
> and to command. It is a mountain air. It is the embalmer of
> the world. It is myrrh and storax, and chlorine and rosemary.
> It makes the sky and the hills sublime, and the silent song of
> the stars is it. By it, is the universe made safe and habitable,
> not by science or power. Thought may work cold and intran-
> sitive in things, and find no end or unity; but the dawn of the
> sentiment of virtue on the heart, gives and is the assurance
> that the Law is sovereign over all natures; and the worlds, time,
> space, eternity, do seem to break out into joy.

For Emerson, mystical awe is intertwined with nature—mountain air, the scent of rosemary, hills, the song of stars. It heals like myrrh (a resin extracted from trees used as incense and medicine). It is the provenance of virtue, more so than cold thought or science. It is a pathway to our highest happiness—of feeling integrated into something larger than the self.

Malcolm would make his way to becoming dean of Grace Cathedral, which sits augustly atop Russian Hill in San Francisco. Over lunch, I ask Malcolm about his earliest experiences of awe, hoping to catch a glimpse of a spiritually inspired child and hear of visions, perhaps, or callings, or premonitions in dreams of a young mystic. After describing his experience by the lake, he smiles broadly and tells me about . . . the first time he dunked in a pickup basketball game.

And then it pours out: Walking around the countryside of Davis, California, where he grew up. Roads at night under expansive skies. Storm systems coming in over that flat Central Valley farmland. Emerson's Harvard Divinity School speech. And moments of awe that day: in prayer, surfing, riding his bike to Grace Cathedral, passages from the Bible, the form-shifting fog that embraces San Francisco in ever-changing geometries.

I ask Malcolm what it is like to work in a career whose bottom line is mystical awe. He has no real interest, he answers, in proof, dogma, definition, or debate over the semantics of terms—"Is there a God?" "Is there a soul?" "What is sin?" "What is the afterlife?" He points his finger outward to some sense of space around us:

> I get to be with people in the most intimate moments in their lives. When someone dies. Or a baby is born. Or I am standing next to two people at the altar. I say this is God, right here, around us. . . .

My last sermon was on decolonizing the mind, in honor of the Kenyan writer Ngũgĩ wa Thiong'o. We have histories of colonialism and slavery. Those histories are rooted in our minds. Gays have felt this self-condemnation for decades. Such shame. But there are no good or evil people. That is what history has given to us.

This Sunday after my talk, an eighty-year-old man came up to me and was crying. He hugged me.

That is awe.

In this moment from Malcolm's life as a minister, we see decay (breaking down the legacy of colonialist and homophobic beliefs), distillation (the feeling that led the elderly man to break down in tears), and growth (that simplest expander of interconnectedness, the hug).

In high school and college, Malcolm carried William James's *The Varieties of Religious Experience* around with him, tucked under his arm, which (for good reason) provoked teasing from his friends. Malcolm Clemens Young was composting William James's experiences of mystical awe from 120 years ago.

James was raised in a nineteenth-century New York family who had the means and free-spiritedness to wander and wonder. He went to experimental schools. He lived with his family in Europe when he was a child and then studied art when he was eighteen. Alongside these privileges, James suffered from anxiety of every kind. Panic. Self-doubt. Generalized anxiety. And a claustrophobia that led him to find window shutters unnerving unless they were opened to just the right degree. In his twenties, James was so beleaguered by severe depression that he contemplated suicide.

James would begin a lifelong search for what he would call the fundamental cosmical IT, or mystical awe:

But it feels like a real fight—as if there were something really wild in the universe which we, with all our idealities and faithfulness, are needed to redeem.

For James, there is an experience to be had, one of mystical awe, that is wild and beyond the ideas of the default self and society's status quo.

Seeking such "wild in the universe," James listened to talks by itinerant spiritualists. He attended seances. Inspired by amateur philosopher Benjamin Paul Blood, James experimented with nitrous oxide. This drug activates the opioid system, which produces feelings of merging, and GABA, a neurotransmitter that energizes thought. In a rush of nitrous oxide, James called out: *Oh my god, oh god, oh god!* The anxieties of his default self were decaying. With the "tattered fragments" of words he described what was distilling as "thought deeper than speech." He had discovered mystical awe through a drug we get at a visit to our dentist today.

These experiences are what led James to gather and curate stories of awe. He compiled personal accounts of encounters with the Divine, so often stories of inexplicable and at times extraordinary experiences, from ministers, writers such as Tolstoy and Whitman, acquaintances, and ordinary citizens. He would present his thinking in the Gifford Lectures in 1901 and 1902 in Edinburgh, Scotland, and from these talks publish *The Varieties of Religious Experience*, the most revolutionary book on religion from the twentieth century and a touchstone for those who study religion today.

In this book, James defines religion as "the feelings, acts, and experiences of men in their solitude. So far as they apprehend themselves to stand in relation to whatever they consider the divine." Religion is about our experience of relating to the Divine, which James describes as vast, primal, and enveloping. We can find these feelings, of bliss, oceanic love, grace, terror, despair, doubt, confusion, and mystical awe—in almost any context. In all religions—Hinduism, Buddhism, Judaism, Jainism, the many forms of Christianity, Islam, Sufism. In nature. In music. In ideas. And even in chemicals that we put into our bodies. His thesis is one of radical pluralism; the pathways to mystical awe are nearly infinite. Everyday mystical awe.

Just over a hundred years later, a new science of religion has concerned itself with this most complex cultural form, focusing on things like beliefs about God, ceremonies and ritual, dogma and explanation, and the historical evolution of religions. And William James's focus and ours, mystical awe.

Mystical awe often originates in inexplicable experiences that transcend the expectations of the default self. Experiences like James's with nitrous oxide or Reverend Jen's upon first entering the sacred space of a church. Or for Mark Twain, a dream of his younger brother's death; two weeks later his brother would die in a riverboat accident, and be buried in Twain's suit as he had dreamed. Or inexplicable visions, such as those of Bernadette, a desperately poor girl living near Lourdes, France, in the nineteenth century, who had eighteen visions of the Virgin Mary in the darkness of a cave that led her to discover a spring whose waters had healing powers (today five million people make the pilgrimage to Lourdes each year to be healed by those waters). In survey research, most people report having had such inexplicable and extraordinary experiences: they have sensed the presence of God or spirits, or heard the voice of God, or felt that remarkable turns of fate are guided by Divine forces. On two different occasions in my early months of grief, I distinctly felt Rolf's large hand on my back.

Mysterious experiences like these require explanation; our minds are impatient with the unexplained. This tendency to explain has given rise in different cultures to spiritual belief systems about illnesses, bodily sensations, sounds and sights, and mysterious forms of consciousness, like dreams or hallucinations. To pick one of many examples, the rich tradition of ghosts, demons, goblins, and spirits in Japan—known collectively as yōkai—offers ever-changing, very local explanations in supernatural forms that make sense of inexplicable sounds, lights, natural events, bodily states, or the feeling of being watched in darkness.

This thesis lies at the heart of the scientific study of religion and spirituality: that we rely on ancient cognitive systems to transform extraordinary experiences into beliefs, images, descriptions, and stories about the Divine. We attribute unusual experiences to the intentions and actions of an extraordinary actor, in this case a deity or deities. An earthquake becomes a god shaking the earth. Remission from cancer is the intervention of God. Moved by wild awe, ten-year-old Malcolm Clemens Young felt that God had given him the beauty of moonlight on a lake.

Our sensory systems shape inexplicable experiences into perceptible, supernatural forms. When we're in the dark, or looking at clouds, or taking in the swirling lines of bark on trees, or marveling at the geological patterns in rocks, regions of our brains may lead us to perceive faces where they are not, and these we take to be images of God. Our deep-rooted tendency to hear the human voice may lead us to hear the Divine in an exceptional wind or an awesome thunderstorm. When alone in an eerie or strange place, most likely at dusk or in the dark, we may feel seen, or touched, or even embraced, by God—reflecting the activation of our ancient attachment-related tactile system. Out of mysterious experiences, our minds construct a sense of the Divine, an all-powerful being that is watching us, hearing us, speaking to us, and embracing us.

As mystical awe unfolds, the default self dissolves, a shift in self-awareness that William James called "surrender." This has been found in studies in which through different means people are led to feel mystical awe, and activation in the DMN is observed with measures of brain response. These studies find that the DMN is quieted when Carmelite nuns recall a mystical experience, devout people pray in the lab, religiously inclined individuals contemplate the Divine, or meditators engage in contemplative practice. Mystical experiences not only deactivate the default mode network; they also activate cortical regions involved in experiences of joy and bliss. When overtaken by mystical awe we may feel goose bumps, tear up, tremble, or shake. We may bow or look upward and raise our arms to the sky, vestiges of seeking embrace. Sometimes we even call out, or quietly observe *wow* or *whoa*, close relatives of the sacred sound *om*.

This experience of mystical awe, this spiritual humus, is deeply shaped by culture, history, place, and ideas of the times. A geographical landscape and local flora and fauna will influence the metaphors, images, and beliefs that are our representations of mystical awe. Mount Fuji's majesty gave birth to a sect of Buddhism that worshipped it, shaping the practices and beliefs of that spiritual community. The well-chronicled mystical experiences of Aua, an Iglulik Inuit, were colored by his frozen, barren physical environment and a reverence for other animals that harsh food scarcity can bring.

Saint Francis of Assisi's mystical experiences arose in the

context of the thirteenth-century fascination with stigmata, the appearance of wounds on the body resembling those suffered by Christ on the cross. While fasting, Saint Francis had a vision of an angel with the stigmata on its hands and feet, and saw similar patterns of blood surfacing at the skin of his own hands and feet. This extraordinary vision led him to an experience of mystical awe, in which he felt himself to be merging with Jesus on the cross. (One wonders, though, about the malaria circulating in Italy at the time, one symptom of which was blood surfacing at the skin.) Mystical awe is shaped by concepts of the self, society, and body at the time.

Advances in science and technology feed into the cultural evolution of mystical awe. Today many people think of their soul in terms of patterns of energy, fields, entanglement, and vibrations, concepts given to us by Einstein and quantum physics. Perhaps our soul is a "quantum self," a pattern of vibrating energy that emanates out of the cells that are our bodies, energy that originated in the big bang and that lives on after we die. Economic ideas about free markets, choice, and hedonic pleasure in relation to mystical awe can be heard at the pulpit on Sundays in certain forms of Christianity, mindfulness movements, and profit-oriented psychedelic retreats. Mystical awe is always composting in the decaying of what we know and the growth of what is new.

Intelligent Design

Extraordinary experiences, and the ways we distill them, can give rise to new spiritual beliefs and practices. Out of mystical awe grow representations, images, symbols, music, and stories about the Divine.

Yuria Celidwen knows this firsthand. Of indigenous Nahua background, Yuria grew up in Chiapas, Mexico, raised by her father, one of Mexico's celebrated poets, and her mother, a professor of clinical psychology. When Yuria was eight, her mother was killed by a teenage driver, leaving her family in deep grief. Her grandmother Celina took her out into the lush forests of Chiapas, some of the most biodiverse in the world, where jaguars roam and enjoy sacred standing. Her grandmother opened Yuria to mystical awe, she tells me, to the songs of "growth" and "breath" in the forest.

In her teens and twenties, Yuria fell into an arty scene in Mexico City, of music, late nights, wild gatherings, and drugs. One evening she nearly died. Studies of near-death experiences find that they follow the patterns of mystical awe, of decay, distilling, and growth. Carefully read Yuria's story of awe, her recollection of what happened, and notice the references to vastness and mystery ("pitch black"; "sky opens"). And the chills ("Lightning fires up my body"). And threat ("Swarms of fiery ants"). And the dissolving self ("I become water"). Here is the beginning of her story.

I blacked out . . .

The earth breaks—pitch black—under my feet.

The sky opens—pristine clear—above my head.

My body is shaken by massive involuntary movements.

Lightning fires up my body.

Swarms of fiery ants, millipedes, worms, tiny roaches . . .

critters of the underground crawling over me.

Light dances behind my eyelids.

It flows . . . never static.

My body also loses form.

I become water.

My limbs have been absorbed into the ground.

I cannot feel my body.

A high-pitched, piercing sound fills my ears.

Water evaporates.

Thirst draws the moisture from my tongue.

I feel cold, burningly, laceratingly cold.

Yuria would regain consciousness but could not move her legs. Her friends could not make out the sounds she was uttering, and hurriedly took her to the hospital. There she would lose consciousness again, and float to a realm of different laws of space, time, and causality.

My eyes dissolve in smoke.

I am falling into thick, dense fog.

I am becoming space . . .

At my arrival to the ER, my body is unresponsive.

It's a mirage of an understaffed health center in a developing country.

No one seems to notice that I am aware.

An eye above my body opens.

It sees nurses, doctors, and the ghosts.

It also sees my parents—far away—and a few relatives and friends.

None of whom knows I am here.

No one can hear.

A few life memories come too,

shortcuts projected in the innermost screen of light.

The nurses strip me of my clothes.

They trade them for a surgical bracelet with no name.

I almost hear their thoughts before they speak.

"No," they say, "no vitals. She's gone."

But I am not!

I am here . . .

am I here?

Everything seems to fade.

Also fades the grip, the anger, the grief.

Instead, only a soothing moonlight peace.

Floating . . .

Melting into twilight . . .

In the liminalities of space

dwells the spirit bare . . .

I had yearned for this feeling so long,

and now it's finally here.

Lucidity

Pre-dawn skies

Luminous, resplendent, bright

. . . love . . .

At the end of this extraordinary experience, Yuria is visited by her grandmother:

She places a seed below my tongue.

"It is a medicine for sorrow and despair," she says, "let it sprout."

It is my grandmother that comes from the dead . . .

A primordial egg cracks and water flows. Lord Chaahk and Bolon Dzacab laugh loud.

The Sun of Wind strikes me with his lightning.

I take my first breath.

The defibrillator sends lightning through my body. My heart beats.

I am awake.

In this decaying and distilling, Yuria would be animated by growth. She would go on pilgrimages to sacred sites around the world, often traveling alone as an Indigenous woman. She carried out PhD scholarship on funerary rites, charting deep patterns in the Day of the Dead ceremonies in Mexico and Tibetan water rituals, in which we touch and hold on to the remains of the dead. Today she works for the United Nations on Indigenous rights. In her spare time she is preserving cloud forests in Chiapas.

When I ask Yuria about her experience, she explains it as a "nekyia," a journey narrative that pays homage to book XI of Homer's *Odyssey* ("nékys" means corpse in Ancient Greek). In most religions, Yuria explains, there are representations, in the form of stories, legends, poems, and myths, about journeys to the afterlife— Hades of ancient Greece, Sheol or hell in the Abrahamic traditions, Valhalla for the Norse, the bardo in Tibetan Buddhism, the Mictlán for the Indigenous Nahua, or Xibalbá for the Indigenous Maya. A nekyia journey, like a near-death experience, involves decay—the dissolution of the self; a distillation—celestial feelings of ascent found in surrender, chaos, and death; and growth—when we return to our waking lives. Understood within the science of mystical awe, nekyia are stories we tell to make sense of the inexplicable—what consciousness is like when we near death. Many religious and spiritual traditions, Yuria tells me, from rituals to iconography, grow from our collective effort to make sense of the mysteries of life.

Grounded in this idea, we can consider how religious and

spiritual practices grow out of experiences of awe, in fact in ways we have already considered. Our awe-related vocalizations become sacred sounds, chanting, and music, allowing us to symbolize and share feelings about the Divine. With visual art—such as that of myriad Mesoamerican traditions—we represent the sacred geometries perceived during mystical awe. We tell symbolic stories of gods in awe-inspiring dance. Yoga offers a series of body postures that often manifest our physical expression of awe, and that bring us the bodily feeling of the Divine, as in this story of awe from twentieth-century yogi and mystic Gopi Krishna:

> The illumination grew brighter and brighter, the roaring louder, I experienced a rocking sensation and then felt myself slipping out of my body, entirely enveloped in a halo of light. . . . I felt the point of consciousness that was myself growing wider, surrounded by waves of light. . . . I was now all consciousness, without any outline, without any idea of a corporeal appendage, without any feeling or sensation coming from the senses, immersed in a sea of light. . . . Bathed in light and in a state of exaltation and happiness impossible to describe.

Moving in unison becomes religious ceremony. Awe-related bowing, shaking, prostration, or looking to the sky give rise to ceremonial acts of reverence. Such rituals bring about a shared physiology, feeling, and attention to being part of something larger than the self. Muslims practicing the salat (the bowing performed five times a day) showed increased activation in the areas of the brain associated with acceptance, reflecting their sense of being connected to a Divine force that is larger than the self.

These many ways of representing mystical awe often come together in community spaces of awe-based intelligent design, of representations, symbols, and rituals that enable the collective experience of awe. The religiously inclined—about 60 percent of Americans—feel mystical awe at church, in prayer, when reading spiritual texts, while listening to sacred music, and when contemplating life and death. People who do not identify with a formal religion create their own "temples," finding mystical awe in nature, or in a collective activity such as singing in a choir, or in dance, as Radha Agrawal does. Or in meditating or practicing yoga. Or in music, as Yumi Kendall does. Today, the Divine comes in many forms.

The shared experience of mystical awe transforms our individual selves in ways that make for stronger groups. For example, empirical studies involving thousands of participants find that feeling a sense of spiritual engagement is associated with increased well-being, a reduced likelihood of depression, and greater life expectancy. And greater humility, collaboration, sacrifice, and kindness that spread through groups. Groups that cultivated these tendencies through forms of religion, a new line of theorizing contends, fared better in competition with other tribes that did not, over the course of our evolution. More intelligent design.

The toxicities of communities that revolve around mystical awe are also well chronicled, and have given the world tribalism, genocide, and the subjugation of those outside of the favored group—historically women, people of color, and Indigenous peoples in more than ninety countries. Extractive and authoritarian forms of power, as well as charismatic sociopaths, often find revered places in communities of mystical awe. This is a truth Reverend Jen Bailey, Malcolm Clemens Young, and Yuria Celidwen know all too well, given their life stories and cultural backgrounds. They are composting religion in ways to allow for the decay of such tendencies, and to distill something essential to power the growth of beliefs and practices that unite rather than divide.

Psychedelic Awe

Bob Jesse used to be an engineer at Oracle. Shortly after arriving at UC Berkeley, I would learn over lunch that Bob had been transformed by experiences with entheogens: chemical substances, typically of plant origin and with deep origins in Indigenous cultures, that include, among many others, psilocybin, ayahuasca, peyote, and the synthesized drugs LSD, MDMA, and DMT. Knowing of my interest in awe, in 2004 Bob invited me to a retreat focusing on the scientific study of psychedelics.

My own psychedelic experiences were fast tracks to mystical awe, attempts to redeem William James's "something really wild in the universe." As if inspired by Emerson's Harvard Divinity School speech, Rolf, our friends, and I threw ourselves into wonders of life while experiencing psychedelics, moving in a throbbing unison in the mosh pit of an Iggy Pop show, marveling at movements of grains of sand amid the loud roar of the Pacific, hearing the sounds of Mozart outdoors merge with the light and scent of eucalyptus trees, wandering through an exhibit of kindergarteners' art in Golden Gate Park, witnessing a shorebird die from an algae infection and move through what we perceived to be the dance of death.

One experience of psychedelic awe stays in the cells of my body to this day, a trip Rolf and I made in our early twenties in

Zihuatanejo, Mexico, where Timothy Leary escaped to when on the run from the law. We went on a journey to "El Faro," the lighthouse, a fitting direction for us: my mom taught Virginia Woolf's transformative *To the Lighthouse* in her classroom. After taking a small boat to the isthmus on whose faraway point El Faro stood, we walked past dozens of red crabs dug into holes, each throwing out radiating balls of sand to mark its territory, which it defended with absurdly large claws, and we absorbed their strangeness and beauty. A fallen tree in the sand, perhaps a small manzanita, now gnarled driftwood, reached out to us, its smoothed branches leaning, yearning, seeking touch, intending and aware.

On the trail, we walked several miles with a precipitous view of the ocean to our left. The Pacific Ocean was illuminated. Magenta bougainvillea pulsated. Arriving at the lighthouse, sweaty and sun warmed, we stood inside in a small circular space with two windows peering out. The ocean's horizon vanished into pure, refracting light. The room's white walls glowed in the brilliant sun of Mexico. A roar of wind and waves surrounded us, echoing, hovering, moving, repeating. On the windowsill sat a piece of pink soap and some rusty nails.

What decayed for me that day was "the interfering neurotic, who . . . tries to run the show." I experienced inexplicable and at times extraordinary sensations—a wind; the embracing, powerful sun; the porous boundaries between Rolf and me; entrained rhythms of breathing, side-by-side strides, and the regular crunching of footsteps. And a sublime laughter about life's absurdities breaking into fragments of sound that vanished in the wind. The distilling of transcendent feelings of brotherhood.

Some fifteen years later in Mill Valley, California, I sat with a cluster of scientists wondering how to study psychedelic awe. One of the first questions we entertained: How do we measure mystical experience? Thankfully, Ralph Hood was on hand. Ralph, it has to be said, bears a striking resemblance to Walt Whitman. He had translated the writings of William James, and scholars of mysticism who followed, into, of all things, a questionnaire—"Hood's Mysticism Scale"—which would figure prominently in the new science of psychedelics.

The next question: Do psychedelics really change people? As with many experiences of awe, people say they have been transformed by psychedelics. The alternative hypothesis, though, is that people *think* they have changed but actually revert to personally ingrained habits of thinking and feeling. William James hinted at this possibility, that mystical awe reveals our individual temperaments: some mystical experiences, he observed, are more optimistic (think Walt Whitman) and others more pessimistic (think Leo Tolstoy). Today, a prominent theory holds that during times of transformation, our identities emerge more forcefully to construct experience in the present moment. This reasoning yields an ironic prediction: Psychedelic experiences make us more like who we are, rather than changing us in any enduring ways. Mystical transformation is an illusion. Out of the decay of these extraordinary experiences, we simply distill who we really are.

My Berkeley colleague Oliver John was in attendance, a specialist in the study of identity change. He had a hunch: psychedelics make us more open to experience. This tendency is captured in statements such as "I come up with new ideas," "I am fascinated by art, music, and literature," and "I am original." People who are open to experience, studies show, are receptive to ideas and new information, are innovative and creative, are often moved to chills and tears by art and music, and are inclined toward empathy and generosity. The defining emotion of openness, you probably already guessed, is awe. Perhaps psychedelics open us up to openness.

Neuroscientist Roland Griffiths listened carefully. Over the course of several years, with Bob Jesse quietly assisting, Griffiths would distill in a first, field-shaping experiment what is at the heart of the psychedelic experience, mystical awe—given to us by Indigenous traditions that are thousands of years old—and see whether it promoted growth in the study's participants. In a double-blind experiment (one in which experimenters and participants alike were unaware of which participants got what), the participant received either psilocybin or a placebo. The participant relaxed on a couch for eight hours during the journey, listening to music with eye covers on, with a therapist and guide nearby. What is called the "set and setting"—how people are oriented to the experience and the comfortable context in which it takes place—were carefully implemented.

In this study, 13 percent of the participants receiving psilocybin reported feeling intense fear. Sixty-one percent of the participants reported a mystical experience that day. That is, on Hood's Mysticism Scale, they reported that they:

- had merged with some kind of force larger than themselves,
- encountered fundamental truths about life,
- felt a sense of reverence for what is sacred,
- experienced intense joy and awe,
- and experienced timelessness and a dissolution of boundaries between themselves and the world around them.

This finding has been replicated: across studies, 50 to 70 percent of participants report that psychedelics produce one of the most significant experiences of mystical awe of their lives.

And, yes, people grew. When compared to their self-assessments before the study, two months later participants who had ingested a small serotonin-altering chemical had become more open to experience, their minds and hearts more open to big ideas, music, art, beauty, mystery, and other people. I don't think there is another experience that produces mystical awe with such reliability except, perhaps, watching the birth of a child, nearly dying, or dancing with the Dalai Lama.

Since Griffiths's breakthrough experiment, one line of studies has looked to psychedelics as an approach to our most complex struggles, such as depression, anxiety, eating disorders, obsessive-compulsive disorder, and PTSD. Psychedelics have been found to reduce levels of depression and anxiety, as well as the fear one might feel when living with a terminal disease. Eighty percent of smokers smoke significantly fewer cigarettes after a guided psychedelic experience. People struggling with alcoholism drink less. Psychedelic experiences make us less likely to commit crimes.

How might psychedelics open our minds to the wonders of life? One straightforward thesis championed by University of Alabama at Birmingham scientist Peter Hendricks and Johns Hopkins scientist David Yaden is that the magic ingredient is awe. In keeping with this thinking, UC San Francisco neuroscientist Robin Carhart-Harris has found that psychedelics consistently deactivate the DMN, thus revealing that a core phenomenological dimension to the psychedelic experience—ego death, or vanishing or disappearing self—has correlates in shifting brain activation. Psychedelics, like awe, reduce activation in threat-related regions of the brain—the amygdala—freeing people from the threat-vigilance of trauma, or obsessive ideas, or addictions, or even the awareness of the certainty of our own mortality. Psychedelics lead people to feel greater common humanity and perceive fewer distinctions with others. These compounds lead us to be more altruistic up to a year after a guided journey, and more curious and open to others. With these plant medicines, given to us by Indigenous cultures thanks to their thousands of years of composting the mystical awe found in these molecules, we do indeed redeem "something really wild in the universe," something very close to our "highest happiness."

Awe Walk in India

In 2010, Nipun and Guri Mehta sold everything they had from their life in Silicon Valley and walked 600 miles through villages in India, in 120-degree heat and monsoon downpours, living on one dollar a day. The married couple was walking in the tradition of Mahatma Gandhi's salt march, when he marched 240 miles to the sea with tens of thousands of fellow protesters to grab a handful of salt in defiance of the British Salt Act of 1882. That protest, powered by moral beauty and moving in unison, would dethrone English colonial rule. Political collective effervescence indeed.

Over lunch one day, Nipun described to me the mystical awe he felt on this pilgrimage. Impoverished villagers would always give them food—humanity's first act of moral beauty. In a graduation speech at the University of Pennsylvania, Nipun distilled what he learned on this awe walk into the acronym WALK: Witness, Accept, Love, and Know thyself. In the vast and mysterious 180-degree view of life one finds at two miles per hour and in Kierkegaard's "chance contacts" with strangers, we discover mystical awe.

In 2020, Nipun invited me to a retreat he named Gandhi 3.0,

to take place in Ahmedabad, India. The invitees included scientists, government officials, tech leaders, and people working in nonprofit organizations. And so, with my twenty-year-old daughter, Serafina, I made the sixteen-hour-flight to be part of Gandhi 3.0, held at the Environmental Sanitation Institute (ESI), a couple of miles from Mahatma Gandhi's ashram. This modest institute was built to bring toilets to India, in reverence of one of Gandhi's most impassioned causes, to champion nationwide toilet access (in his era, so-called untouchables composted the feces of people in castes above them). The entrance to ESI is a museum of toilets, with annotated photos, models, flow charts, and histories of toilet and sewer systems. Posters provide lessons about the life cycles of composting. The toilets in our rooms composted our waste, feeding the lush grounds of the ESI.

One day, at Gandhi's ashram, we sat quietly in the sand-filled square near the Sabarmati River, where Gandhi meditated each day. We reflected in the room where he wrote at a small desk, spun wool, and took in the view of a courtyard outside. From such a modest room came vast ideas that would inspire Martin Luther King Jr. to acts of courage, which would stir Berkeley students in 1964 to free speech protests of moving in unison, which would nourish the student antiwar movement, which would pave the way in the swinging pendulum of history for Ronald Reagan's rise to power. History so often follows the ebbs and flows of awe.

On one day of the retreat, I interviewed two sisters under the warm surround of a banyan tree, the national tree of India. Trupti Pandya, the younger sister, had read of Nipun and Guri's pilgrimage and decided to set out on her own. Her older sister, Swara Pandya, begrudgingly came along, worried what her younger sister might do. Over five months, Trupti and Swara walked 1,600 miles along the Narmada River, called "mother," like many rivers in India. Along the way they were fed and housed by strangers. For Trupti, our greatest illusion—the scarcity mindset of modern life—began to decay. Extraordinary experiences distilled each day. The river—its currents, reflections, swirling light, and rushes and hisses—sounded like the voice of God, telling Trupti that life is guided by "a gentle, kind force, every step of the way." She and Swara created rituals: greeting the river each day, expressing gratitude to families who opened their cupboards to feed them. In visits to temples, Trupti held pebbles that had been touched by the feet of pilgrims. She felt moved, empowered, fearless, and alive. She now works in a shelter for young women who have been battered and abandoned. Decay, distilling, and growth.

On the last day of Gandhi 3.0, we took part in an awe walk that composted beliefs and practices from around the world. We walked around a dark, leaf-covered pool where rainwater was collected. Following Buddhist tradition, we took four steps and then bowed and touched our foreheads to the ground. Many of us touched trees as we passed by. Toward the end of this thirty minutes of silent moving in unison, volunteers invited us to take a handful of salt from a large pile—mimicking Gandhi's own act of righteous courage. Bowing with forehead on the ground and eyes looking to the side, I made eye contact with Jayesh Patel, who directs the ESI built by his father, who was raised by two women who caught Gandhi in their arms when he was assassinated.

We then moved to a clearing where we all sat in silence. I felt touched by the sun on my right cheek and forehead. In nearby lush plants and trees, growing out of my composted waste, birds sang a web of sound; I could almost hear in their songs *woo-hoo* and *whoa.* A gentle breeze rushed down from the trees and over the grounds. I could feel myself dissolving into the bright sky, surrounded and embraced. I sensed Rolf smiling and spread out in the sky and distributed in the light. In relation to something beyond words. Redeeming something wild in the universe. And kind.

Living a Life
of Awe

TEN

LIFE AND DEATH

How Awe Helps Us Understand the Cycle of Life and Death

What do you think has become of the young and old men?

And what do you think has become of the women and children?

They are alive and well somewhere,

The smallest sprout shows there is really no death,

And if ever there was it led forward life, and does not wait at the end to arrest it,

And ceased the moment life appeared.

All goes onward and outward. . . . And nothing collapses,

And to die is different from what any one supposed, and luckier.

· WALT WHITMAN

I n our twenty-six-culture study, no matter their religion, politics, culture, level of medical care, or life expectancy, people told stories about being awestruck by the beginning of life and its early unfolding—and about being moved in transcendent ways by watching the end of life.

Life

Our cycle of life, compared to that of other primates, is a defining feature of our evolution. Because of the narrowing of the female pelvis, brought about by our species' shift to walking upright, and the disproportionate size of the human head to accommodate our large, language-producing brain, our infants are born premature. In fact, wildly premature, taking ten to fifty-two years to reach semifunctioning independence, if there is such a thing. Our hypervulnerable babies require years of intensive face-to-face, skin-to-skin care, networks of caregivers, a safe home, and enculturation just to survive.

Childbirth is the most undervalued act of courage in human history. Our twenty-six-culture study revealed just how extraordinary the appearance of new life is, giving rise to epiphanies of different kinds. People were struck by the raw fact of how a sperm and ovum create life, one emerging from a mother's womb, as hinted at in this story from Russia:

> It was the birth of my daughter. The appearance in light of another person. It is a miracle! Life, which you gave, pains which passed for the appearance of a new person. The first cry. Facing that new life. I froze, dumbfounded. It is difficult to convey the feelings I felt at that moment.

Some wrote of their amazement at their baby's sublime beauty, as in this forgivably hubristic example from Mexico.

The birth of my second daughter, and she was a very pretty girl when she was first born, contrary to all other babies who don't look good recently born.

Babies have a transfixing physicality: a baby's hypnotically large forehead, anime-like eyes, little lips, and small chin capture onlookers in awe-like absorption. In this astonished state, the besotted caregiver forgets about the spit-up on their new blouse, the years of sleep deprivation, the involuntary sexual asceticism, and the disappearance of evenings out for dinner or with friends. I can still recall with awe the first time I looked at my daughter Natalie's face, just as she emerged from Mollie's womb, and how in her eyes and mouth and cheekbones and forehead—a system of facial morphology built up by sixty genes—I could see the geometries of generations of grandmothers, grandfathers, aunts, uncles, and a mother, shaping the features and contours of her face.

People spoke of the arrival of a new life as a gift, as in this example from Indonesia:

Witnessing the birth of my firstborn. It had been a long wait, about eight hours, from eleven p.m. to seven a.m. I was there with my wife throughout her painful labor. But when he finally emerged, I just couldn't believe what a beautiful and wonderful gift God has bestowed on my wife, and I just couldn't stop smiling and feeling awe and grateful to God for giving us a son.

For some, the arrival of a child triggered epiphanies about time, as in this story from South Korea:

That vague wonder that I felt when I was pregnant turned into wonder and awe of life as I gave birth. I also felt the expectations and joy for the next generation, as it is the law of nature. It was also an opportunity to realize how precious life is.

And about the responsibilities of protecting a new life, as in this story from Japan:

When I gave birth to a child for the first time, I was deeply moved by the realization and responsibility of becoming a parent, as well as the preciousness of life. From now on I felt that I would desperately live just to protect this life.

Many narratives referred to the bodily responses of awe, the tears, chills, tingling, and the urge to hold and touch and feel skin-to-skin warmth. Common to the narratives were references to a sense of transcendent, boundary-dissolving connection whose neurophysiology is now becoming understood. Recent research finds that both parents show elevated levels of oxytocin, that neuropeptide that promotes boundary-dissolving openness and connection, six months after the birth of their first child. And a region of the mammalian hypothalamus, the MPOA, activates patterns of parenting in both women and men, whether heterosexual or gay. The MPOA is responsive to the sights and sounds of infants—the skin, cooing, cuddling, touch, mutual gaze, and fragrance and softness of the tops of their heads. This region of the brain activates dopamine release and deactivates the threat-sensitive amygdala. This synchronized neurophysiology of parent and child underpins the shared attention and intersubjectivity so common in experiences of awe across the wonders of life.

In many stories, people found their own moral beauty in the birth of a child, as in these narratives from Russia and China:

The birth of my son. It was nine years ago. I was happy with the maternity ward. I wanted to hug the entire world.

The birth of my child made me truly have the sense of awe. It made me see the miracle of life and it also made me more tough and tolerant when I interacted with people around me.

Some stories revealed how the arrival of a child triggers the nesting instinct humans express as childbirth approaches, which this Brazilian dad finds in, of all things, buying new furniture and filling out forms!

The birth of my first son. In 1992. I was in Natal Rio Grande do Norte. With me was my first wife. Before, I bought new furniture to welcome him! Right after, I took care of making him a health insurance plan.

There are a limited number of species, outside of bird species, that "nest" like we do. The nests they create are where offspring are born, and out of which community members forage for food and return and eat together in safety. The "nests" we create often contain cultural archives of awe—music, lullabies, books, images of people of moral beauty, mobiles with beautiful geometries, wallpaper with life patterns. Those nests become home, an entrance into a culture's ways of awe.

And what is true of new caregivers is true of grandparents, so often awestruck by the arrival of grandchildren, as in this story from France:

> The birth of my grandchild was a moment of awe and full of emotion. I was present during the ultrasound scan and I saw this wonderful tiny human being. Even though I am a mother of six children, I lived this moment with awe. I was moved, full of joy, I cried as for the birth of my children. I left the maternity ward overexcited, I wanted to shout my joy to the whole world and was overwhelmed at the same time. These moments were very rich in emotion.

We are the only primate species in which women live significantly beyond the age of menopause. This shift in life expectancy over the history of our species ensured that grandmothers, experts in giving birth and raising offspring, lived long enough to share their wisdom and physical talents with young women having children at the average age of nineteen years or so in hunter-gatherer times and more recently in our history. The vulnerability of our offspring requires intensive care from many quarters, including aging grandparents, who hopefully find new forms of awe in this next wave of loving support for children.

The wonders and horrors of childbirth led Nancy Bardacke to a remarkable career in promoting more awe-filled births. Bardacke was transformed in the late 1960s by the natural childbirth work of Fernand Lamaze. At that time, U.S. culture had overmedicalized childbirth, so much so that laboring women were often drugged to full unconsciousness while giving birth. They often didn't recognize their new babies upon first seeing them. Nancy worked as a midwife, and then created a mindful birthing program that has brought thousands of humans into the world. She has seen it all, from placing a neonate she knew was soon to die in the arms of his parents, to thousands of high vagal, oxytocin-rich births. When we spoke, she described her work as follows.

> The birth . . .
> You see the head crown, and then the eyes and face slowly appear. WOW. Each time I don't believe that the baby will come out. And each time it does. It is a miracle. It is a privilege to witness life become.
> My work is like a child . . . it didn't belong to me . . . it came through me . . .
> Birth and death are metaphors for everything.
> Breathe in, I am here.
> Breathe out, I expire.
> WONDER!

In the right circumstances, childbirth is the very beginning of years of exploration of the eight wonders of life. The way in which we play introduces children to wonders of different kinds—moving in unison in dance, camping, music, painting and drawing wild forms, and discovering sacred geometries. Childhoods rich with awe are good for the child. In one illustrative study, five-year-olds who watched an awe-inspiring nature video, compared to children in a control condition, were more imaginative in how they played with a new toy and chose smaller circles—another way to measure the small self—to describe themselves. My collaborators Dante Dixson, a professor at Michigan State University; Craig Anderson;

and I have found that as children develop, regular feelings of awe animate their curiosity in school and predict better academic performance for students in underresourced neighborhoods.

One of the most alarming trends in the lives of children today is the disappearance of awe. We are not giving them enough opportunities to discover and experience the wonders of life. Art and music classes do not make the school budget. The free-form play of recess and lunchtime is being replaced with drills to boost scores on tests that have only modest relation to how well kids do in school. Teachers must teach to those tests rather than engage students in open-ended questioning and discovery, where the unknown is the centerpiece of the lesson. Every minute is scheduled. And the natural world children are experiencing is undergoing mass extinctions. It's no wonder that stress, anxiety, depression, shame, eating disorders, and self-harm are on the rise for young people. They are awe-deprived.

Rachel Carson saw what was happening as early as the 1950s. She knew the importance of awe, and over her life she fought pharmaceutical companies and the gender and sex biases of science and journalism, and transcended the early death of her sister, her own cancer, and near-continual financial hardship to write about her favorite systems in nature, warning the world of pesticides like DDT and launching in important ways today's efforts in the United States to save our planet.

When she realized the ways in which young people were being deprived of awe, she offered an alternative approach in a remarkable essay from *Woman's Home Companion*, placed in between recipes for mayonnaise and potato salad and ads for Best Foods. In her essay "Help Your Child to Wonder," Carson lays out an awe-based approach to raising children.

It begins with a story of awe about her twenty-month-old nephew, Roger, whom she would raise because of her sister's early death. They wander down to the Atlantic Ocean one wild, stormy night. Getting soaked and risking colds, they laugh at the frothy waves, finding a "spine-tingling response to the vast, roaring ocean and the wild night around us." Later, on a rain-drenched walk in Maine woods, Roger delights in the now spongy texture of the lichen on rocks: "getting down on chubby knees to feel it and running from one patch to another . . . with squeals of pleasure." I bet they sounded like *weee* and *wow* amid longer periods of open-mouthed, wide-eyed silence.

Carson observes "that true instinct for what is beautiful and awe-inspiring is dimmed and even lost before we reach adulthood." She wishes that each child would live according to "a sense of wonder so indestructible that it would last throughout life, as an unfailing antidote against the boredom and disenchantments of later years, the sterile preoccupation of things that are artificial, the alienation from the sources of our strength."

How can we live a life of awe with young children? How can we do it by ourselves? First, Carson suggests, find awe and wonder in our senses. In simple, unfettered, slowed-down acts of looking. At clouds. Up at the sky. In listening to the natural world. The wind. There you will find, in Carson's words, "living music," "insects playing fiddles" in "insect orchestras."

She, like Edmund Burke, suggests opening our minds to vastness. Here's one way: trace an insect sound to its source. We can do the same for other systems of nature—thunder, waves, rain, the wind, a cloud, pine needles lying glistening on the ground, a bird call, the outlines of hills or mountains.

Distrust acts of labeling and classifying—the currency of the default self. Avoid reducing natural phenomena to words. Instead begin with mysteries. Where does an insect's sound go? What is the mystery of a seed? Approach the natural world (and life) with this question: What if I had never seen this before?

Mysteries awaken us to systems. Look to the sky and listen for migrations of birds. Follow the tides. Watch the growth of a seedling and its relationship to the earth. Take in the ground of a forest, the humus, fungi, and tree roots, which we now know to be communicating via slow neurochemical signals, intertwined in ecosystems of collaborating species.

In these wonder-filled explorations, we encounter the epiphany that in "those who dwell . . . among the beauties and mysteries of the earth are never alone or weary of life." Carson ends this astonishing essay, written while she herself was battling cancer, by quoting oceanographer Otto Pettersson, a person of moral beauty for her. Pettersson made groundbreaking discoveries in the study of the biology of fish, tides, ocean depths, and large waves underneath the surface of the sea. Nearing his own death at ninety-two, Pettersson observed: "What will sustain me in my last moments is an infinite curiosity as to what is to follow."

Death

Roshi Joan Halifax is a hero of twentieth- and twenty-first-century stories of awe. In her early twenties, she protested in the U.S. civil rights movement. For her PhD work, she studied the Indigenous Dogon people in Mali, and later the Huichol of Mexico, and witnessed how mystical awe is archived in story, ritual, ceremony, music, and visual design in Indigenous traditions thousands of years old. Frustrated with graduate school, though, in the 1960s she did what most alienated PhD students only think about doing: she bought a Volkswagen bus, took it on a ferry to North Africa, and drove by herself through villages and countryside, in search of a more communal spirit. Talk about an awe walk.

During her brief marriage to Stanislav Grof in the 1970s, she carried out some of the early experiments with LSD therapy. She collaborated with Joseph Campbell in his work on mythologies. Inspired by Buddhist monk Thich Nhat Hanh, she trained for years to become a roshi, or monk, very uncommon for a woman. Today Roshi Joan leads the Upaya Zen Center in New Mexico, which trains people in contemplative approaches to death.

Roshi Joan's book *Being with Dying* tells the story of what she learned from more than four decades of this work, in particular with young men dying of AIDS. It is well chronicled how dying has been overmedicalized, moved into sterile, fluorescent-lit hospital rooms with machines and televisions and half-eaten trays of "food" nearby. The rituals, ceremonies, stories, music, song, touch, and contemplative practices that enable the dying and those they love through this transition do not make their way into hospital rooms—the antithesis of awe-based, intelligent design. Roshi Joan's life work is to return us to the wonders of watching others die.

In being with the dying, a first principle is *not knowing*. Quiet the chatter of the default self. We don't truly know what dying is like. Nor, really, what happens after. Be open. Observe. Wonder.

A second is *bearing witness*. Let the dying guide the experience. When facing the uncertainty, fear, and horrors of dying, our tendency is to take action, provide a hopeful interpretation, reframe, or turn away. Instead, Roshi Joan says, just be there. Listen. Sit in silence. Rest your hand on the arm of the dying. Breathe. And follow where the dying will take you.

Finally, find *compassionate action*. Be open to suffering and its companion, kindness. Studies show that we respond to others' pain in one of two general ways: either with our own distress, which leads us to turn away in cortisol-fueled flight, or with compassion, the latter being better for those who suffer and those who witness such suffering. In a practice Roshi Joan teaches, you breathe in a person's suffering, and then breathe it out transformed. The cycle of life and death is one of many, like that of our breathing.

In watching Rolf pass that last night of his cycle of life, with pulsating fields of light pulling him away into something vast, I was guided by this wisdom, thanks to reading Roshi Joan's book and being in conversation with her. I felt open to witnessing this part of the cycle of life. I wondered about the thoughts and feelings that were to be the last of his living brain and body, what Virginia Woolf called the "flickerings of that innermost flame which flashes its myriad messages through the brain."

Seeking to understand those "flickerings," scientists today are studying the cellular activity in the brain that follows death. Others with a historical bent have compiled stories about consciousness after decapitation, like that attributed to Charlotte Corday. After being beheaded at the guillotine in 1793, Corday showed flushed indignation upon being slapped by her executor. I searched the literature, seeking I know not what exactly, and found solace in the new science of near-death experiences (NDEs).

This science is based on stories of people like Yuria Celidwen who have come back from the brink of death. These are narratives of people who have survived near-fatal heart attacks, strokes, the trauma of a car wreck, or lying broken on a slab of granite after a fall while rock climbing. NDE stories sound like stories of awe, and in fact surfaced in our twenty-six-culture study, as in this story from Australia:

> In childbirth I was declared as deceased. While I was in a state of altered consciousness I felt the most incredible sense of peace and calmness. I was watching what was being done to my body to revive me and I remember thinking "Why don't they stop . . . I am at peace with myself and the world." My then husband rushed in and I knew that it wasn't my time as my two young daughters needed me. I immediately returned to my body. It then took around seven hours to deliver my son Kyle.

In the scientific literature on NDEs, as in the story above, people report a vanishing of their default selves. They are merging with a larger force or form of consciousness that feels infinite, pure, fundamental, and benevolent. The unfolding of experience does not seem governed by the temporal and spatial laws of our default mind. Transcendent emotions wash over them, like compassion, love, and bliss. And awe. I sensed this in my brother's face that last night he was alive.

Months after Rolf's death, I traveled to Japan with Mollie. In the dusk of our first day in Kyoto, amid heavy rains that followed a record typhoon, I made my way to a cemetery on a hill outside the city. Japanese families honor the deceased in plots of granite tombstones, which stand next to one another, gather moss, and slowly lean and fall to the ground with time—the Japanese principle of wabi-sabi, that the evolution of all forms, from the natural to "man-made," follows a cycle of creation, birth, growth, decay, and death. Near an earthy, tangled bank of overgrown hills, I stood in front of an arrangement of about fifteen tombstones, three rows in total, each about two feet tall, some inscribed in Japanese, all uniquely patterned. One, a smaller marker with a plain granite face, leaned and tilted into a taller one just next to it. They rested together, touching in the rain.

That night watching my brother's life cycle end left me awe-struck, and then deeply awe-deprived. I went in search of awe to find how to make my way again. In experiences of awe across the eight wonders of life, I learned that there is more to our existence than what ends with the last breath of the body. That I could feel and hear Rolf in gentle breezes and in being embraced by a powerful, warming sun. And that he and I shared some kind of awareness in spaces of feeling beyond what we ordinarily see and hear. And that the people we love, and our companions in a life of awe, remain with us in even more mysterious ways after they leave, enabling an opening to new wonders of life. And that these lessons can be found in seeking awe—which leads us to our last chapter.

ELEVEN

EPIPHANY

The Big Idea of Awe: We Are Part of Systems Larger than the Self

> *Whilst this planet has gone cycling on according to the fixed law of gravity, from so simple a beginning endless forms most beautiful and most wonderful have been, and are being, evolved.*
>
> · CHARLES DARWIN

C harles Darwin's emotions so often gave rise to his big ideas, including the science of emotion, of which the story of awe is but one chapter. Caring for his ten-year-old daughter Annie until her death shaped his thinking about the evolutionary benefits of sympathy. His humble curiosity about fellow human beings brought Darwin, of a privileged background, into conversations with working-class pigeon breeders, opening his eyes to their science of breeding species for signature qualities, or adaptations. His kind cheerfulness on the *Beagle* held the crew together as Captain Robert FitzRoy suffered a nervous breakdown, and enabled a five-and-a-half-year voyage of incomparable and inexplicable wonders.

Might awe have shaped Darwin's thinking about evolution?

In *The Descent of Man* in 1871 and *The Expression of the Emotions in Man and Animals* in 1872, Darwin locates the emotions we experience today in the vast story of mammalian evolution. Reading his descriptions of more than forty emotional expressions is an epiphany, as rich a portrayal of emotional expression as any, except perhaps that of Japanese artist Kobayashi Kiyochika's print series *100 Faces* from 1883. But Darwin never used the word "awe" in these descriptions.

Perhaps awe—so often a religious emotion—was a psychic battleground for him. To tell a story about the mammalian evolution of awe would challenge the creationist dogma of his era, one his devout wife, Emma, hewed to. That dogma held that our self-transcendent emotions, emotions like bliss, joy, sympathy, gratitude, and awe, are the handiwork of God, placed into human anatomy and our social lives by some form of intelligent design. Perhaps Darwin was avoiding awe to keep the peace at home.

Frank Sulloway knows the details of Darwin's life and work better than just about any scholar you might encounter, so I dropped by his office to solve a mystery, the mystery of Darwin's awe. Frank's office is the outward expression of his mind. On the walls hang framed photographs he took during his eighteen trips to the Galápagos, arresting images of tortoises, pink flamingos, and cacti-dotted volcanic landscapes. Yellow Post-it notes on his computer contain scribblings of statistical equations. Most prominent of all is a three-foot-tall stack of *Darwin and His Bears: How Darwin Bear and His Galápagos Islands Friends Inspired a Scientific Revolution,* Frank's new children's book, whose main character, a bear, tells the story of how he guided Darwin to his discoveries.

For his senior thesis at Harvard in 1969, Frank wrote about the eight-person film expedition he organized the previous summer to retrace Darwin's footsteps in South America, during his voyage with HMS *Beagle*, and focused on the role that the *Beagle* voyage had in Darwin's scientific development and conversion to the theory of evolution. This thesis included a computer-aided content analysis of all the letters written by Darwin during the voyage, to his family and his mentor, John Stevens Henslow.

For his PhD in the history of science at Harvard, Frank wrote his thesis on Freud, which would become *Freud, Biologist of the Mind* and garner Frank a MacArthur genius award. But Freud's allure, Frank tells me, quickly wore off—his thinking seemed closed and arrogantly unfalsifiable.

Frank kept returning to Darwin. His intellectual courage, humility, and kindness drew Frank, the scholar, into Darwin's life. In the course of his graduate work and forty years of scholarship after, Frank has retraced Darwin's footsteps on the Galápagos based on the ship's log of the *Beagle* and Darwin's own sketches. He wrote the bestselling book *Born to Rebel*, which profiles how Darwin's status as a latter-born child—he was the fifth of six siblings— accounts for his open-minded, polymath, risky, and awe-inspired revolutionary life and thought. He now is revising Darwin's *On the Origin of Species*, integrating tens of thousands of new scientific studies. In his spare time Frank spearheads conservation efforts on the Galápagos to limit a goat population, an invasive species disrupting the islands' ecosystems. Other people's moral beauty can become a moral compass in our own lives, and for Frank, Darwin is a life-altering person of moral beauty.

Over Indian food, Frank ate sparsely, like the competitive miler he was at Harvard. I asked him about Darwin's awe.

"Frank, why did Darwin write about 'astonishment,' 'admiration,' and 'devotion/reverence' but not 'awe'? Was he worried about writing about a religious emotion? Or creating conflict with Emma?"

Frank shakes his head.

"That's silly. . . . It's more likely that people didn't use the word 'awe' during the mid-nineteenth century. Try Google Trends and see what you find . . ."

Sure enough, Google Trends finds that the use of the word "awe" has risen dramatically since 1990. Darwin's use of "admiration," "reverence," and "devotion" was simply in keeping with linguistic conventions of the day. This small piece of detective work, though, led Frank to other thinking. He continued.

"But Darwin did experience the chills. One had to do with listening to the organ in King's College at Cambridge."

Later that night Frank sent me Darwin's story of musical chills, which we relied on earlier as a guide to musical awe. He added this passage from Darwin's autobiography about feeling awe—"a sense of sublimity"—toward painting:

I frequently went to the Fitzwilliam Gallery, and my taste must have been fairly good, for I certainly admired the best pictures, which I discussed with the old curator. . . . This taste, though not natural to me, lasted for several years, and many of the pictures in the National Gallery in London gave me much pleasure; that of Sebastian del Piombo exciting in me a sense of sublimity.

In his office, Frank continued wondering.

"And of course, in the Amazonian rain forest when he spoke of the 'temple of nature.'"

Frank continued.

"And now that I think about it, in his Diaries he writes about waking from a dream in Chiloé, Chile. When he awoke, Darwin was awestruck at intertwined vines on the bank of a river, which would appear in the last sentences from *Origins*, some of my favorites in all of Darwin's writings."

Frank then paused, and in reverential tones that can only be compared to those of a radio personality from the 1940s, quoted those last sentences from *On the Origin of Species*:

It is interesting to contemplate a tangled bank, clothed with many plants of many kinds, with birds singing on the bushes, with various insects flitting about, and with worms crawling through the damp earth, and to reflect that these elaborately constructed forms, so different from each other, and dependent upon each other in so complex a manner, have all been produced by laws acting around us. These laws, taken in the largest sense, being Growth with Reproduction; Inheritance which is almost implied by reproduction; Variability from the indirect and direct action of the conditions of life, and from use and disuse; a Ratio of Increase so high as to lead to a Struggle for Life, and as a consequence to Natural Selection, entailing Divergence of Character and the Extinction of less improved forms. Thus, from the war of nature, from famine and death, the most exalted object which we are capable of conceiving, namely, the production of the higher animals, directly follows. There is grandeur in this view of life, with its several powers, having been originally breathed by the Creator into a few forms or into one; and that, whilst this planet has gone cycling on according to the fixed law of gravity, from so simple a beginning endless forms most beautiful and most wonderful have been, and are being, evolved.

There, in one paragraph, is Darwin's epiphany—that life has evolved and is ever evolving. I take this moment in Darwin's life and writing to be a story of awe. It is grounded in a new way of seeing some essential truth about the world. This passage follows awe's familiar unfolding: there is wonder ("It is interesting to contemplate"), vastness ("many plants of many kinds," "endless forms"), mystery ("complex a manner"), and kindness ("most beautiful"). As in other stories of awe we have read, Darwin turns to metaphor—"clothed with many plants," the Creator "breathes" life into existence. As in traditional ecological knowledge, Darwin sees the profound interdependence of species. We find reconciliation of the awesome and awful, that the "war of nature" gives birth to "endless forms most beautiful." In taking in a tangled bank near a river, of birds singing, insects flitting about, and worms doing their composting work in damp earth, Darwin saw the laws of evolution, growth, reproduction, inheritance, variability, and extinction. In awe, Darwin found "grandeur in this view of life."

Tangled Bank of Life

Awe is about knowing, sensing, seeing, and understanding fundamental truths, and leads to epiphanies across the eight wonders of life—transforming how we see the essential nature of the world. William James called this the "noetic" dimension of mystical awe. Emerson's spiritual experiences in nature revealed "the law of laws," the deepest truth for him in his understanding of the meaning of life. Reverend Jen's epiphany in a church told her that she is loved by God. Literary studies speak of epiphanies, such as those in Virginia Woolf's *To the Lighthouse*, or that of Stephen Dedalus in James Joyce's *A Portrait of the Artist as a Young Man*, in which status quo meanings of society are stripped away and essential truths about our social lives are illuminated. For Toni Morrison, in the epiphanies found by allowing goodness its own speech, we come to understand ourselves.

What is the substance and structure of awe's epiphany? Its big idea? What form of self-knowledge do we gain in experiences of awe? In our studies and the stories of awe we have encountered, people most reliably say something like: "I am part of something larger than myself." For Belinda Campos, it was a great chain of sacrifices made by her predecessors that enabled her to attain a PhD. For Stacy Bare, it was being a small cog in a misguided military operation. For Louis Scott, it was seeing his life being imprisoned by a history of racism this country was "founded upon." For Yumi Kendall, it was feeling part of the history of music. Awe locates us in forces larger than ourselves.

The English language does not offer up a rich vocabulary to capture this sense of being connected to things larger than the self, so individualistic are we. (That task is much easier for speakers of Japanese, for in Japanese one translation of "self"—jibun—means "shared life space.") As a result, English speakers turn to abstraction, to metaphor, to neologism, or to mystical language to describe this big idea of awe. William James called it "the fundamental IT."

Margaret Fuller "the all." Walt Whitman and Henry David Thoreau "the scheme." Ralph Waldo Emerson called it the "transparent eyeball," to public scorn. For Yumi Kendall it was a cashmere blanket of sound. For Rose-Lynn Fisher a sacred geometry. For Reverend Jennifer Bailey it is a timeless cycle of religious composting. And many of the people we have heard stories of awe from, ordinarily articulate and well practiced in describing matters of mind and spirit, like Claire Tolan, Robert Hass, Steve Kerr, Yuria Celidwen, and Malcom Clemens Young, simply gesture to a kind of space in which awe touches them, surrounds them, embraces them, embeds them.

What is it that awe connects us to that is larger than the self? That is initially invisible, but in the experience of awe becomes visible? That resists description and formulation, but appears like an image, or holistic pattern, like Darwin's dreamlike awakening to a vision of a tangled bank of life, as the default self's grip upon perception is loosened and dissolves?

My answer is this: it's a system. I realize "system" doesn't have the mystery of "numinous," or wild-eyed excess of "transparent eyeball," never mind the poetic beauty of "cashmere blanket of sound" or the metaphorical depth of "composting religion." In almost every realm of inquiry, though, from the study of the cell to formal analyses of dance, music, ritual, and art; to studies of religion, prisons, politics, and intellectual movements; to studies of our brains that make sense of these things, people turn to the idea of systems to make sense of the deep structures of the wonders of life. Systems thinking, it's worth noting, is at the heart of an Indigenous science now thousands of years old. It is an old, big idea. It may be our species' big epiphany.

Systems are entities of interrelated elements working together to achieve some purpose. When we look at life through this systems lens, we perceive things in terms of *relations* rather than separate objects. In feeling inspired at a political march, we may take note of how our calls of protest and fists thrust into the air are linked to those of others and synchronized with the words of a speaker. In noting how a song might bring us the chills, we sense how the notes relate to one another in dynamic, unfolding patterns.

In thinking in this way we perceive patterns of *interdependent* relationships. Here it is worth quoting Darwin: "these elaborately constructed forms, so different from each other, and dependent upon each other." Various forms of life, we are now learning, from the DNA in our cells to the individuals in our communities, are perpetually engaged in mutual influence, interdependent collaboration, and cooperation. In looking at the flow of people crossing a street, or the movements of five teammates on a court, or the interplay of color, line, form, and texture in a painting, or in marveling at life in an ecosystem, we holistically perceive how the parts of the whole are working together toward achieving some end.

In systems thinking, we note how phenomena are *processes* that evolve and unfold. Life is change. Our communities are always evolving. Nature is about growth, change, death, and decay. Music and art are continually transforming, in the changes they stir in our minds and bodies. Our spiritual beliefs and practices are continually decaying, distilling, and growing.

Our default mind gravitates to the certain and predictable—fixed, reliable essences in the world. Awe arises when we perceive change. When we sense a sunset changing from oranges to deep purplish blues, how clouds transform as they move across the horizon, how a knee-high two-year-old one day is speaking to you in sentences when only a moment ago they were babbling and cooing, how a nonviolent salt march can transform history. And in the recognition that that which is born and grows also ages and dies.

Finally, through a systems lens, phenomena, both living and created, are animated by *qualities* that unite their disparate elements according to a unifying purpose. This might be the moral beauty of someone whose life brings you to tears. Or the rhythm of music that synchronizes us with others in dance. Or beliefs about the human soul. Or the vying for life in nature that gives rise to the endless forms most beautiful that are the world's species. Or the feeling of awe expressed in art.

We sense the animating quality of a system holistically, in intuition, image, and metaphor—Steve Kerr's golden wave of light, Yumi Kendall's cashmere blanket of sound, Reverend Jen Bailey's composting religion, Yuria Celidwen's poetic account of the consciousness of nearly dying. And Charles Darwin's tangled bank, which, along with the tree, would become his central metaphor in his writings, uniting his observations into his understanding of the evolution of living forms. Awe enables us to see the systems underlying the wonders of life and locate ourselves in relation to them.

Wonders of Systems

The eight wonders of life are themselves systems. Acts of moral beauty instantiate our ethical systems. Forms of moving in unison like dance, everyday ritual, and basketball are systems of movement animated by ideas, and unite people in collective effervescence. The natural world is made up of interlocking systems, from the cells of our bodies to gardens, forests, oceans, and mountains. Music, art, film, and architecture are systems of creation that deploy their symbols and modes of representation to express the big ideas of identity and culture. Religion is a system of belief, rituals, symbols, images, music, stories, and ceremonies that bring people together in community. Life is a system, its animating quality following dynamics of growth and decay. The idea of a system is a system, an abstract set of propositions that organizes observations and explanations into a coherent whole.

We developed a systems view of life to adapt to the central challenges in our hypersocial evolution. Systems thinking allowed us to track the shared caregiving of our vulnerable young, the network of coalitions that defined our relations with friends, the more fluid social hierarchies we shifted to, and all the forms of collective activity that made up our daily life—food sharing, collaborative labor, defense, and celebration. Systems thinking emerged in our relation to nature and underlies traditional ecological knowledge. Our survival depended on our understanding of the social system— community—we are part of, and our relation to ecosystems; our minds developed a systems way of understanding, grounded in a new neural architecture of our social brains. Many Indigenous peoples developed this view of the grandeur of life thousands of years ago.

As Andrea Wulf tells it in her wondrous *The Invention of Nature*, the centrality of systems thinking to awe, science, and art is embodied in the life story of nineteenth-century scientist Alexander von Humboldt. Humboldt would be drawn to the Andes in the spirit of wonder and write about nature as a web of life—each living form exists within "a network of forces and interrelationships." His drawings of the maps of flora, fauna, climates, and geology of the twenty-thousand-foot Ecuadorian mountain Chimborazo would give birth in Western thinking to the idea of an ecosystem. System was Humboldt's big idea, shaping Darwin, who traveled on the HMS *Beagle* with Humboldt's books; Thoreau and Emerson in their writings about nature; Gaudí's organic and architectural wonders like the Sagrada Família; environmentalists and revolutionaries like Simón Bolívar (Humboldt abhorred the system of slavery); and poets like Coleridge and Wordsworth. Systems thinking is always composting.

Our default mind blinds us to this fundamental truth, that our social, natural, physical, and cultural worlds are made up of interlocking systems. Experiences of awe open our minds to this big idea. Awe shifts us to a systems view of life.

New studies are documenting how. The pattern to these results is that awe shifts our minds from a more reductionistic mode of seeing things in terms of separateness and independence to a view of phenomena as interrelating and dependent. For example, brief experiences of awe shift us from the illusions of the twentieth- and twenty-first-century thinking that we are separate selves to realize that we are embedded in complex social networks of interdependent individuals. Awe moves us to a sense that we are part of the natural world, one of many species, in an ecosystem of species dependent upon one another for survival. Awe opens our eyes to the idea that complex systems of interdependent adaptations gave rise to the millions of species that make up the living world. Awe even leads us to see systems-like patterns of agency organizing random sequences of digits.

Awe enables us to see that life is a process, that all endless forms most beautiful are deeply interconnected, and involve change, transformation, impermanence, and death.

Finding Our Place in the Systems of Life

Since that day on Paul Ekman's deck when he pointed me in the direction of awe, I have charted the systems of awe to tell its scientific story.

Awe begins with our miraculous eyes, ears, nose, tongue, and skin responding to the images, sounds, scents, tastes, and touches of the eight wonders of life. Our sensory systems represent these encounters in neurochemical patterns that make their way to the prefrontal cortex, where we interpret the wonders of life with the symbolic systems that are language and culture. Being moved by awe triggers the release of oxytocin and dopamine, a calming of stress-related physiology, and vagus nerve response, systems of millions of cells working to enable us to connect, be open, and explore. The complex systems of muscles in the face, body, and vocal apparatus enable us to convey to others what we find wonderful. Tears and chills, themselves end results of systems behind our eyes and under our skin, signal to our conscious minds the presence of vast forces that require we merge with others to adapt and understand. Being cultural animals, we turn to ever-evolving cultural systems, of chanting, song, and music; painting, carving, sculpture, and design; poetry, fiction, and drama; and supernatural explanation and spiritual practice—our archives of awe—to bring others into a shared understanding of the wonders of life.

But what is the end of awe, its unifying purpose? Here's my answer. Awe integrates us into the systems of life—communities, collectives, the natural environment, and forms of culture, such as music, art, religion, and our mind's efforts to make sense of all its webs of ideas. The epiphany of awe is that its experience connects our individual selves with the vast forces of life. In awe we understand we are part of many things that are much larger than the self.

Being part of this scientific story of awe has taught me that the evolution of our species built into our brains and bodies an emotion, our species-defining passion, that enables us to wonder together about the great questions of living: What is life? Why am I alive? Why do we all die? What is the purpose of it all? How might we find awe when someone we love leaves us? Our experiences of awe hint at faint answers to these perennial questions and move us to wander toward the mysteries and wonders of life.

Acknowledgments

I feel such warmth when thinking about my vast network of collaborators in the science of awe: Craig Anderson, Yang Bai, Belinda Campos, Serena Chen, Daniel Cordaro, Rebecca Corona, Alan Cowen, Dante Dixson, Amie Gordon, Sara Gottlieb, Kristophe Green, Jon Haidt, Oliver John, Neha John-Henderson, Michael Kraus, Daniel Loew, Laura Maruskin, Galen McNeil, Maria Monroy, Joseph Ocampo, Chris Oveis, Paul Piff, Disa Sauter, Lani Shiota, Emiliana Simon-Thomas, Eftychia Stamkou, Daniel Stancato, Jennifer Stellar, Todd Thrash, Jessica Tracy, Ozge Ugurlu, Everett Wetchler, David Yaden, Felicia Zerwas, and Jia Wei Zhang. This science was enabled in profound ways by the bold support of Christopher Stawski and the John Templeton Foundation. For the awe pioneers who shared their time and stories of awe with me, I bow my head in appreciation here. For careful readings of my writing, I am grateful to Barry Boyce, Yuria Celidwen, Natalie Keltner-McNeil, Mollie McNeil, Michael Pollan, and Andrew Tix. I found such joy in talking about awe with Chris Boas, Nathan Brostrom,

ACKNOWLEDGMENTS

Danielle Krettek Cobb, Chip Conley, Claire Ferrari, Roshi Joan Halifax, Jeff Hamaoui, Serafina Keltner-McNeil, Casper ter Kuile, Michael Lewis, Evan Sharp, Dan Siegel, Jason Silva, Matias Tarnopolsky, Jon Tigar, and Nick U'Ren. Thank you, Jason Marsh, for creating so many conversations about awe at the Greater Good Science Center. I had deep hesitations about writing this book, and upon starting had no idea what form it would take. My agent, Tina Bennett, guided me in finding the structure and soul of the book; she pointed me in regular missives to currents of awe in history, literature, and culture and challenged me in different drafts. Thinking of this brings a current of goose bumps to me now. To work on this book with my editor, Ann Godoff—all I can say is *wow*. What a humbling and mind-opening experience it has been. Thank you, Ann, for your interest in the transcendent, for guiding my writing with lightning-bolt epiphanies about this mysterious emotion, and for pushing me toward an understanding of the essence of awe beyond the data and figures and hypotheses.

Credits

Page 21: Map of emotional experiences evoked by video, copyright © Alan S. Cowen, 2017.

Page 34: Research materials and findings from study of vanishing sense of awe, courtesy of Yang Bai.

Page 107: Selfies from participants in the "awe walk" study, courtesy of Virginia E. Sturm.

Page 123: The sculpture of the skinless man, from Galerie de Paléontologie et D'anatomie Comparée, courtesy of the author.

Page 132: Participants in a study of wild awe, courtesy of Craig Anderson and Maria Monroy.

Page 134: Participants in a study of study, photos courtesy of Paul Piff.

Page 176: *The pull between attachment and release* from *The Topography of Tears* © Rose-Lynn Fisher, published by Bellevue Literary Press 2017, blpress.org.

Page 182: Berlin street art, courtesy of the author.

Page 189: "Transmigración del moderno Maya-Pipil" (1997) mix media on blueprint paper. Artist Leda Ramos. Leda Ramos Collection, Central American Memoria Histórica Archive, Special Collections and Archives, Cal State LA University Library.

Notes

ix **"From wonder into wonder":** Tzu, Lao. *Tao Te Ching*. Translated by Witter Bynner. New York: Perigee, 1944.

Introduction

xxii **I ached physically:** For an explanation of how the pain of loss activates different branches of the nervous system, see Eisenberger, Naomi I., and Matthew D. Lieberman. "Why Rejection Hurts: A Common Neural Alarm System for Physical and Social Pain." *Trends in Cognitive Sciences* 8 (2004): 294–300.

xxii **hallucinations that Joan Didion describes:** For a compelling account of how grief can lead to altered patterns of thought and perception, bordering, at least in experience, on the hallucinatory, see Didion, Joan. *The Year of Magical Thinking*. New York: Vintage Books, 2007.

xxii **Our minds are relational:** Andersen, Susan, and Serena Chen. "The Relational Self: An Interpersonal Social-Cognitive Theory." *Psychological Review* 109 (2002): 619–45.

xxii **vastest mystery I had encountered:** In his book *A Brief History of Death*, historian W. M. Spellman charts how death is the instigator of great thought and cultural forms. Across history, Spellman observes, cultures resort to one of three broad systems of beliefs to make sense of death. For the strict reductionists, the death of the body is it; it is the end of the individual. The agnostics throw up their hands, or keep open their minds, to the possibility that there is something beyond life, but they are noncommittal. And then there is most of humanity, which tells stories about some kind of afterlife, in different religious traditions. Spellman, W. M. *A Brief History of Death*. London: Reaktion Books, 2014. For more on the cultural history of how we approach death, see: Kerrigan, Michael. *The History of Death*. London: Amber Books, 2017.

Chapter 1: Eight Wonders of Life

3 **"our passions are uncharted":** Woolf, Virginia. *Jacob's Room*. London: Hogarth Press, 1922, 105.

4 **every human experience:** I was a graduate student at Stanford University, an epicenter of this cognitive revolution. My classmates Rich Gonzalez and Dale Griffin and I carried around the books just coming out by our faculty advisers about judgment and decision-making. There was buzz that someday this work, so challenging to accounts in economics of rational choice theory, would win Nobel Prizes, which proved to be the case for Daniel Kahneman and Richard Thaler. This work would make its way some thirty years later to popular books like: Kahneman's *Thinking, Fast and Slow*

and my friend Michael Lewis's *The Undoing Project* from 2016. In the mid-1980s, our bibles were: Kahneman, Daniel, Paul Slovic, and Amos Tversky. *Heuristics and Biases: Judgments under Uncertainty.* Cambridge, UK: Cambridge University Press, 1982. Nisbett, Richard, and Lee Ross. *Human Inference: Strategies and Shortcomings.* Englewood Cliffs, NJ: Prentice Hall, 1980.

4 **termed "System 1" thinking:** Kahneman, Daniel. *Thinking, Fast and Slow.* New York: Farrar, Strauss and Giroux, 2011.

4 **Ekman, though, would soon publish:** Early in the science of emotion, Paul Ekman and, across the Atlantic in Switzerland, Klaus Scherer oriented the field to these elements of emotions: the quality of their experience, their expression, how they influence thought and action, and their neurophysiological patterning. These arguments underlie many of the studies that examine how awe differs from states like fear, interest, the feeling of beauty, and surprise. Ekman, Paul. "An Argument for Basic Emotions." *Cognition and Emotion* 6, no. 3–4 (1992): 169–200. https://doi.org/10.1080/02699939208411068. Scherer, Klaus R. "The Dynamic Architecture of Emotion: Evidence for the Component Process Model." *Cognition & Emotion* 23, no. 7 (2009): 1307–51. https://doi.org/10.1080/02699930902928969.

5 **scientists mapped anger:** For a superb review of the science of the six states Ekman drew our attention to, see: Lench, Heather C., Sarah A. Flores, and Shane W. Bench. "Discrete Emotions Predict Changes in Cognition, Judgment, Experience, Behavior, and Physiology: A Meta-analysis of Experimental Emotion Elicitations." *Psychological Bulletin* 137 (2011): 834–55.

5 **restore our standing:** Tangney, June P., Rowland S. Miller, Laura Flicker, and Deborah H. Barlow. "Are Shame, Guilt, and Embarrassment Distinct Emotions?" *Journal of Personality and Social Psychology* 70 (1996): 1256–64.

5 **Sensing that there is more:** Barbara Fredrickson was the first to note this bias in the science of emotion, its focus on fight-or-flight states like anger, disgust, or fear, to the neglect of the positive emotions. Fredrickson, Barbara L. "The Value of Positive Emotions." *American Scientist* 91 (2003): 330–35.

5 **"the emotional brain":** LeDoux, Joseph E. *The Emotional Brain.* New York: Simon & Schuster, 1996.

5 **the secrets of love:** Gottman, John M. *Why Marriages Succeed or Fail.* New York: Simon & Schuster, 1993.

5 **moral issues of our times:** Haidt, Jonathan. *The Righteous Mind: Why Good People Are Divided by Politics and Religion.* New York: Vintage Books, 2012. Haidt, Jonathan. "The Moral Emotions." In *Handbook of Affective Sciences*, edited by Richard J. Davidson, Klaus R. Scherer, and H. H. Goldsmith, 852–70. London: Oxford University Press, 2003.

6 **cultivating our "emotional intelligence":** Mayer, John D., and Peter Salovey. "The Intelligence of Emotional Intelligence." *Intelligence* 17, no. 4 (1993): 433–42.

6 **"an age of emotion":** Dukes, Daniel, et al. "The Rise of Affectivism." *Nature Human Behaviour* 5 (2021): 816–20.

6 **survival-of-the-selfish-genes view:** In the late twentieth century, evolutionary thinking and the science of emotion were shaped by Richard Dawkins's selfish gene hypothesis, and its privileging of the gene as the unit of analysis and assumptions that humans have evolved competitive, self-serving traits that led to the reproduction of those selfish genes. This thinking produced a self-preservation bias in my field: emotions are about individual survival. In the twenty-first century, evolutionary thought shifted to the group and culture as the units of analysis. Discoveries of the cooperative tendencies of young children; our universal inclination to share; our instinct to attach, belong, and be tribal; and the neurophysiology of empathy,

contagion, mirroring, connection, compassion, and exploration were revealing a new lens upon human nature: we are a hypersocial species who accomplished almost all survival-related tasks, from the raising of vulnerable offspring to the provision of food, in collaborative, often altruistic groups. Groups that collaborate well and build a sense of shared identity, this reasoning would advance, are more likely to prevail and survive. And culture—the system of beliefs and practices that unite individuals into community—is an ever-evolving repository of shared knowledge and experience, a collective mind that enables us to adapt together to the challenges and opportunities in our natural and social environments.

7 **articulate a definition of awe:** Keltner, Dacher, and Jonathan Haidt. "Approaching Awe, a Moral, Aesthetic, and Spiritual Emotion." *Cognition & Emotion* 17 (2003): 297–314.

7 **We read treatments:** Kaufman, Scott B. *Transcend: The New Science of Self-Actualization.* New York: TarcherPerigee, 2020.

7 **mobs whipped up by demagogues:** Weber, Max. *Economy and Society: An Outline of Interpretive Sociology.* (Based on 4th German ed., various translators.) Edited by Guenther Roth and Claus Wittich. Berkeley: University of California Press, 1978.

9 **perceived threat also flavors experiences:** Our thinking was grounded in part in neuroscience: upon detecting threat, a small, almond-shaped region of the brain known as the amygdala revs up your body's fight-or-flight response and, if activated during awe, should blend fear into the experience. For an excellent review of this fight-or-flight physiology, see: Rodrigues, Sarina M., Joseph E. LeDoux, and Robert M. Sapolsky. "The Influence of Stress Hormones on Fear Circuitry." *Annual Review of Neuroscience* 32 (2009): 289–313. For recent thinking on the amygdala, see: FeldmanHall, Oriel, Paul Glimcher, Augustus L. Baker, NYU PROSPEC Collaboration, and Elizabeth A. Phelps. "The Functional Roles of the Amygdala and Prefrontal Cortex in Processing Uncertainty." *Journal of Cognitive Neuroscience* 11 (2019): 1742–54. In terms of threat-based awe, Amie Gordon found that when awe does involve perceived threat, it feels less good, increases your heart rate, and diminishes your well-being. In this and other work, we find that threat-based awe amounts to about a quarter of our experiences of awe. Gordon, Amie M., Jennifer E. Stellar, Craig L. Anderson, Galen D. McNeil, Daniel Loew, and Dacher Keltner. "The Dark Side of the Sublime: Distinguishing a Threat-Based Variant of Awe." *Journal of Personality and Social Psychology* 113, no. 2 (2016): 310–28.

9 **Perceptions of threat:** Nakayama, Masataka, Yuki Nozaki, Pamela Taylor, Dacher Keltner, and Yukiko Uchida. "Individual and Cultural Differences in Predispositions to Feel Positive and Negative Aspects of Awe." *Journal of Cross-Cultural Psychology* 51, no. 10 (2020): 771–93. For an excellent treatment of this respect-based, fear-colored awe in Japan, see: Muto, Sera. "The Concept Structure of Respect-Related Emotions in Japanese University Students." *Shinrigaku Kenkyu* 85, no. 2 (2014): 157–67. https://doi.org/10.4992/jjpsy.85.13021. PMID: 25016836.

10 **Emotions are like stories:** I really owe this thinking to Keith Oatley. Keith is not only a world-class cognitive scientist and leading theorist in the science of emotion but a prizewinning novelist as well. Out of his love of literature and study of emotion, he has made the case that emotions have storylike structures. Oatley, Keith. *Emotions: A Brief History.* Malden, MA: Blackwell, 2004.

10 **Having defined awe:** For excellent stories of awe fitting for our digital age, see Jason Silva's "Shots of Awe." https://www.thisisjasonsilva.com/.

10 **understanding mystical awe:** James, William. *The Varieties of Religious Experience: A Study in Human Nature: Being the Gifford Lectures on Natural Religion Delivered at Edinburgh in 1901–1902.* New York; London: Longmans, Green, 1902.

10 stories of awe: Bai, Yang, and Dacher Keltner. "Universals and Variations in Awe" (manuscript under review).

10 concern about "WEIRD" samples: Studies involving only WEIRD samples do not generalize to non-WEIRD individuals, namely most people of the world. Henrich, Joseph, Steve Heine, and Ara Norenzayan. "The Weirdest People in the World?" *Behavioral and Brain Sciences* 33, no. 2–3 (2010): 61–83.

12 a stirring theme: Edmundson, Mark. *Self and Soul: A Defense of Ideals.* Cambridge, MA: Harvard University Press, 2015.

13 *collective effervescence:* Durkheim, Émile. *The Elementary Forms of the Religious Life.* Translated by J. W. Swain. New York: Free Press, 1912.

13 Many mentioned night skies: Marchant, Jo. *Human Cosmos: Civilization and the Stars.* New York: Dutton Press, 2020.

13 our capacity to wonder: Drake, Nadia. "Our Nights Are Getting Brighter, and Earth Is Paying the Price." *National Geographic,* April 3, 2019. https://www.nationalgeo graphic.com/science/2019/04/nights-are-getting-brighter-earth-paying-the-price -light-pollution-dark-skies/.

14 Common to experiences of natural awe: Pollan, Michael. "The Intelligent Plant: Scientists Debate a New Way of Understanding." *New Yorker,* December 16, 2013.

14 *Music* offered up: For an excellent summary of the kinds of chanting found in different cultures and religions, and their place in ritual and ceremony, see: Gass, Robert. *Chanting: Discovering Spirit in Sound.* New York: Broadway Books, 1999. Chanting worldwide was and is a way in which people communicate about their encounters with mystical forces. It is interesting to observe how many of the sounds by which we communicate emotions like compassion and awe weave their way into chanting. Through influences on breathing, and in particular exhalation, which usually accompanies the production of the sounds of speech and emotional communication, chanting can slow the heart rate, activate the vagus nerve, reduce blood pressure, and enable a physical state of openness and wonder.

16 visual design of jewels: Huxley, Aldous. *The Doors of Perception: And Heaven and Hell.* New York: Harper & Row, 1963.

18 No one mentioned their laptop: This really shouldn't surprise us, for in general the time we spend on smartphones, Facebook, and other digital platforms tends to mildly depress our well-being. Tangmunkongvorakul, Arunrat, Patou M. Musumari, Kulvadee Thongpibul, Kriengkrai Srithanaviboonchai, Teeranee Techasrivichien, S. P. Suguimoto, Masako Ono-Kihara, and Masahiro Kihara. "Association of Excessive Smartphone Use with Psychological Well-Being among University Students in Chiang Mai, Thailand." *PloS ONE* 14, no. 1 (2019): e0210294. https://doi.org/10.1371 /journal.pone.0210294.

19 a realm beyond the profane: Many scholars have differentiated what we might think of as what is sacred from the mundane and profane. For Mary Douglas, this distinction centers on what is clean and pure (the sacred), and what is unclean and dirty. Douglas, Mary. *Purity and Danger: An Analysis of Concepts of Pollution and Taboo.* New York: Routledge, 2004. Rudolf Otto differentiated between the phenomenal—our sensory experiences of the immediate physical world—and the numinous—what lies beyond the senses. Otto, Rudolf. *The Idea of the Holy.* Translated by J. W. Harvey. 2nd ed. New York: Oxford University Press, 1950. Philip Tetlock, Jennifer Lerner, and their colleagues have done fascinating work showing that people become morally outraged when offered money for things that they deem sacred in their lives. Tetlock, Philip E., Orie Kristel, Beth Elson, Melanie C. Green, and Jennifer S. Lerner. "The Psychology of the Unthinkable: Taboo Trade-Offs, Forbidden Base Rates and Heretical Counterfactuals." *Journal of Personality and Social Psychology* 78, no. 5 (2000): 853–70.

19 **The study of emotional experience:** For a summary of the origins of this narrow focus in the science of emotion, and the considerable statistical and inferential problems that arise from this narrow focus, see: Cowen, Alan, Disa Sauter, Jessica Tracy, and Dacher Keltner. "Mapping the Passions: Toward a High-Dimensional Taxonomy of Emotional Experience and Expression." *Psychological Science in the Public Interest* 20, no. 1 (2019): 69–90. https://doi.org/10.1177/1529100619850176.

20 **widely used emotional experience questionnaire:** Watson, David, Lee A. Clark, and Auke Tellegen. "Development and Validation of Brief Measures of Positive and Negative Affect: The PANAS Scales." *Journal of Personality and Social Psychology* 54, no. 6 (1988): 1063–70.

20 **emotionally rich GIFs:** Cowen, Alan S., and Dacher Keltner. "Self-Report Captures 27 Distinct Categories of Emotion with Gradients between Them." *Proceedings of the National Academy of Science* 114, no. 38 (2017): E7900-E7909.

22 **In subsequent mapping studies:** Cowen, Alan, and Dacher Keltner. "Emotional Experience, Expression, and Brain Activity Are High-Dimensional, Categorical, and Blended." *Trends in Cognitive Science* 25, no. 2 (2021): 124–36.

23 **everyday awe:** Bai, Yang, Laura A. Maruskin, Serena Chen, Amie M. Gordon, Jennifer E. Stellar, Galen D. McNeil, Kaiping Peng, and Dacher Keltner. "Awe, the Diminished Self, and Collective Engagement: Universals and Cultural Variations in the Small Self." *Journal of Personality and Social Psychology* 113, no. 2 (2017): 185–209. Gordon, A. M., J. E. Stellar, C. L. Anderson, G. D. McNeil, D. Loew, and D. Keltner. "The Dark Side of the Sublime: Distinguishing a Threat-Based Variant of Awe." *Journal of Personality and Social Psychology* 113, no. 2 (2016): 310–28.

28 *self-transcendent* **states:** Stellar, Jennifer E., Amie M. Gordon, Paul K. Piff, Craig L. Anderson, Daniel Cordaro, Yang Bai, Laura Maruskin, and Dacher Keltner. "Self-Transcendent Emotions and Their Social Functions: Compassion, Gratitude, and Awe Bind Us to Others through Prosociality." *Emotion Review* 9, no. 3 (2017): 200–7.

Chapter 2: Awe Inside Out

29 **"The most beautiful experience":** Einstein, Albert. *Ideas and Opinions, Based on Mein Weltbild.* Edited by Carl Seelig. New York: Bonzana Books, 1954, 11.

29 **"A sense of wonder":** Carson, Rachel. "Help Your Child to Wonder." *Woman's Home Companion,* July 1956, 46.

29 **an eleven-year-old girl:** For a broader discussion of how the science of emotion played out in *Inside Out*, see: Keltner, Dacher, and Paul Ekman. "The Science of Inside Out." *New York Times,* July 6, 2015.

30 *how* **emotions work:** For a summary of the science of emotion, see: Keltner, Dacher, Keith Oatley, and Jennifer Jenkins. *Understanding Emotions.* 4th ed. Hoboken, NJ: Wiley & Sons, 2018.

30 **spider on a computer screen:** For a review of how emotions influence the elements of decision-making, see: Lerner, Jennifer S., Ye Li, Piercarlo Valdesolo, and Kassam S. Karim. "Emotion and Decision Making." *Annual Review of Psychology* 66 (2015): 799–823.

30 **our mind is attuned:** Transient feelings of fear also lead people to support more conservative policies toward immigration and terrorism. People who report more conservative attitudes on social issues tend to feel more fear in general, have more nightmares, and show a stronger startle response (an eye blink) when startled. Oxley, Douglas R., Kevin B. Smith, John R. Alford, Matthew V. Hibbing, Jennifer L. Miller, Mario Scalora, Peter K. Hatemi, and John R. Hibbing. "Political Attitudes Vary with Physiological Traits." *Science* 321, no. 5896 (2008): 1667–70. https://doi.org/10.1126/science.1157627. PMID:18801995.

NOTES

30 **The "out" of** *Inside Out*: This notion underlies Charles Darwin's influential account of emotional expression. He viewed the expressions we observe today—such as the tightened lips and clenched jaw of anger—as vestiges of actions from our mammalian past—the biting of attack. Darwin, Charles. *The Expression of Emotions in Man and Animals.* 3rd ed. New York: Oxford University Press, 1872/1998.

30 **it is the five emotions:** These ideas were part of a conversation Pete, Ronnie, and I had about sadness and its role in the film. Pete had begun thinking about the film in witnessing the sadness his own daughter showed as she entered adolescence, a time of surprising sadness as the ease and delights of childhood fade. Pete and Ronnie wanted the hero of the film to be the character of Sadness, but were getting pushback from the executive team, who thought sadness would be too depressing and discourage ticket sales. In that conversation, we talked about distinctions between sadness and depression; unlike sadness, depression is often flat, colorless, and devoid of passion and concern. We delved into the "inside" of sadness, how sadness slows life down, allows for reflection, and reorients us to what matters in life, given the loss we are facing. We considered the "out" of sadness, how tears bring others close to us. Pete and Ronnie prevailed and placed Sadness at the center of *Inside Out*.

30 **sequences of actions:** This view of emotion has its roots in anthropological and sociological analyses of emotion. These ideas, often rooted in rich observations of how emotions unfold in the dramas of social life, reveal emotions to be much more than fleeting states in the mind; they involve sequences of actions between individuals as they negotiate social relationships. Lutz, Catherine, and Geoffrey M. White. "The Anthropology of Emotions." *Annual Review of Anthropology* 15 (1986): 405–36. Clark, Candace. "Emotions and the Micropolitics in Everyday Life: Some Patterns and Paradoxes of 'Place.'" In *Research Agendas in the Sociology of Emotions,* edited by Theodore D. Kemper, 305–34. Albany: State University of New York Press, 1990. Shields, Stephanie A. "The Politics of Emotion in Everyday Life: 'Appropriate' Emotion and Claims on Identity." *Review of General Psychology* 9 (2005): 3–15. Parkinson, Brian, Agneta H. Fischer, and Anthony S. R. Manstead. *Emotion in Social Relations: Cultural, Group, and Interpersonal Processes.* Philadelphia: Psychology Press, 2004.

31 **our individual self gives way:** For an archive of first-person narratives about experiences with psychedelics, visit https://www.erowid.org/.

31 *Revelations of Divine Love:* Norwich, Julian. *The Revelations of Divine Love of Julian of Norwich.* Translated by John Skinner. New York: Doubleday, 1996. For an excellent history of Julian of Norwich's life, theology, and influence upon the world, see: Turner, Denys. *Julian of Norwich, Theologian.* New Haven, CT: Yale University Press, 2011.

31 **This dissolving of the self:** Popova, Maria. *Figuring.* New York: Pantheon Press, 2019.

32 **"there was no self":** Fuller, Margaret. Edited by Michael Croland. *The Essential Margaret Fuller.* Mineola, NY: Dover Thrift Edition, 2019, 11.

32 **The vanishing self, or "ego death":** Pollan, Michael. *How to Change Your Mind: What the New Science of Psychedelics Teaches Us about Consciousness, Dying, Addiction, Depression, and Transcendence.* New York: Penguin Books, 2019, 263.

32 **Aldous Huxley called it:** Huxley, Aldous. *The Doors of Perception: And Heaven and Hell.* New York: Harper Perennial Classics, 2009, 53.

33 **this default self:** Vohs, Katherine D., and Roy R. Baumeister, eds. *The Self and Identity, Volumes I–V.* Thousand Oaks, CA: Sage, 2012.

33 **When our default self reigns:** Twenge, Jean M. *iGen: Why Today's Super-Connected Kids Are Growing Up Less Rebellious, More Tolerant, Less Happy—and Completely Unprepared for Adulthood.* New York: Atria Books, 2017.

33 **An overactive default self:** Keltner, Dacher, Aleksandr Kogan, Paul K. Piff, and Sarina R. Saturn. "The Sociocultural Appraisal, Values, and Emotions (SAVE) Model of Prosociality: Core Processes from Gene to Meme." *Annual Review of Psychology* 65 (2014): 425–60.

33 **she approached more than 1,100 travelers:** Bai, Yang, Laura A. Maruskin, Serena Chen, Amie M. Gordon, Jennifer E. Stellar, Galen D. McNeil, Kaiping Peng, and Dacher Keltner. "Awe, the Diminished Self, and Collective Engagement: Universals and Cultural Variations in the Small Self." *Journal of Personality and Social Psychology* 113, no. 2 (2017): 185–209.

33 **"It was like lying":** "Theodore Roosevelt and Conservation." National Parks Service, U.S. Department of the Interior, April 10, 2015, https://nps.gov/thro/learn/his toryculture/theodore-roosevelt-and-conservation.htm.

35 **awe expands our sense of self:** Shiota, Michelle N., Dacher Keltner, and Amanda Mossman. "The Nature of Awe: Elicitors, Appraisals, and Effects on Self-Concept." *Cognition & Emotion* 21 (2007): 944–63.

35 **People feeling awe named qualities:** Fiske, Alan. P. *Structures of Social Life.* New York: Free Press, 1991.

35 **the Campanile tower:** Stellar, Jennifer E., Amie M. Gordon, Craig L. Anderson, Paul K. Piff, Galen D. McNeil, and Dacher Keltner. "Awe and Humility." *Journal of Personality and Social Psychology* 114, no. 2 (2018): 258–69.

36 **"the earth as a giant organism":** Holmes, Richard. *The Age of Wonder: The Romantic Generation and the Discovery of the Beauty and Terror of Science.* New York: Vintage Books, 2008.

36 **the overview effect:** Yaden, David B., Jonathan Iwry, Kelley J. Slack, Johannes C. Eichstaedt, Yukun Zhao, George E. Vaillant, and Andrew B. Newberg. "The Overview Effect: Awe and Self-Transcendent Experience in Space Flight." *Psychology of Consciousness: Theory, Research, and Practice* 3, no. 1 (2016): 1–11.

36 **Here is astronaut Ed Gibson:** White, Frank. *The Overview Effect: Space Exploration and Human Evolution.* 2nd ed. Reston, VA: American Institute for Aeronautics and Astronautics, 1998, 41.

36 **the default mode network:** Hamilton, J. P., Madison Farmer, Phoebe Fogelman, and Ian H. Gotlib. "Depressive Rumination, the Default-Mode Network, and the Dark Matter of Clinical Neuroscience." *Biological Psychiatry* 78, no. 4 (2016): 224–30. https://doi.org/10.1016/j.biopsych.2015.02.020. Epub February 24, 2015. PMID: 25861700; PMCID: PMC4524294. In more specific terms, the DMN includes the ventromedial prefrontal cortex, which is engaged when people evaluate progress toward their personal goals, and the posterior cingulate cortex, which is active when we think about memories of our past or how to navigate space from our own point of view.

36 **threat-filled awe:** Takano, Ryota, and Michio Nomura. "Neural Representations of Awe: Distinguishing Common and Distinct Neural Mechanisms." *Emotion.* Advance online publication. https://doi.org/10.1037/emo0000771.

36 **reduced activation in the DMN:** In a similar vein, Fang Guan and colleagues found in a study in China reporting that people who feel more everyday awe and are open-minded and wonder-filled in how they approach life showed lower activation in the posterior cingulate cortex, an important part of the DMN. Guan, Fang, Yanhui Xiang, Chen Outong, Weixin Wang, and Jun Chen. "Neural Basis of Dispositional Awe." *Frontiers of Behavioral Neuroscience* 12 (2018): 209. https://doi.org/10.3389 /fnbeh.2018.00209.

37 **DMN and the amygdala:** Converging with these brain findings, Amie Gordon has found that threat-based awe triggers fight-or-flight physiology in the body, as

indexed in the release of sweat in the glands in the hands and a boost in heart rate. Gordon, Amie M., Jennifer E. Stellar, Craig L. Anderson, Galen D. McNeil, Daniel Loew, and Dacher Keltner. "The Dark Side of the Sublime: Distinguishing a Threat-Based Variant of Awe." *Journal of Personality and Social Psychology* 113, no. 2 (2016): 310–28.

37 **It is worth noting:** Barrett, Frederick S., and Roland R. Griffiths. "Classic Hallucinogens and Mystical Experiences: Phenomenology and Neural Correlates." *Current Topics in Behavioral Neurosciences* 36 (2018): 393–430. https://doi.org/10.1007/7854.

37 **As our default self vanishes:** Bai, Yang, Laura A. Maruskin, Serena Chen, Amie M. Gordon, Jennifer E. Stellar, Galen D. McNeil, Kaiping Peng, and Dacher Keltner. "Awe, the Diminished Self, and Collective Engagement: Universals and Cultural Variations in the Small Self." *Journal of Personality and Social Psychology* 113, no. 2 (2017): 185–209.

37 **"I celebrate myself":** Whitman, Walt. *Song of Myself: 1892 Edition.* Glenshaw, PA: S4N Books, 2017, 1.

37 **In *The Age of Wonder*:** Holmes, Richard. *Age of Wonder: The Romantic Generation and the Discovery of the Beauty and Terror of Science.* New York: Vintage Books, 2008.

38 **"Astronomy has enlarged":** Holmes, Richard. *Age of Wonder: The Romantic Generation and the Discovery of the Beauty and Terror of Science.* New York: Vintage Books, 2008, 106.

39 **Wonder, the mental state:** Philosopher Jesse Prinz has written in illuminating ways about the evolutionary and cultural history of wonder: Prinz, Jesse. "How Wonder Works." *Aeon*, June 21, 2013. https://aeon.co/essays/why-wonder-is-the-most-human-of-all-emotions. For an earlier historical consideration, see: Keen, Sam. *Apology for Wonder.* New York: HarperCollins, 1969.

39 **living with wonder:** Shiota, Michelle N., Dacher Keltner, and Oliver P. John. "Positive Emotion Dispositions Differentially Associated with Big Five Personality and Attachment Style." *Journal of Positive Psychology* 1, no. 2 (2006): 61–71.

39 **To the strengths and virtues:** Stellar, Jennifer E., Amie M. Gordon, Craig L. Anderson, Paul K. Piff, Galen D. McNeil, and Dacher Keltner. "Awe and Humility." *Journal of Personality and Social Psychology* 114, no. 2 (2018): 258–69.

39 **our experience of color:** Steve Palmer has done outstanding work mapping the emotional meaning of colors. Palmer, Steve E., and Karen B. Schloss. "An Ecological Valence Theory of Color Preferences." *Proceedings of the National Academy of Sciences* 107, no. 19 (2010): 8877–82. https://doi.org/10.1073/pnas.0906172107.

39 **Laboratory studies have captured:** Griskevicius, Vlad, Michelle N. Shiota, and Samantha L. Neufeld. "Influence of Different Positive Emotions on Persuasion Processing: A Functional Evolutionary Approach." *Emotion* 10 (2010): 190–206.

40 **We perceive natural phenomena:** Gottlieb, Sara, Dacher Keltner, and Tania Lombrozo. "Awe as a Scientific Emotion." *Cognitive Science* 42, no. 6 (2018): 2081–94. https://doi.org/10.1111/cogs.12648. This study found that people who feel more everyday awe are less likely to engage in what is called teleological reasoning; they are less likely to attribute phenomena to the narrow purposes they might serve. The teleological mind says that "bees exist in order to facilitate pollination in plants," that "lightning releases electricity in order to travel," and that the enticing quality of sap lures us into protecting a tree. See also: Valdesolo, Piercarlo, Jun Park, and Sara Gottlieb. "Awe and Scientific Explanation." *Emotion* 16, no. 7 (2016): 937–40. In his superb book, philosopher Daniel Dennett suggests that this insight is perhaps Darwin's most revolutionary idea, that the world is evolving not as the result of some transcendent or Divine purpose, but due to complex systems of evolutionary forces.

Dennett, Daniel. *Darwin's Dangerous Idea: Evolution and the Meanings of Life.* New York: Simon & Schuster, 1995.

40 **the circle of care:** Singer, Peter. *The Expanding Circle: Ethics and Sociobiology.* Oxford: Clarendon Press, 1981.

41 **Other participants watched the hilarious:** Piff, Paul K., Pia Dietze, Matthew Feinberg, Daniel M. Stancato, and Dacher Keltner. "Awe, the Small Self, and Prosocial Behavior." *Journal of Personality and Social Psychology* 108, no. 6 (2015): 883–99.

41 **Memphis University professor Jia Wei Zhang:** Zhang, Jia W., Paul K. Piff, Ravi Iyer, Spassena Koleva, and Dacher Keltner. "An Occasion for Unselfing: Beautiful Nature Leads to Prosociality." *Journal of Environmental Psychology* 37 (2014): 61–72.

42 **her hero, Jane Goodall:** I would like to thank the wonderful primatologist Frans de Waal, so influential to my thinking about the human capacity for kindness and sociality, for directing me to this video. "Waterfall Displays." *Jane Goodall's Good for All News,* http://bit.ly/2r2iZ3t, accessed February 15, 2022.

Chapter 3: Evolution of the Soul

43 **"And if the body were":** Whitman, Walt. "I Sing the Body Electric." In *Walt Whitman: Selected Poems.* New York: Dover, 1991, 12.

44 **I felt overcome:** That tears mark our recognition of sacred forces in our lives, and in particular sacred people, is revealed in a stunning video worth watching. It is a one-minute film of a nine-month-old infant who, with new hearing aids, hears her mother's voice for the first time. In the short clip the mom vocalizes in the musical intonations of motherese—"Hi . . ." "Are you going to cry?" "I love you." The infant first smiles with bright eyes, and then tears up and emits a few high pitched *aah*s, quite clearly overwhelmed in hearing her mother's voice for the first time. Christy Keane Can. "My baby hears me for the first time and is almost moved to tears!" YouTube video, 1:05, October 14, 2017. https://www.youtube.com/watch?v=-_Q5kO4YXFs.

44 **Our guides will be Charles Darwin:** For an astonishing biography of Darwin's life, his thoughts, and how he shaped the world, a must read is: Browne, Janet. *Charles Darwin.* Vol. 1, *Voyaging.* New York: Alfred Knopf; London: Jonathan Cape, 1995. Browne, Janet. *Charles Darwin.* Vol. 2, *The Power of Place.* New York: Alfred Knopf, 2002.

45 **Whitman observed:** Wineapple, Brenda, ed. *Walt Whitman Speaks: His Final Thoughts on Life, Writing, Spirituality, and the Promise of America as Told to Horace Traubel.* New York: Random House, 2019.

46 **taxonomy of the tears of emotion:** Lutz, Tom. *Crying: The Natural and Cultural History of Tears.* New York: W. W. Norton, 1999. This book is an outstanding study of how to trace an emotional behavior through its biological and cultural history.

46 **Alan Fiske has proposed:** Fiske, Alan P. *Structures of Social Life.* New York: Free Press, 1991. Fiske argues that we relate to others in one of four basic ways (and their combinations): in a communal fashion; a market-based fashion of exchange; a hierarchical fashion, as one would in a military or religious organization; and in equality-based ways, as in good friendships. This thinking has had a profound influence upon our study of emotion. It led us to think about how emotions, through their shaping of social interactions like flirtation, teasing, or ceremony, are the basic language of our relationships.

46 **So vital is this way of relating:** These studies are part of Alan Fiske's search to understand *kama muta,* the feeling of being moved by being connected to others or seeing evidence of others moving closer to one another in connection. Seibt, Beate, Thomas W. Schubert, Janis H. Zickfeld, and Alan P. Fiske. "Touching the Base:

Heart-Warming Ads from the 2016 U.S. Election Moved Viewers to Partisan Tears." *Cognition and Emotion* 33 (2019): 197–212. https://doi.org/10.1080/02699931.2018 .1441128. Zickfeld, Janis H., Patricia Arriaga, Sara V. Santos, Thomas W. Schubert, and Beate Seibt. "Tears of Joy, Aesthetic Chills and Heartwarming Feelings: Physiological Correlates of Kama Muta." *Psychophysiology* 57, no. 12 (2020): e13662. https:// doi.org/10.1111/psyp.13662. Blomster Lyshol, Johanna K., Lotte Thomsen, and Beate Seibt. "Moved by Observing the Love of Others: Kama Muta Evoked through Media Fosters Humanization of Out-Groups." *Frontiers in Psychology* (June 24, 2020). https://doi.org/10.3389/fpsyg.2020.01240.

47 **Tears, then, arise:** Vingerhoets, Ad. *Why Only Humans Weep: Unravelling the Mysteries of Tears*. New York: Oxford University Press, 2013.

47 **Children cry to signal hunger:** Parsons, Christine E., Katherine S. Young, Morten Joensson, Elvira Brattico, Jonathan A. Hyam, Alan Stein, Alexander Green, Tipu Aziz, and Morten L. Kringelbach. "Ready for Action: A Role for the Human Midbrain in Responding to Infant Vocalizations." *Social Cognitive and Affective Neuroscience* 9 (2014): 977–84. http://dx.doi.org/10.1093/scan/nst076.

48 **that twenty-first-century malaise:** Surgeon General Vivek Murthy calls loneliness a "social recession," and treats it as comparable in its influence upon the health of nations with economic recessions. Murthy, Vivek. *Together: The Healing Power of Connection in a Sometimes Lonely World*. New York: HarperCollins, 2020.

48 **She often found herself wide awake:** For an account of the essential place that sleep has in our lives and why we are not getting enough, and what to do about it, see: Walker, Matthew. *Why We Sleep*. New York: Scribner, 2017.

49 **Videos of caregiving acts:** A year out of graduate school, in 1990, I read a short story by John Updike in the *New Yorker*, "Tristan and Iseult," my first encounter with a literary portrayal of ASMR. In the story, the narrator gets his molars, "corrupt wrecks just barely salvaged from the ruin of his years of unthinking consumption," cleaned by a dental assistant, working with gloves in an AIDS era. Through the assistant's fleshy touches and close inspection, hovering, gazing intently, only inches away, the narrator feels seen, forgiven, known, even spiritual. The intimacy they share during the dental visit is "like something from a supermarket tabloid or a Harlequin romance"; he notes that "her spirit intertwined with his." Updike, John. "Tristan and Iseult." *New Yorker*, December 3, 1990.

50 **originate in bodily sensations:** For an excellent line of work on our bodily maps of emotion, see Nummenmaa, Lauri, Enrico Glerean, Riitta Hari, and Jari K. Hietanen. "Bodily Maps of Emotions." *Proceedings of the National Academy of Sciences* 111, no. 2 (2014): 646–51. Bud Craig has devoted his career to understanding how our subjective experience of emotion arises in bodily sensations and discovered how such embodiment involves the anterior insular cortex. Craig, A. D. *How Do You Feel?: An Interoceptive Moment with Your Neurobiological Self*. Princeton, NJ: Princeton University Press, 2015. One of the early and influential statements about embodiment was made by George Lakoff, a linguistics and philosophy professor at Berkeley. He suggested that our metaphorical tendencies, so prominent in how we understand the world, often arise out of bodily experiences. We talk about "waves," "surges," and "ebbs and flows" of emotion, to pick one example, because these metaphorical descriptions arise out of making sense of the sensations associated with emotion-related shifts in cardiovascular physiology and the distribution of blood through the body. Lakoff, George, and Mark Johnson. *Metaphors We Live By*. Chicago: Chicago University Press, 1980.

50 **For James:** James, William. "What Is an Emotion?" *Mind* 9 (1884): 188–205.

50 **correlates in bodily responses:** Winkielman, Piotr, Paula Niedenthal, Joseph Wiel-gosz, Jiska Wielgosz, and Liam C. Kavanagh. "Embodiment of Cognition and Emo-tion." In *APA Handbook of Personality and Social Psychology.* Vol. 1, *Attitudes and Social Cognition,* edited by Mario Mikulincer, Philip R. Shaver, Eugene E. Borgida, and John A. Bargh, 151–75. Washington, DC: American Psychological Association, 2015.

50 **shifts in your systolic blood pressure:** This careful work has been carried out by Sarah Garfinkel and Hugo Critchley, who painstakingly measured systolic and dia-stolic blood pressure and cognitive activities like assessing risk, tracking down to the millisecond how the heart's contraction and distribution of blood through the body (systolic blood pressure) influences perceptions of risk. Garfinkel, Sarah N., and Hugo D. Critchley. "Threat and the Body: How the Heart Supports Fear Processing." *Trends in Cognitive Sciences* 20, no. 1 (2016): 34–46. Garfinkel, Sarah N., Miranda F. Manassei, Giles Hamilton-Fletcher, Yvo In den Bosch, Hugo D. Critchley, and Mir-iam Engels. "Interoceptive Dimensions across Cardiac and Respiratory Axes." *Philo-sophical Transactions of the Royal Society B* 371, no. 1708 (2016): 20160014. Garfinkel, Sarah N., Claire Tiley, Stephanie O'Keeffe, Neil A. Harrison, Anil K. Seth, and Hugo D. Critchley. "Discrepancies between Dimensions of Interoception in Autism: Impli-cations for Emotion and Anxiety." *Biological Psychology* 114 (2016): 117–26.

50 **configuration of the related emotion:** Niedenthal, Paula M., Piotr Winkielman, Laurie Mondillon, and Nicolas Vermeulen. "Embodiment of Emotional Concepts: Evidence from EMG Measures." *Journal of Personality and Social Psychology* 96 (2009): 1120–36.

50 **Simply adopting the furrowed brow:** Keltner, Dacher, Phoebe C. Ellsworth, and Kari Ellsworth. "Beyond Simple Pessimism: Effects of Sadness and Anger on Social Perception." *Journal of Personality and Social Psychology* 64 (1993): 740–52.

50 **sensations in your gut:** For a review of the surprisingly accurate nature of such gut feelings, see: Hertenstein, Matthew. *The Tell: The Little Clues That Reveal Big Truths about Who We Are.* New York: Basic Books, 2013.

51 **The chills also arise when:** Konečni, Vladimir J. "The Aesthetic Trinity: Awe, Being Moved, Thrills." *Bulletin of Psychology and the Arts* 5 (2005): 27–44.

51 **"Although we read":** Nabokov, Vladimir. *Lectures on Literature.* Boston, MA: Hough-ton Mifflin Harcourt, 2017, 64.

51 **"Oh my god":** Vignola, Michael, and Stuart Gwynedd. "If Carl Bernstein Has Chills About the Trump Impeachment, He's Not Saying So." *Los Angeles Magazine,* October 29, 2019, https://www.lamag.com/citythinkblog/carl-bernstein-trump/.

51 **encounters with the Divine:** Job 4: 12–17. King James Version (KJV).

52 **Within the Yogic tradition:** Vasu, S. C., trans. *The Gheranda Samhita: A Treatise on Hatha Yoga.* Bombay: Theosophical, 1895.

52 **the meanings of "the chills":** Maruskin, Laura A., Todd M. Thrash, and Andrew J. Elliot. "The Chills as a Psychological Construct: Content Universe, Factor Structure, Affective Composition, Elicitors, Trait Antecedents, and Consequences." *Journal of Personality and Social Psychology* 103, no. 1 (2012): 135.

52 **reminiscent of Dante's hell:** Ehrman, Bart D. *Heaven and Hell: A History of the After-life.* New York: Simon & Schuster, 2020.

53 **a strange and unexpected emptiness:** For a terrific discussion of the eerie and the strange, read: Fisher, Mark. *The Weird and the Eerie.* London: Sheperton House, 2016. In this book, Fisher details distinctions between the weird (which is based in the presence of the strange) and the eerie (which is rooted in the sense of absence). Grounded in this distinction, Fisher then takes the reader on a tour of the impor-tance of these states in the works of people like H. G. Wells, Margaret Atwood,

David Lynch, Stanley Kubrick, Brian Eno, and Philip K. Dick (author of the book *Do Androids Dream of Electric Sheep?*, basis of the awe-inspiring film *Blade Runner*, and of whom many who live in Berkeley are proud, because he graduated from Berkeley High School in the same era as Ursula K. Le Guin).

53 **Highly social mammals:** Hans IJzerman, James A. Coan, Fieke M. A. Wagemans, Marjolein A. Missler, Ilja van Beest, Siegwart Lindenberg, and Mattie Tops. "A Theory of Social Thermoregulation in Human Primates." *Frontiers in Psychology* 6 (2015): 464. https://doi.org/10.3389/fpsyg.2015.00464.

53 **lean in and coordinate:** Social mammals often respond to threat and peril by bonding with other mammals nearby. This thesis was first championed by Shelley E. Taylor and her colleagues and had a profound influence upon our understanding of our emotional lives. Taylor would argue that there is much more to our response to peril and threat than fight or flight, which was the predominant focus until her thinking. She would argue that when facing peril, humans, perhaps with greater frequency women, "tend and befriend": we collaborate, care for, and bond with others to face peril. Taylor, Shelley E., Laura C. Klein, Brian P. Lewis, Tara L. Gruenewal, Regan A. R. Gurung, and John A. Updegraff. "Biobehavioral Responses to Stress in Females: Tend-and-Befriend, not Fight-or-Flight." *Psychological Review* 107 (2000): 411–29.

54 **the release of oxytocin:** For excellent reviews of the oxytocin literature, revealing how much oxytocin release depends on the context and varies according to the individual's personality, see Bartz, Jennifer. A. "Oxytocin and the Pharmacological Dissection of Affiliation." *Current Directions in Psychological Science* 25 (2016): 104–10. Bartz, Jennifer. A., Jamil Zaki, Nial Bolger, and Kevin N. Ochsner. "Social Effects of Oxytocin in Humans: Context and Person Matter." *Trends in Cognitive Sciences* 15 (2011): 301–9.

54 **activation of the vagus nerve:** Gordon, Amie M., Jennifer. E. Stellar, Craig. L. Anderson, Galen D. McNeil, Daniel Loew, and Dacher Keltner. "The Dark Side of the Sublime: Distinguishing a Threat-Based Variant of Awe." *Journal of Personality and Social Psychology* 113, no. 2 (2016): 310–28. For evidence concerning the vagus nerve and compassion, see: Stellar, Jennifer E., Adam Cowen, Christopher Oveis, and Dacher Keltner. "Affective and Physiological Responses to the Suffering of Others: Compassion and Vagal Activity." *Journal of Personality and Social Psychology* 108 (2015): 572–85.

54 **His trembling and shuddering:** Sartre, Jean-Paul. *Nausea*. Norfolk, CT: New Directions, 1949.

54 **"beautiful laws of physiology":** Wrobel, Arthur. "Whitman and the Phrenologists: The Divine Body and the Sensuous Soul." *PMLA* 89, no. 1 (1974): 24.

55 **Rainbows stirred Newton and Descartes:** Fisher, Philip. *Wonder, the Rainbow, and the Aesthetics of Rare Experiences*. Cambridge, MA: Harvard University Press, 1998.

55 **double rainbow:** Yosemitebear62. "Yosemitebear Mountain Double Rainbow 1-8 -10." YouTube video, 3:29, January 8, 2010. https://www.youtube.com/watch?v= OQSNhk5ICTI.

55 **we alert others to the wonders:** Expressions of emotion in the face, voice, and body do more than just signal emotions to others; they are a language of social interaction. Emotional expressions provide important *information* about the individual's feelings, intentions, and attitudes. They *evoke* responses in others; a cry, for example, will often stir others to sympathetic response. Emotion-related facial displays and vocalizations also provide information about whether the environment poses threats or is worthy of exploration. Keltner, Dacher, and Ann M. Kring. "Emotion, Social Function, and Psychopathology." *Review of General Psychology* 2 (1998): 320–42.

56 **Darwin detailed the evolution:** Darwin, Charles. *The Expression of the Emotions in Man and Animals*. Chicago: University of Chicago Press, 1965.

56 **my Yale collaborator Daniel Cordaro:** Cordaro, Daniel T., Rui Sun, Dacher Keltner, Shanmukh Kamble, Niranjan Huddar, and Galen McNeil. "Universals and Cultural Variations in 22 Emotional Expressions across Five Cultures." *Emotion* 18, no. 1 (2018): 75–93.

57 **repertoires of vocal bursts:** For a review of the parallels between human emotion and nonhuman expressive behavior, see: Cowen, Alan, and Dacher Keltner. "Emotional Experience, Expression, and Brain Activity Are High-Dimensional, Categorical, and Blended." *Trends in Cognitive Science* 25, no. 2 (2021): 124–36.

57 **When we played these sounds:** Cordaro, Daniel T., Dacher Keltner, Sumjay Tshering, Dorji Wangchuk, and Lisa M. Flynn. "The Voice Conveys Emotion in Ten Globalized Cultures and One Remote Village in Bhutan." *Emotion* 1 (2016): 117–28.

58 **an early hominid profile of awe:** Stanley Kubrick's "Dawn of Man" montage from *2001: A Space Odyssey* is an artistic rendering of this idea. In the montage, inspired by Jane Goodall's studies, our hominid predecessors on the African savannah encounter another group at a watering hole. They respond with a waterfall dance: they pilo-erect and, moving in unison, transform into a collective wave of threat expressed in fierce shrieks and roars. Later, waking from a sleep huddled in a cave, they are visited by a smooth gray obelisk—perhaps the idea of culture or religion—which they explore with touch, in a reverential way. In the next scene a member of this tribe discovers a bone, and its power to destroy, which he uses to kill a rival in the next encounter between the two tribes at the watering hole. That bone is thrown into the air and transforms into a space station. We transform moments of awe into culture, both beneficent and violent.

58 **the archaeological record reveals:** Pagel, Mark. *Wired for Culture: Origins of the Human Social Mind*. New York: W. W. Norton, 2012.

59 **awe-related bodily tendencies:** Dutton, Dennis. *The Art Instinct: Beauty, Pleasure, and Human Evolution*. London: Bloomsbury, 2009.

60 **the legendary poet Bashō:** Matsuo, Bashō, and Makoto Ueda. *Bashō and His Interpreters: Selected Hokku with Commentary*. Stanford, CA: Stanford University Press, 1995, 102.

60 **this haiku about a neighbor:** Matsuo, Bashō, and Makoto Ueda. *Bashō and His Interpreters*, 411. Like many, I count Alfred Hitchcock's *Rear Window* among my top ten movies, in large part, I believe, for its portrayal of the awe we experience in wondering about the lives of others. Its main character, played by James Stewart, is housebound due to a foot injury and spends his days wondering about the various characters he can see through a rear window off a courtyard in his New York apartment complex. We can find a form of everyday awe in wondering about other people's lives and minds.

61 **He notes her abiding interest:** Dickinson, Emily. *Final Harvest: Emily Dickinson's Poems*. Selections and introduction by Thomas H. Johnson. New York: Little Brown, 1961.

61 **"Winter afternoons":** Dickinson, Emily. *The Poems of Emily Dickinson: Reading Edition*. Cambridge, MA: Harvard University Press, 2005, 142.

62 **Literature, drama, essay, and poetry:** Ashfield, Andrew, and Peter de Bolla. *Sublime: A Reader in British Eighteenth-Century Aesthetic Theory*. Cambridge, UK: Cambridge University Press, 1996. Kim, Sharon. *Literary Epiphany in the Novel, 1850–1950: Constellations of the Soul*. New York: Palgrave Macmillan, 2012.

62 **students were first presented:** Thrash, Todd M., Laura A. Maruskin, Emil G. Moldovan, Victoria C. Oleynick, and William C. Belzak. "Writer-Reader Contagion

of Inspiration and Related States: Conditional Process Analyses within a Cross-Classified Writer × Reader Framework." *Journal of Personality and Social Psychology.* Advance online publication. http://dx.doi.org/10.1037/pspp0000094.

64 **This archiving of mystical awe:** For summaries, see: Walter Stace's excellent surveys of mysticism across religions. Stace, Walter T. *Mysticism and Philosophy.* New York: St. Martin's Press, 1960. Stace, Walter T. *The Teachings of the Mystics.* New York: Mentor, 1960.

64 **a largely religious emotion:** Armstrong, Karen. *The Great Transformation: The Beginning of Our Religious Traditions.* New York: Alfred Knopf, 2006.

64 **Shakespeare's plays, for example:** Platt, Peter. *Reason Diminished: Shakespeare and the Marvelous.* Lincoln: University of Nebraska Press, 1997.

64 **They would inspire American transcendentalists:** For a deep study of the contributions of Margaret Fuller to nineteenth-century culture and our understanding of the transcendent, see: Popova, Maria. *Figuring.* New York: Pantheon Press, 2019.

Chapter 4: Moral Beauty

69 **"Over time":** Morrison, Toni. "Toni Morrison: 'Goodness: Altruism and the Literary Imagination,'" *New York Times,* August 7, 2019, https://www.nytimes.com/2019/08/07/books/toni-morrison-goodness-altruism-literary-imagination.html.

69 **inmate-led restorative justice:** For a summary of the application of restorative justice in prisons around the world, see: Johnstone, Gerry. "Restorative Justice in Prisons: Methods, Approaches and Effectiveness." Report to the European Committee on Crime Problems, September 29, 2014. https://rm.coe.int/16806f9905. For some of the evidence concerning how RJ reduces victim anger and offender recidivism, see: McCullough, Michael E. *Beyond Revenge: The Evolution of the Forgiveness Instinct.* San Francisco: Jossey-Bass, 2008.

71 **"It ain't a secret":** 2Pac. "Changes." *Greatest Hits.* Amaru, Death Row, and Interscope Records, 1998.

73 **adverse childhood experiences:** In your first eighteen years of life: 1. Did a parent or adult figure swear at you or humiliate you? 2. Did a parent or adult figure grab or hit you? 3. Did someone over the age of five touch you sexually? 4. Did you feel that people in your family did not love you or support one another? 5. Did you not have enough to eat or have to wear dirty clothes, or were your parents often too high or drunk to take you to a doctor when you needed one? 6. Were your parents separated or divorced? 7. Was your mother or stepmother punched, grabbed, thrown to the floor, or threatened with a gun or knife? 8. Was an adult family member addicted to alcohol or hard drugs? 9. Was an adult figure in your home depressed or did one suffer from other serious mental illness? 10. Did an adult figure in your home go to prison?

73 **dampening prospects and shortening lives:** For an excellent review, see: Miller, Gregory E., Edith Chen, and Karen J. Parker. "Psychological Stress in Childhood and Susceptibility to the Chronic Diseases of Aging: Moving toward a Model of Behavioral and Biological Mechanisms." *Psychological Bulletin* 137 (2011): 959–97. I review some of this evidence in Keltner, Dacher. *The Power Paradox: How We Gain and Lose Influence.* New York: Penguin Press, 2016.

74 **people who have less wealth:** Piff, Paul K., and Jake P. Moskowitz. "Wealth, Poverty, and Happiness: Social Class Is Differentially Associated with Positive Emotions." *Emotion* 18, no. 6 (2018): 902–5. In this study involving a nationally representative sample, low-income participants were more likely to report feeling more everyday love, compassion, and awe, and the well-to-do were more likely to feel pride and amusement.

74 In our daily diary studies: Bai, Yang, Laura A. Maruskin, Serena Chen, Amie M. Gordon, Jennifer E. Stellar, Galen D. McNeil, Kaiping Peng, and Dacher Keltner. "Awe, the Diminished Self, and Collective Engagement: Universals and Cultural Variations in the Small Self." *Journal of Personality and Social Psychology* 113, no. 2 (2017): 185–209.

79 In solitary confinement: Shakespeare, William. *Julius Caesar.* Edited by Roma Gill. 4th edition. Oxford School Shakespeare. London: Oxford University Press, 2001. For an illuminating treatment of the value of honor and how it plays out in an individual's sense of morality and action, see: Nisbett, Richard E., and Dov Cohen. *Culture of Honor: The Psychology of Violence in the South (New Directions in Social Psychology).* Boulder, CO: Westview Press, 1996.

79 Underground Scholars Initiative: MacFarquhar, Larissa. "Building a Prison-to-School Pipeline." *New Yorker*, December 4, 2016. https://www.newyorker.com/magazine/2016/12/12/the-ex-con-scholars-of-berkeley.

79 these unlikely college students: Forty percent of the approximately 2 million incarcerated people in the United States don't finish high school. About one in eight takes a shot at college, one-fourth the rate of the United States population as a whole.

79 we find our moral compass: Jonathan Haidt transformed the study of morality by highlighting how our moral judgments are rooted in emotions like compassion and awe, and in how we communicate about these moral passions with others. Haidt, Jonathan. "The Emotional Dog and Its Rational Tail: A Social Intuitionist Approach to Moral Judgment." *Psychological Review* 108 (2001) 814–34. Haidt, Jonathan. "The Moral Emotions." In *Handbook of Affective Sciences*, edited by Richard J. Davidson, Klaus R. Scherer, and H. H. Goldsmith, 852–70. London: Oxford University Press, 2003. Haidt, Jonathan. "The New Synthesis in Moral Psychology." *Science* 316 (2007): 998–1002. Greene, Joshua, and Jonathan Haidt. "How (and Where) Does Moral Judgment Work?" *Trends in Cognitive Science* 6 (2002): 517–23. Haidt, Jonathan, and Jesse Graham. "When Morality Opposes Justice: Conservatives Have Moral Intuitions That Liberals May Not Recognize." *Social Justice Research* 20 (2007): 98–116.

79 "moral law within": Kant, Immanuel, and John H. Bernard. *Kant's Critique of Judgement.* London: Macmillan, 1914.

80 health professionals get burned out: Berg, Sara. "Physician Burnout: Which Medical Specialties Feel the Most Stress." American Medical Association, January 21, 2020. https://www.ama-assn.org/practice-management/physician-health/physician-burnout-which-medical-specialties-feel-most-stress. This survey finds upward of 50 percent of physicians reporting feeling burned out at their work.

81 the power of an epiphany: Kim, Sharon. *Literary Epiphany in the Novel, 1850–1950: Constellations of the Soul.* New York: Palgrave Macmillan, 2012.

81 the power of witnessing: Thomson, Andrew L., and Jason T. Siegel. "Elevation: A Review of Scholarship on a Moral and Other-Praising Emotion." *Journal of Positive Psychology* 12, no. 6 (2017): 628–38. https://doi.org/10.1080/17439760.2016.1269184.

81 These encounters lead people: Aquino, Karl, Dan Freeman, Americus Reed II, Vivien K. G. Lim, and Will Felps. "Testing a Social Cognitive Model of Moral Behavior: The Interaction of Situational Factors and Moral Identity Centrality." *Journal of Personality and Social Psychology* 97 (2009): 123–41. Johnson, Sara K., et al. "Adolescents' Character Role Models: Exploring Who Young People Look Up To as Examples of How to Be a Good Person." *Research in Human Development* 13 (2016): 126–41. https://doi.org/10.1080/15427609.2016.1164552.

81 they often imitate others' acts: A philosophical argument for this is found in Jesse Prinz's essay in this book: Prinz, Jesse J. "Imitation and Moral Development." In

Perspectives on Imitation: From Neuroscience to Social Science. Vol. 2, *Imitation, Human Development, and Culture*, edited by Susan E. Hurley and Nick E. Chater, 267–82. Cambridge, MA: MIT Press, 2005. A recent review of eighty-eight studies involving 25,000 participants from around the world documents how robust our tendency is to imitate the prosocial behaviors of others, sharing, cooperation, and assisting in need. Jung, Haesung, Eunjin Seo, Eunjoo Han, Marlone D. Henderson, and Erika A. Patall. "Prosocial Modeling: A Meta-analytic Review and Synthesis." *Psychological Bulletin* 146, no. 8 (2020): 635–63. https://doi.org/10.1037/bul0000235.

81 **share stories of moral beauty:** Song, Hyunjin, Homero G. de Zúñiga, and Hajo G. Boomgaarden. "Social Media News Use and Political Cynicism: Differential Pathways through 'News Finds Me.'" *Perception, Mass Communication and Society* 23, no. 1 (2020): 47–70. https://doi.org/10.1080/15205436.2019.1651867.

82 **In their grief:** Freeman, Dan, Karl Aquino, and Brent McFerran. "Overcoming Beneficiary Race as an Impediment to Charitable Donations: Social Dominance Orientation, the Experience of Moral Elevation, and Donation Behavior." *Personality and Social Psychology Bulletin* 35 (2009): 72–84. This study used a portrayal of the Amy Biehl story as an elicitor of the feelings of moral beauty, or awe.

82 **"social dominance orientation":** Pratto, Felicia, Jim Sidanius, and Shana Levin. "Social Dominance Theory and the Dynamics of Intergroup Relations: Taking Stock and Looking Forward." *European Review of Social Psychology* 17 (2006): 271–320.

82 **Witnessing others' acts of courage:** Wang, Tingting, Lei Mo, Ci M. Li, Hai Tan, Jonathan S. Cant, Luojin Zhong, and Gerald Cupchik. "Is Moral Beauty Different from Facial Beauty? Evidence from an fMRI Study." *Social Cognitive and Affective Neuroscience* 10, no. 6 (2015): 814–23. https://doi.org/10.1093/scan/nsu123.

83 **the release of oxytocin:** Piper, Walter T., Laura R. Saslow, and Sarina R. Saturn. "Autonomic and Prefrontal Events during Moral Elevation." *Biological Psychology* 108 (2015): 51–55. https://doi.org/10.1016/j.biopsycho.2015.03.004. Epub March 23, 2015. PMID: 25813121.

84 **Yuyi's most recent book:** Morales, Yuyi. *Dreamers.* New York: Neal Porter Books, 2019.

84 **When I spoke with Yuyi:** Yuyi's gratitude letter is a powerful practice in the science of happiness. Brown, Joshua, and Joel Wong. "How Gratitude Changes You and Your Brain." *Greater Good*, June 6, 2017. "A Thank-You to Librarians Who Make Everyone Feel Welcome." Gratefulness.org. Greater Good Science Center. Accessed March 4, 2022. https://gratefulness.org/resource/a-thank-you-to-librarians-who-make-every one-feel-welcome/.

84 **Yuyi's letter of gratitude:** Woodruff, Paul. *Reverence: Renewing a Forgotten Virtue.* New York: Oxford University Press, 2002.

84 **Subtle is everyday reverence:** Brown, Penelope, and Steven J. Levinson. *Politeness: Some Universals in Language Usage.* Cambridge, UK: Cambridge University Press, 1987.

85 **convey reverential deference:** Keltner, Dacher, Randall C. Young, and Brenda N. Buswell. "Appeasement in Human Emotion, Personality, and Social Practice." *Aggressive Behavior* 23 (1997): 359–74. Gordon, Amie M., Emily A. Impett, Aleksandr Kogan, Christopher Oveis, and Dacher Keltner. "To Have and to Hold: Gratitude Promotes Relationship Maintenance in Intimate Bonds." *Journal of Personality and Social Psychology* 103 (2012): 257–74.

85 **With a simple warm clasp:** Gordon, Amie M., Emily A. Impett, Aleksandr Kogan, Christopher Oveis, and Dacher Keltner. "To Have and to Hold: Gratitude Promotes Relationship Maintenance in Intimate Bonds." *Journal of Personality and Social Psychology* 103 (2012): 257–74.

85 editing a movie review: Algoe, Sara B., Patrick C. Dwyer, Ayana Younge, and Christopher Oveis. "A New Perspective on the Social Functions of Emotions: Gratitude and the Witnessing Effect." *Journal of Personality and Social Psychology* 119, no. 1 (2019): 40–74. https://doi.org/10.1037/pspi0000202.

85 Others' acts of reverence: For an explanation of such mimicry and imitation, see: Preston, Stephanie, and Frans de Waal. "Empathy: Its Ultimate and Proximate Bases." *Behavioral and Brain Sciences* 25 (2002): 1–20. https://doi.org/10.1017/S0140525X02000018.

87 For those who've been subjugated: Mendoza-Denton, Rodolfo, Geraldine Downey, Valerie J. Purdie, Angelina Davis, and Janina Pietrzak. "Sensitivity to Status-Based Rejection: Implications for African American Students' College Experience." *Journal of Personality and Social Psychology* 83 (2002): 896–918. https://doi.org/10.1037/00223514.83.4.896. Rheinschmidt-Same, Michelle, Neha A. John-Henderson, and Rodolfo Mendoza-Denton. "Ethnically-Based Theme House Residency and Expected Discrimination Predict Downstream Markers of Inflammation among College Students." *Social Psychological and Personality Science* 8 (2017): 102–11.

87 He is the only prisoner: Louis has a website at http://www.louisavilscott.com/.

87 RJ is grounded: Hand, Carol A., Judith Hankes, and Toni House. "Restorative Justice: The Indigenous Justice System." *Contemporary Justice Review* 15, no. 4 (2012): 449–67. https://doi.org/10.1080/10282580.2012.734576. De Waal, Frans. *Peacemaking among Primates*. Cambridge, MA: Harvard University Press, 1989.

88 a white prisoner named Chris: For Louis's interview with Chris: "When Loyalty Is Misguided." San Quentin Public Radio, June 3, 2015. https://www.kalw.org/post/sqpr-when-loyalty-is-misguided#stream/0.

89 the blush is a manifestation: Keltner, Dacher. "The Signs of Appeasement: Evidence for the Distinct Displays of Embarrassment, Amusement, and Shame." *Journal of Personality and Social Psychology* 68 (1995): 441–54.

89 *Ashker v. Governor of California*: "Ashker v. Governor of California." Center for Constitutional Rights. Updated February 3, 2022. https://ccrjustice.org/home/what-we-do/our-cases/ashker-v-brown. Center for Constitutional Rights. "The United States Tortures before It Kills: An Examination of the Death Row Experience from a Human Rights Perspective." Position paper, October 10, 2011, https://ccrjustice.org/sites/default/files/assets/files/deathrow_torture_postition_paper.pdf.

90 One inmate summed it up: Haney, Craig. "Mental Health Issues in Long-Term Solitary and 'Supermax' Confinement." *Crime & Delinquency* 49 (2003): 124–56. Haney, Craig. "The Psychological Effects of Solitary Confinement: A Systematic Critique." In *Crime and Justice: A Review of Research*, edited by Michael Tonry, 365–16. Vol. 47. Chicago: University of Chicago Press, 2018.

90 how hard solitary was: Here is a video of Ashker talking about the SHU and his hunger strike. Thee L.A. Timez. "ALLEGED A.B. MEMBER TODD ASHKER INTERVIEW ON PELICAN BAY SOLITARY EFFECTS, HUNGER STRIKE AND SHU." YouTube video, 36:47, February 25, 2020. https://www.youtube.com/watch?v=GuFwEKr5XOs.

Chapter 5: Collective Effervescence

94 "Once the individuals are gathered": Alexander, Jeffrey C., and Philip Smith, eds. *The Cambridge Companion to Durkheim*. Cambridge, UK: Cambridge University Press, 2005, 183.

94 Burning Man: Ehrenreich, Barbara. *Dancing in the Streets: A History of Collective Joy*. New York: Holt, 2007.

96 **report suffering from loneliness:** For a synthesis of statistics like these, see: Murthy, Vivek H. *Together: The Healing Power of Human Connection in a Sometimes Lonely World.* New York: HarperCollins, 2020.

96 **This dissolving of our sense:** Eisenberger, Naomi I., and Matthew D. Lieberman. "Why Rejection Hurts: A Common Neural Alarm System for Physical and Social Pain." *Trends in Cognitive Sciences* 8 (2004): 294–300.

97 **In his 1912 work:** Durkheim, Émile. *The Elementary Forms of the Religious Life: A Study in Religious Sociology.* London; New York: G. Allen & Unwin; Macmillan, 1915.

98 **our social inhibitions:** Zimbardo, Philip G. "The Human Choice: Individuation, Reason, and Order versus Deindividuation, Impulse, and Chaos." In *1969 Nebraska Symposium on Motivation,* edited by W. J. Arnold and D. Levine, 237–307. Lincoln: University of Nebraska Press, 1970.

98 **Like ocean waves:** Fisher, Len. *The Perfect Swarm: The Science of Complexity in Everyday Life.* New York: Basic Books, 2007. One striking discovery in this new science of moving in unison, or swarms, is how simple it is mathematically. For example, many forms of collective movement—birds in flight, herds of wildebeests running, humans walking in a parade or political march—are explained by a few simple principles: keep your distance constant to those moving in front of you and to the side of you, and orient toward the direction of where the person in front of you is going.

99 **heavy metal show:** Silverberg, Jesse L., Matthew Bierbaum, James P. Sethna, and Itai Cohen. "Collective Motion of Humans in Mosh and Circle Pits at Heavy Metal Concerts." *Physical Review Letters* 110 (May 31, 2013): 228701.

99 **four-month-olds mirror:** Bernieri, Frank, and Rachel Rosenthal. "Coordinated Movement in Human Interaction." In *Fundamentals of Nonverbal Behavior,* edited by R. S. Feldman and B. Rime, 401–32. New York: Cambridge University Press, 1991.

99 **As adults, we mirror:** Lakin, Jessica, Valerie Jefferis, Clara Cheng, and Tanya Chartrand. "The Chameleon Effect as Social Glue: Evidence for the Evolutionary Significance of Nonconscious Mimicry." *Journal of Nonverbal Behavior* 27 (2003): 145–62. https://doi.org/10.1023/A:1025389814290.

99 **"porosity" of human bodies:** Gay, Ross. *The Book of Delights.* Chapel Hill, NC: Algonquin Books, 2019, 56.

99 **our biological rhythms synchronize:** McClintock, Martha K. "Synchronizing Ovarian and Birth Cycles by Female Pheromones." In *Chemical Signals in Vertebrates 3,* edited by D. Muller-Schwarze and R. M. Silverstein, 159–78. New York: Plenum Press, 1983.

99 **Sports fans' heart rhythms:** Maughan, Ronald, and Michael Gleeson. "Heart Rate and Salivary Cortisol Responses in Armchair Football Supporters." *Medicina Sportiva* 12, no. 1 (2008): 20–24. https://doi.org/10.2478/v10036-008-0004-z.

100 **villagers in San Pedro Manrique:** Konvalinka, Ivana, Dimitris Xygalatas, Joseph Bulbulia, Uffe Schjødt, Else-Marie Jegindø, Sebastian Wallot, Guy Van Orden, and Andreas Roepstorff. "Synchronized Arousal between Performers and Related Spectators in a Fire-Walking Ritual." *Proceedings of the National Academy of Sciences* 108, no. 20 (May 2011): 8514–19. https://doi.org/10.1073/pnas.1016955108.

100 **The study of emotional contagion:** Anderson, Cameron, Dacher Keltner, and Oliver P. John. "Emotional Convergence between People over Time." *Journal of Personality and Social Psychology* 84 (2003): 1054–68.

100 **synchronized social behaviors during childhood:** Tomasello, Michael. *Becoming Human. A Theory of Ontogeny.* Cambridge, MA: Belknap Press of Harvard University Press, 2019.

100 **a collective consciousness:** Paul, Annie M. *The Extended Mind: The Power of Thinking outside of the Brain.* New York: Houghton Mifflin Harcourt, 2021. This book provides

an excellent discussion of the philosophy and new science related to the idea that our minds' operations don't solely reside within the skull but extend to the context and environment.

101 **This convergence in mind:** Rimé, Bernard, Dario Páez, Nekane Basabe, and Francisco Martínez. "Social Sharing of Emotion, Post-traumatic Growth, and Emotional Climate: Follow-Up of Spanish Citizen's Response to the Collective Trauma of March 11th Terrorist Attacks in Madrid." *European Journal of Social Psychology* 40 (2010): 1029–45. https://doi.org/10.1002/ejsp.700.

102 **Our evolutionary shift:** Solnit, Rebecca. *Wanderlust: A History of Walking.* New York: Penguin, 2001.

103 **our actions within a human wave:** Hill, Michael R. *Walking, Crossing Streets and Choosing Pedestrian Routes: A Survey of Recent Insights from the Social/Behavioral Sciences* (University of Nebraska Studies, no. 66). Lincoln: University of Nebraska, 1984.

103 **study of walking in unison:** Jackson, Joshua C., Jonathan Jong, David Bilkey, Harvey Whitehouse, Stefanie Zollmann, Craig McNaughton, and Jamin Halberstadt. "Synchrony and Physiological Arousal Increase Cohesion and Cooperation in Large Naturalistic Groups." *Science Reports* 8 (2018): 127. https://doi.org/10.1038/s41598-017-18023-4.

103 **Walking in unison gives rise:** Collective movement also can generate, in certain conditions, more conformity and less creative thought, it's worth noting. Gelfand, Michele J., Nava Caluori, Joshua C. Jackson, and Morgan K. Taylor. "The Cultural Evolutionary Trade-Off of Ritualistic Synchrony." *Philosophical Transactions of the Royal Society B* 375 (2020): 20190432. http://dx.doi.org/10.1098/rstb.2019.0432.

104 **Celebrants spoke of being part:** Khan, Sammy S., Nick Hopkins, Stephen Reicher, Shruti Tewari, Narayanan Srinivasan, and Clifford Stevenson. "How Collective Participation Impacts Social Identity: A Longitudinal Study from India." *Political Psychology* 37 (2016): 309–25. https://doi.org/10.1111/pops.12260.

104 **military units marching:** McNeill, William H. *Keeping Together in Time: Dance and Drill in Human History.* Cambridge, MA: Harvard University Press, 2008.

104 **cultural history of walking:** Solnit. *Wanderlust.*

104 **awe-like form of consciousness:** Sturm, Virginia E., et al. "Big Smile, Small Self: Awe Walks Promote Prosocial Positive Emotions in Older Adults." *Emotion.* September 2020. Advance online publication, https://doi.org/10.1037/emo0000876.

105 **We were simply naming:** O'Mara, Shane O. *In Praise of Walking: A New Scientific Exploration.* New York: W. W. Norton, 2019. This book provides a compelling synthesis of all the mental and physical benefits of walking.

105 **starting in our midfifties:** Graham, Carol, and Julia Ruiz Pozuelo. "Happiness, Stress, and Age: How the U-Curve Varies across People and Places." Forthcoming in the *Journal of Population Economics*, 30th Anniversary Issue. *Journal of Population Economics* 30, no. 1 (2017): 611. https://doi.org/10.1007/s00148-016-0611-2.

106 **the law of hedonic adaptation:** Lyubomirsky, Sonja. "Hedonic Adaptation to Positive and Negative Experiences." In *Oxford Library of Psychology: The Oxford Handbook of Stress, Health, and Coping*, edited by S. Folkman, 200–204. New York: Oxford University Press, 2011.

108 **Walking gave him:** *Søren Kierkegaard's Journals and Papers*, ed. and trans. Howard V. Hong and Edna H. Hong. Bloomington, IN: Indiana University Press, 1978, 6:113.

108 **Jane Jacobs's thesis:** Jacobs, Jane. *The Death and Life of Great American Cities.* New York: Random House, 1961.

108 **coaching the Golden State Warriors:** Jackson, Phil. *Sacred Hoops: Spiritual Lessons of a Hardwood Warrior.* New York: Hachette Book Group, 2006. In our conversations, it was clear that Steve learned a lot about team play from Phil Jackson.

111 **Flocks of flying birds:** Fisher, Len. *The Perfect Swarm: The Science of Complexity in Everyday Life*. New York: Basic Books, 2007.

111 **This is true for humans:** Gelfand, Caluori, Jackson, and Taylor. "The Cultural Evolutionary Trade-Off of Ritualistic Synchrony."

111 **Cricket teammates whose laughter:** Totterdell, Peter. "Catching Moods and Hitting Runs: Mood Linkage and Subjective Performance in Professional Sport Teams." *Journal of Applied Psychology* 85 (2000): 848–59. https://doi.org/10.1037/0021-9010.85.6.848.

111 *shared feeling* **of success:** Mukherjee, Satyam, Yun Huang, Julia Neidhardt, Brian Uzzi, and Noshir Contractor. "Prior Shared Success Predicts Victory in Team Competitions." *Nature Human Behaviour* 3, no. 1 (2019): 74–81. https://doi.org/10.1038/s41562-018-0460-y. For an up-close account of this idea of team chemistry, see: Ryan, Joan. *Intangibles: Unlocking the Science and Soul of Team Chemistry*. New York: Little, Brown and Company, 2020.

111 **And outside of sports:** Chang, Andrew, Steven R. Livingstone, Dan J. Bosnyak, and Laurel J. Trainor. "Body Sway Reflects Leadership in Music Performance." *Proceedings of the National Academy of Sciences* 114, no. 21 (2017): E4134–41. https://doi.org/10.1073/pnas.1617657114.

112 **Pittsburgh Steelers fans:** Cottingham, Marci. "Interaction Ritual Theory and Sports Fans: Emotion, Symbols, and Solidarity." *Sociology of Sport Journal* 29 (2015): 168–85. https://doi.org/10.1123/ssj.29.2.168.

112 **"A man with a stern face":** Cottingham. "Interaction Ritual Theory and Sports Fans: Emotion, Symbols, and Solidarity."

113 **When European colonialists first traveled:** Ehrenreich, Barbara. *Dancing in the Streets: A History of Collective Joy*. New York: Holt, 2007.

114 **A sophisticated answer:** Muni, Bharata. *Natyasastra: English Translation with Critical Notes*, translated by A. Rangacharya. Bangalore: IBH Prakashana, 1986.

115 **In a study from Brazil:** Tarr, Bronwyn, Jacques Launay, Emma Cohen, and Robin Dunbar. "Synchrony and Exertion during Dance Independently Raise Pain Threshold and Encourage Social Bonding." *Biological Letters* 11 (2015): 20150767. http://doi.org/10.1098/rsbl.2015.0767.

115 **Even twelve-month-old babies:** Trainor, Laurel, and Laura Cirelli. "Rhythm and Interpersonal Synchrony in Early Social Development." *Annals of the New York Academy of Sciences* 1337 (2015). https://doi.org/10.1111/nyas.12649.

115 **Western Europeans had no trouble:** Hejmadi, Ahalya, Richard J. Davidson, and Paul Rozin. "Exploring Hindu Indian Emotion Expressions: Evidence for Accurate Recognition by Americans and Indians." *Psychological Science* 11 (2000): 183–87.

Chapter 6: Wild Awe

117 **"Those who dwell, as scientists":** Carson, Rachel. "Help Your Child to Wonder." *Woman's Home Companion*, July 1956, 48.

117 **cytokines heat up your body:** Eisenberger, Naomi I., Mona Moieni, Tristen K. Inagaki, Keely A. Muscatell, and Michael R. Irwin. "In Sickness and in Health: The Co-regulation of Inflammation and Social Behavior." *Neuropsychopharmacology* 42, no. 1 (2017): 242. Dickerson, Sally S., Margaret E. Kemeny, Najib Aziz, Kevin H. Kim, and John L. Fahey. "Immunological Effects of Induced Shame and Guilt." *Psychosomatic Medicine* 66 (2017): 124–31.

118 **like an invading pathogen:** This linkage between social rejection and increased inflammation has profound implications for how we think about things like racism, bullying, sexism, sexual harassment, and the stigma of coming from a lower social class background, suggesting that these social processes have direct influences on biological pathways that give rise to disease. John-Henderson, Neha A., Jennifer E.

Stellar, Rodolfo Mendoza-Denton, and Darlene D. Francis. "Socioeconomic Status and Social Support: Social Support Reduces Inflammatory Reactivity for Individuals Whose Early-Life Socioeconomic Status Was Low." *Psychological Science* 26, no. 10 (2015): 1620–29. John-Henderson, Neha A., Jennifer E. Stellar, Rodolfo Mendoza-Denton, and Darlene D. Francis. "The Role of Interpersonal Processes in Shaping Inflammatory Responses to Social-Evaluative Threat." *Biological Psychology* 110 (2015): 134–37. Muscatell, Keely A., Mona Moeini, Tristen K. Inagaki, Janine D. Dutcher, Ivana Jevtic, Elizabeth C. Breen, Michael R. Irwin, and Naomi I. Eisenberger. "Exposure to an Inflammatory Challenge Enhances Neural Sensitivity to Negative and Positive Social Feedback." *Brain, Behavior, and Immunity* 57 (2016): 21–29. Muscatell, Keely A., Katarina Dedovic, George M. Slavich, Michael R. Jarcho, Elizabeth C. Breen, Julienne E. Bower, Michael R. Irwin, and Naomi I. Eisenberger. "Neural Mechanisms Linking Social Status with Inflammatory Responses to Social Stress." *Social Cognitive and Affective Neuroscience* 11 (2016): 915–22. Marsland, Anna L., Catherine Walsh, Kimberly Lockwood, and Neha A. John-Henderson. "The Effects of Acute Psychological Stress on Circulating and Stimulated Inflammatory Markers: A Systematic Review and Meta-analysis." *Brain Behavioral Immunology* 64 (August 2017): 208–19. https://doi.org/10.1016/j.bbi.2017.01.011. Epub January 12, 2017. PMID: 28089638; PMCID: PMC5553449.

118 **predicted lower levels of inflammation:** Stellar, Jennifer E., Neha John-Henderson, Craig L. Anderson, Amie M. Gordon, Galen D. McNeil, and Dacher Keltner. "Positive Affect and Markers of Inflammation: Discrete Positive Emotions Predict Lower Levels of Inflammatory Cytokines." *Emotion* 15, no. 2 (2015): 129.

119 **getting very close to human suffering:** Angell, Marcia. "The Epidemic of Mental Illness: Why?" *New York Review of Books*, June 23, 2011. Angell, Marcia. "The Illusions of Psychiatry. *New York Review of Books*, July 14, 2011.

121 **quarter of veterans binge-drink:** "State of Veteran Mental Health and Substance Abuse." American Addiction Centers, 2019, https://americanaddictioncenters.org/learn/state-of-veterans/, accessed on February 15, 2022.

122 **Romanticism was born:** Blanning, Tim. *The Romantic Revolution*. New York: Random House, 2012, 7.

123 **a holistic kind of science:** Holmes, Richard. *The Age of Wonder: The Romantic Generation and the Discovery of the Beauty and Terror of Science*. New York: Vintage Books, 2008.

123 **Ralph Waldo Emerson was moved:** Richardson, Robert D. *Emerson: The Mind on Fire*. Berkeley: University of California Press, 1995.

124 **"I will be a naturalist":** Emerson, Ralph W. *The Journals and Miscellaneous Notebooks of Ralph Waldo Emerson*. Volume IV, 1832–1834. Edited by Alfred R. Ferguson. Cambridge, MA: Belknap Press of Harvard University Press, 1964, 272–75.

125 **"endless forms most beautiful":** Ball, Philip. *Patterns in Nature: Why the Natural World Looks the Way It Does*. Chicago: University of Chicago Press, 2016. This book offers a stunning example of the sacred geometries of nature and their deep evolutionary design, and how they engage sophisticated patterns of reasoning, a long-standing interest of Emerson's. Fractal patterns in nature, such as in mountain ranges, reveal how repetition of forms at different scales is a law of life. Spiral patterns evoke thinking about temporal patterns of growth, that so much in life, and life itself, begins in some germinal moment and spirals outward into vastness. Nature's part-whole relations may reveal how we are always part of larger systems.

125 **the "strange sympathies":** Wilson, E. O. *Biophilia: The Human Bond with Other Species*. Cambridge, MA: Harvard University Press, 1984.

125 **There are robust communities:** The awe we feel for different parts of the natural world has stirred scientific discovery, lifelong passion, and deep community. Out of

his awe and wonder for clouds, Gavin Pretor-Pinney has created a society that tracks their marvels, the Cloud Appreciation Society, and this awe-inspiring book: Pretor-Pinney, Gavin. *The Cloudspotter's Guide: The Science, History, and Culture of Clouds.* New York: Penguin Books, 2006. Out of his love of water and surfing, Wallace J. Nichols has created a movement that enables and studies the benefits of being near water. Nichols, Wallace J. *Blue Mind: The Surprising Science That Shows How Being Near, In, On, or Under Water Can Make You Happier, Healthier, More Connected, and Better at What You Do.* New York: Little Brown and Company, 2014.

126 **And gardens:** Through her work in the 1850s with injured soldiers in the Crimean War, Florence Nightingale came to view gardens as a form of health care. Today, scientists have documented many of gardening's benefits, from increased vitamin D to reduced stress-related EEG activity of the brain. Thompson, Richard. "Gardening for Health: A Regular Dose of Gardening." *Clinical Medicine (London)* 18, no. 3 (June 2018): 201–5. https://doi.org/10.7861/clinmedicine.18-3-201. PMID: 29858428; PMCID: PMC6334070.

126 **Should you encounter flowers:** Haviland-Jones, Jeanette, Holly H. Rosario, Patricia Wilson, and Terry R. McGuire. "An Environmental Approach to Positive Emotions: Flowers." *Evolutionary Psychology* 3 (2005): 104–32.

126 **The scents in the garden:** Soudry, Y., Cedric Lemogne, D. Malinvaud, S. M. Consoli, and Pierre Bonfils. "Olfactory System and Emotion: Common Substrates." *European Annals of Otorhinolaryngology, Head and Neck Diseases* 128, no. 1 (2011): 18–23. https://doi.org/10.1016/j.anorl.2010.09.007. Epub January 11, 2011. PMID: 21227767.

126 **Or the more social needs:** Anderson, Cameron, John A. D. Hildreth, and Laura Howland. "Is the Desire for Status a Fundamental Human Motive? A Review of the Empirical Literature." *Psychological Bulletin* 141, no. 3 (2015): 574–601.

126 **Basic, evolved needs:** Baumeister, Roy, and Mark Leary. "The Need to Belong: Desire for Interpersonal Attachments as a Fundamental Human Motivation." *Psychological Bulletin* 117 (1995): 497–529. https://doi.org/10.1037/0033-2909.117.3.497.

126 **our biological need to belong:** Julianne Holt-Lunstad has carried out groundbreaking reviews of vast literatures, finding that healthy social relationships with friends, families, and colleagues contribute as robustly to our physical health as any risk factor that would concern your MD. This is in part why awe leads to health benefits, for we so often experience it with people we consider community. Holt-Lunstad, Julianne, Timothy B. Smith, Mark Baker, Tyler Harris, and David Stephenson. "Loneliness and Social Isolation as Risk Factors for Mortality: A Meta-analytic Review." *Perspectives on Psychological Science* 10, no. 2 (2015): 227–37. Holt-Lunstad, Julianne, Timothy B. Smith, and J. B. Layton. "Social Relationships and Mortality Risk: A Meta-analytic Review." In *PLoS Medicine* 7, no. 7 (2010): e1000316. https://doi.org/10.1371/journal.pmed.1000316.

127 **Our remarkably long childhood:** Gopnik, Alison. *The Gardener and the Carpenter.* New York: Farrar, Strauss and Giroux, 2016.

127 **the neurophysiology of wild awe:** Kuo, Ming. "How Might Contact with Nature Promote Human Health? Promising Mechanisms and a Possible Central Pathway." *Frontiers in Psychology* 6 (2016): 1093. https://doi.org/10.3389/fpsyg.2015.01093.

127 **our need for wild awe:** The evidence for this hypothesis runs throughout Florence Williams's *The Nature Fix*, which synthesizes all the ways in which being in nature is good for your mind and body. Williams, Florence. *The Nature Fix: Why Nature Makes Us Happier, Healthier, and More Creative.* New York: W. W. Norton, 2017.

128 **When we satisfy our need:** Berman, Marc G., John Jonides, and Stephen Kaplan. "The Cognitive Benefits of Interacting with Nature." *Psychological Science* 19 (2008): 1207. https://doi.org/10.1111/j.1467-9280.2008.02225.x.

128 **Frances Kuo, a pioneer:** Kuo, Frances E., and Taylor A. Faber. "A Potential Natural Treatment for Attention-Deficit/Hyperactivity Disorder: Evidence from a National Study." *American Journal of Public Health* 94, no. 9 (2004): 1580–86.

128 **Getting outdoors in nature:** James, William. *The Principles of Psychology.* Vol. 1. New York: H. Holt, 1890, 424.

128 **beautiful green spaces:** Green, Kristophe, and Dacher Keltner. "What Happens When We Reconnect with Nature." *Greater Good*, March 1, 2017.

128 **finding awe outdoors:** Frumkin, Howard, et al. "Nature Contact and Human Health: A Research Agenda." *Environmental Health Perspectives* 125, no. 7 (2017): 075001. https://doi.org/10.1289/EHP1663.

129 **Moved by this idea:** One of my favorite books on wild awe is this one rich with personal narrative, cultural history, naturalistic description, and the science of mountaineering: Macfarlane, Robert. *Mountains of the Mind: Adventures in Reaching the Summit.* New York: Vintage Books, 2004.

129 **a study of wild awe:** Anderson, Craig L., Maria Monroy, and Dacher Keltner. "Emotion in the Wilds of Nature: The Coherence and Contagion of Fear during Threatening Group-Based Outdoors Experiences." *Emotion* 18, no. 3 (2017): 355–68. Anderson, Craig L., Maria Monroy, and Dacher Keltner. "Awe in Nature Heals: Evidence from Military Veterans, At-Risk Youth, and College Students." *Emotion* 18, no. 8 (2018): 1195–202.

130 **Growing up in poverty:** I review this science in chapter 5 of *The Power Paradox: How We Gain and Lose Influence.* New York: Penguin Press, 2017.

133 **"In the woods, we return":** Emerson, Ralph W. "Nature." In *Ralph Waldo Emerson, Selected Essays.* New York: Penguin, 1982, 39.

133 **In many ways, "mean egotism":** Twenge, Jean M. *Generation Me: Why Today's Young Americans Are More Confident, Assertive, and Entitled—and More Miserable Than Ever Before.* New York: Atria, 2006. Sansone, Randy A., and Lori A. Sansone. "Rumination: Relationships with Physical Health." *Innovations in Clinical Neuroscience* 9, no. 2 (2012): 29–34.

133 **world has become more narcissistic:** Twenge, Jean M., and W. Keith Campbell. *The Narcissism Epidemic: Living in the Age of Entitlement.* New York: Atria, 2010.

133 **Emerson's mean egotism hypothesis:** Piff, Paul K., Pia Dietze, Matthew Feinberg, Daniel M. Stancato, and Dacher Keltner. "Awe, the Small Self, and Prosocial Behavior." *Journal of Personality and Social Psychology* 108, no. 6 (2015): 883–99. I cannot help but report a telling limitation of this study: eucalyptus trees, as awe-inspiring as they are, are an invasive species in Northern California and cause many problems due to their oily leaves and seeds. We can feel awe, and often do, for wonders— invasive species, authoritarian leaders, false prophets, and disseminators of false information—that lead us astray.

134 **Out in the trees:** Wohlleben, Peter. *The Hidden Life of Trees: What They Feel, How They Communicate—Discoveries from a Hidden World.* Vancouver; Berkeley: Greystone Books, 2016. Haskell, David G. *The Songs of Trees: Stories from Nature's Great Connectors.* New York: Viking, 2017. Sheldrake, Merlin. *Entangled Life: How Fungi Make Our Worlds, Change Our Minds, and Shape Our Futures.* New York: Random House, 2020.

135 **Our participants feeling wild awe:** In another relevant study, simply viewing ten awe-inspiring images of nature led participants to share more of a resource with a stranger in a trust game. Zhang, Jia W., Paul K. Piff, Ravi Iyer, Spassena Koleva, and Dacher Keltner. "An Occasion for Unselfing: Beautiful Nature Leads to Prosociality." *Journal of Environmental Psychology* 37 (2014): 61–72.

135 **experiences of awe lead us:** Stellar, Jennifer E., Amie M. Gordon, Craig L. Anderson, Paul K. Piff, Galen D. McNeil, and Dacher Keltner. "Awe and Humility." *Journal of Personality and Social Psychology* 114, no. 2 (2018): 258–69.

135 **Some backpackers completed:** Atchley, Ruth A., David L. Strayer, and Paul Atchley. "Creativity in the Wild: Improving Creative Reasoning through Immersion in Natural Settings." *PLoS ONE* 7, no. 12 (2012): e51474. https://doi.org/10.1371/journal .pone.0051474.

135 **Polarization:** Jesse Shapiro has documented the rise of political polarization in the United States and its sources (internet use is not one!). Here's a recent piece of his: Boxell, Levi, Matthew Gentzkow, and Jesse Shapiro. "Cross-Country Trends in Affective Polarization." NBER Working Paper No. 26669, June 2020, revised November 2021. https://doi.org/10.3386/w26669.

136 **We assume that we are reasonable:** Robinson, Robert, Dacher Keltner, Andrew Ward, and Lee Ross. "Actual versus Assumed Differences in Construal: 'Naive Realism' in Intergroup Perception and Conflict." *Journal of Personality and Social Psychology* 68 (1995): 404–17.

136 **wild awe might defuse:** Stancato, Daniel, and Dacher Keltner. "Awe, Ideological Conviction, and Perceptions of Ideological Opponents." *Emotion* 21, no. 1 (2021): 61–72. https://doi.org/10.1037/emo0000665.

136 **Americans often sense the Divine:** Froese, Paul, and Christopher D. Bader. *America's Four Gods: What We Say about God—and What That Says about Us.* New York: Oxford University Press, 2010.

136 **people reported spiritual experiences:** Marsh, Paul, and Andrew Bobilya. "Examining Backcountry Adventure as a Spiritual Experience." *Journal of Outdoor Recreation, Education, and Leadership* 5 (2013): 74–95. https://doi.org/10.7768/1948-5123.1188.

137 **sociologists assessed the natural beauty:** Ferguson, Todd W., and Jeffrey A. Tamburello. "The Natural Environment as a Spiritual Resource: A Theory of Regional Variation in Religious Adherence." *Sociology of Religion* 76, no. 3 (Autumn 2015): 295–314. https://doi.org/10.1093/socrel/srv029.

137 **traditional ecological knowledge, or TEK:** Pierotti, Raymond. *Indigenous Knowledge, Ecology, and Evolutionary Biology.* New York: Routledge, 2011.

137 **During experiences of wild awe:** Today, plant biologists are documenting how plants show evidence of communication, adaptation, and even intention in how they communicate with other plants through root systems or in the chemicals they release when preyed upon by insects. For a skeptical view of plant consciousness, see: Taiz, Lincoln, Daniel Alkon, Andreas Draguhn, Angus Murphy, Michael Blatt, Chris Hawes, Gerhard Thiel, and David Robinson. "Plants Neither Possess nor Require Consciousness." *Trends in Plant Science* 24, no. 8 (2019): 677–87. For another perspective, see: Simard, Suzanne. *Finding the Mother Tree: Discovering the Wisdom of the Forest.* New York: Alfred Knopf, 2020.

138 **experiences of awe:** Zhao, Huanhuan, Heyun Zhang, Yan Xu, Jiamei Lu, and Wen He. "Relation between Awe and Environmentalism: The Role of Social Dominance Orientation." *Frontiers in Psychology* 9 (2018): 2367. https://doi.org/10.3389/fpsyg .2018.02367.

138 **Steven Chu observed:** McMahon, Jeff. "Meat and Agriculture Are Worse for the Climate than Power Generation, Steven Chu Says." *Forbes*, April 4, 2019. https:// www.forbes.com/sites/jeffmcmahon/2019/04/04/meat-and-agriculture-are-worse-for -the-climate-than-dirty-energy-steven-chu-says/?sh=12fb475611f9.

138 **"The soul ascends":** Blanning, Tim. *The Romantic Revolution.* New York: Random House, 2012, 139.

139 Book 6 of his epic: Wordsworth, William. *The Prelude—an Autobiographical Poem.* Bristol, UK: Ragged Hand, 2020, 9.

Chapter 7: Musical Awe

145 "I listen with my body": Sontag, Susan. *Reborn: Journals and Notebooks, 1947–1963.* Edited by David Rieff. New York: Farrar, Straus, and Giroux, 2008.

146 This is true for infants: Bainbridge, Constance M., Mila Bertolo, Julie Youngers, S. Atwood, Lidya Yurdum, Jan Simson, Kelsie Lopez, Feng Xing, Alia Martin, and Samuel A. Mehr. "Infants Relax in Response to Unfamiliar Foreign Lullabies." *Nature Human Behaviour* 5 (2021): 256–64. https://doi.org/10.1038/s41562-020-00963-z.

146 Lullabies integrate parent and child: Collins, Anita. *The Lullaby Effect: The Science of Singing to Your Child.* Self-published, Publicious, 2019.

147 Beethoven, a hero of Romanticism: Hoffman, E. T. A. *Allgemeine musikalische Zeitung (Leipzig), 1810.* Translated by Martyn Clarke. In David Charlton, ed., *E. T. A. Hoffmann's Musical Writings.* Cambridge, UK: Cambridge University Press, 1989, 96–97, 98. This was Hoffmann writing about Beethoven's Fifth Symphony in 1810. It isn't just critics and musicians of "highbrow" music who consider music to be a medium of awe. Musician Nick Cave, lead singer of the post-punk band Nick Cave and the Bad Seeds, offers one of the best compact analyses of why we feel awe in music: "What a great song makes us feel is a sense of awe. . . . A sense of awe is almost exclusively predicated on our limitations as human beings. It is entirely to do with our audacity as humans to reach beyond our potential." Cave, Nick. "Considering Human Imagination the Last Piece of Wilderness, Do You Think AI Will Ever Be Able to Write a Good Song?" The Red Hand Files, Issue 22, blog post, January 2019. Accessed on February 16, 2022. https://www.theredhandfiles.com/considering-human-imagination-the-last-piece-of-wilderness-do-you-think-ai-will-ever-be-able-to-write-a-good-song/.

147 The local flora and fauna: Although "wonder" and "wander" have different etymologies, the first referring to curiosity and the second to walking in a wending and winding way, they both become ways in which we characterize the mind and feeling, no doubt because of their shared connection to awe. "Are 'Wonder' and 'Wander' Etymologically Related?" English Stack Exchange, May 8, 2013. https://english.stackexchange.com/questions/113411/are-wonder-and-wander-etymologically-related.

147 "I acquired a strong taste": Darwin, Charles. *The Autobiography of Charles Darwin, 1809–1882.* Edited by Nora Barlow. New York: W. W. Norton, 1958, 61–62.

147 Scholars of music: In Rentfrow, Peter J., and Daniel J. Levitin, eds. *Foundations of Music Psychology: Theory and Research.* Cambridge, MA: MIT Press, 2000. For a leading voice in the study of music and feeling, see: Huron, David. *Sweet Anticipation: Music and the Psychology of Expectation.* Cambridge, MA: MIT Press, 2006. For a classic book in the scientific study of emotion and music: Meyer, Leonard B. *Emotion and Meaning in Music.* Chicago: University of Chicago Press, 1956. For work more focused on distinct emotions, see: Gabrielsson, Alf, and Patrik N. Juslin. "Emotional Expression in Music." In *Handbook of Affective Sciences,* edited by Richard J. Davidson, Klaus R. Scherer, and H. H. Goldsmith, 503–34. London: Oxford University Press, 2003. Scherer, Klaus R., and Evandro Coutinho. "How Music Creates Emotion: A Multifactorial Approach." In *The Emotional Power of Music,* edited by Tom Cochrane, Bernardino Fantini, and Klaus R. Scherer, 122–45. Oxford, UK: Oxford University Press, 2013.

148 "'What? What is this?'": Davis, Miles, and Quincy Troupe. *Miles: The Autobiography.* New York: Simon & Schuster, 1990, 7.

148 **"Listening to Beethoven":** Popova, Maria. *Figuring.* New York: Pantheon Press, 2019, 462. Popova provides revelatory accounts of the roles of many queer women in great intellectual movements very relevant to awe, including Margaret Fuller and Rachel Carson.

149 **Her face moved through expressions:** For new work on some of these expressions, see: Cowen, Alan S., and Dacher Keltner. "What the Face Displays: Mapping 28 Emotions Conveyed by Naturalistic Expression." *American Psychologist* 75, no. 3 (2020): 349–64. https://doi.org/10.1037/amp0000488.

151 **This neural representation of music:** Trost, Wiebke, Thomas Ethofer, Marcel Zentner, and Patrik Vuilleumier. "Mapping Aesthetic Musical Emotions in the Brain." *Cerebral Cortex* 22 (2012): 2769–83.

152 **music shifts our bodies:** Byrne, David. *How Music Works.* New York: Three Rivers, 2012.

152 **Melodious, slow music:** Loomba, Rohit S., Rohit Arora, Parinda H. Shah, Suraj Chandrasekar, and Janos Molnar. "Effects of Music on Systolic Blood Pressure, Diastolic Blood Pressure, and Heart Rate: A Meta-analysis." *Indian Heart Journal* 64, no. 3 (2012): 309–13. https://doi.org/10.1016/S0019-4832(12)60094-7.

152 **Faster, louder music:** Trappe, Hans-Joachim, and Gabriele Voit. "The Cardiovascular Effect of Musical Genres." *Deutsches Ärzteblatt International* 113, no. 20 (2016): 347. PMID: 27294814; PMCID: PMC4906829.

152 **the dopaminergic circuitry:** Ferreri, Laura, et al. "Dopamine Modulates the Reward Experiences Elicited by Music." *Proceedings of the National Academy of Sciences* 116, no. 9 (2019): 3793–98. https://doi.org/10.1073/pnas.1811878116. PMID: 3067 0642; PMCID: PMC6397525.

152 **bodily state of musical awe:** Konečni, Vladimir J., Rebekah A. Wanic, and Amber Brown. "Emotional and Aesthetic Antecedents and Consequences of Music-Induced Thrills." *American Journal of Psychology* 120 (2007): 619–43.

152 **their brains synchronize:** Abrams, Daniel A., Srikanth Ryali, Tianwen Chen, Parag Chordia, Amirah Khouzam, Daniel J. Levitin, and Vinod Menon. "Inter-subject Synchronization of Brain Responses during Natural Music Listening." *European Journal of Neuroscience* 37 (2013): 1458–69. Trost, Wiebke, Sascha Frühholz, Tom Cochrane, Yann Cojan, and Patrik Vuilleumier. "Temporal Dynamics of Musical Emotions Examined through Intersubject Synchrony of Brain Activity." *Social Cognitive and Affective Neuroscience* 10, no. 12 (2015): 1705–21. https://doi.org/10.1093/scan/nsv060.

152 **shared brain activation:** Henry, Molly J., D. J. Cameron, Dana Swarbick, Dan Bosnyak, Laurel Trainor, and Jessica Grahn. "Live Music Increases Intersubject Synchronization of Audience Members' Brain Rhythms." Presentation to the Cognitive Neuroscience Society Annual Conference, Boston, March 27, 2018.

153 **Some 2,500 years ago:** NASA has transformed the patterns of energy emitted by different planets into sounds that you can hear, and there are devices that transform the very slow sounds that plants emit into songs.

154 **She feels touched:** To read of Oliver Sacks's speculations about the underlying neurophysiology of bright lights and out-of-body experiences in musical and mystical awe and that of near-death experiences, see: Sacks, Oliver. "Seeing God in the Third Millennium." *Atlantic*, December 12, 2012. https://www.theatlantic.com /health/archive/2012/12/seeing-god-in-the-third-millennium/266134/.

155 **purpose is to objectify feeling:** Langer, Susanne K. *Feeling and Form: A Theory of Art.* New York: Macmillan, 1953, 374.

155 **"the pattern of life":** Haidt, Jonathan. "The Emotional Dog and Its Rational Tail: A Social Intuitionist Approach to Moral Judgment." *Psychological Review* 108 (2001): 814–34. https://doi.org/10.1037//0033-295X.108.4.814. Graham, Jesse, Brian A.

Nosek, Jonathan Haidt, Ravi Iyer, Spassena Koleva, and Peter H. Ditto. "Mapping the Moral Domain." *Journal of Personality and Social Psychology* 101, no. 2 (2011): 366–85, https://doi.org/10.1037/a0021847.

155 **our experience of aesthetic emotion:** Immanuel Kant called the realm of aesthetics the "free play of the imagination." Kant, Immanuel. *Critique of Judgment.* Translated by J. H. Bernard. New York: Hafner Press, 1951, 190. By "free," he meant that in the arts we are free from the constraints of society and the demands of the default self. By "play," he meant that we can explore and try out ideas; we can imagine what *might be* at the safe distance that art forms allow us.

155 **The realm of meaning:** Langer, Susanne. *Feeling and Form.* New York: Charles Scribner's Sons, 1953, 27.

156 **Swiss emotion scientist Klaus Scherer:** Banse, Rainer, and Klaus R. Scherer. "Acoustic Profiles in Vocal Emotion Expression." *Journal of Personality and Social Psychology* 70 (1996): 614–36. Scherer, Klaus R. "Vocal Affect Expression: A Review and a Model for Future Research." *Psychological Bulletin* 99 (1986): 143–65.

156 **These bodily changes alter:** In studies in this literature, scientists focus on different parameters of sound. This includes the *pitch*, or frequency, of the sound wave, which is perceived as notes in a piece of music; joyful music, for example, has higher pitches, while sad music has lower ones. *Rhythm* refers to the duration of the notes and how they group into units of sound. *Tempo* is the speed of the piece of music; is it fast like the Ramones or a high-spirited polka, or slow like Brian Eno's ambient music? *Contour* refers to the shape of the sound; does it rise toward the end of notes, in moments of exhilaration, or fall in acoustic movements of despair? *Timbre* refers to the particular sounds of different instruments or singers' voices. Great singers—Aretha Franklin, Joni Mitchell, Johnny Cash, Bob Dylan, Tom Waits, Drake, David Byrne, and Nicki Minaj—have timbres that you can detect within a note or two. *Loudness* refers to the amplitude, or energy, of the sound waves, and how much sound one perceives. *Beat* is where the song places percussive emphasis, and is registered in where you are inclined to tap your foot, sway your body, bump, or, if you are a teenager and the chaperones aren't looking, twerk.

156 **when in an anxious state:** Cowen, Alan S., Petri Laukka, Hillary A. Elfenbein, Runjing Liu, and Dacher Keltner. "The Primacy of Categories in the Recognition of 12 Emotions in Speech Prosody across Two Cultures." *Nature Human Behaviour* 3 (2019): 369–82.

157 **The musical expression of joy:** Historians have likewise noted how the sounds of music convey the life patterns of the times. During the era of slavery, African Americans transformed Christian psalms and hymns into songs about the conditions of slavery and their hope for freedom. Many songs were deep and slow in their pitch and rhythm, symbolizing the disempowerment and suffering of slavery. The contours of these songs lifted upward, stirring hope, inspiration, empowerment, and awe in imagining a new Black collective identity. This chapter in African American music represented the life patterns of subjugation, resolve, protest, and transformation of identity at the very heart of U.S. history. See: Barker, Thomas P. "Spatial Dialectics: Intimations of Freedom in Antebellum Slave Song." *Journal of Black Studies* 46, no. 4 (2015): 363–83. https://doi.org/10.1177/0021934715574499. See also: Southern, Eileen. *The Music of Black Americans: A History.* 3rd ed. New York: W. W. Norton, 1997. Michael Eric Dyson has charted how rap emerged in the 1980s in urban areas like Philadelphia and the South Bronx, expressing a pattern of social life. Rap originated out of the rhythms, beats, pitches, and contours of the street corner banter of young African American men, known as "playing the dozens," which allowed young men to cultivate a toughness and a voice of protest in a racist culture.

Rap transformed the sounds of this life pattern into an art form that billions of people around the world turn to in order to understand their own sense of oppression, freedom, identity, and power. Dyson, Michael E. *Know What I Mean?: Reflections on Hip Hop*. New York: Basic Civitas Books, 2007.

157 **how music expresses awe:** Cowen, Alan, Xia Fang, Disa Sauter, and Dacher Keltner. "What Music Makes Us Feel: At Least 13 Dimensions Organize Subjective Experiences Associated with Music across Different Cultures." *Proceedings of the National Academy of Sciences* 117, no. 4 (2020): 1924–34. See also: Schindler, Ines, Georg Hosoya, Winfried Menninghaus, Ursula Beermann, Valentin Wagner, Michael Eid, and Klaus R. Scherer. "Measuring Aesthetic Emotions: A Review of the Literature and a New Assessment Tool." *PLoS ONE* 12, no. 6 (2017): e0178899. https://doi.org/10.1371/journal.pone.0178899.

158 **We imagine emotion-specific actions:** Overy, Katie, and Istvan Molnar-Szakacs. "Being Together in Time: Musical Experience and the Mirror Neuron System." *Music Perception* 26, no. 5 (2009): 489–504. https://doi.org/10.1525/mp.2009.26.5.489.

158 **the power of sacred music:** Beck, Guy L. *Sacred Sound: Experiencing Music in World Religions*. Waterloo, CAN: Wilfrid Laurier University Press, 2006. This book provides a superb scholarly account of the sacred sounds in different religions.

158 **the provenance of the music:** Bellah, Robert. *Religion in Human Evolution: From the Paleolithic to the Axial Age*. Cambridge, MA: Harvard University Press, 2011.

159 **humans walked out of Africa:** Morley, Iain. *The Prehistory of Music: Human Evolution, Archaeology, and the Origins of Musicality*. Oxford, UK: Oxford University Press, 2013. Wallin, Nils L., Bjorn Merker, and Steven Brown. *The Origins of Music*. Cambridge, MA: MIT Press, 2000.

159 **Our most basic social interactions:** Tomlinson, Gary. *A Million Years of Music: The Emergence of Human Modernity*. New York: Zone Books, 2015. In this fascinating and complex book, Tomlinson proposes that music emerged as hominids created the Acheulean biface hand axe some 1.8 million years ago in East Africa, a tool that was vital to hunting, carving carcasses, digging, cutting wood, and defense. Archaeological evidence reveals that the individual production of these axes required a sequence of six to eight specific physical actions. Our hominid predecessors likely made these axes in groups, synchronizing their bodily actions through gesture and sound. Associations between sounds—grunts, groans, and even *ooh*s and *aah*s at a truly symmetrical axe and *whoa*s upon seeing others' efforts—and specific outcomes in the knapping of the stone into an axe were common. From this, Tomlinson suggests, tool makers learned the basic cognitive architecture of music: that different sounds signify different actions and different outcomes in the world, and that variations in sounds fit within a larger system of people making sounds together.

159 **Music became a medium:** This is the central thesis of neuroscientist and musician Daniel Levitin's writing about music. Levitin, Daniel. *This Is Your Brain on Music: The Science of a Human Obsession*. New York: Penguin Press, 2013. For a recent assessment of this hypothesis, see: Savage, Patrick, Psyche Loui, Bronwyn Tarr, Adena Schachner, Luke Glowacki, Steven Mithen, and W. Fitch. "Music as a Coevolved System for Social Bonding." *Behavioral and Brain Sciences* 44 (2021): 1–42. https://doi.org/10.1017/S0140525X20000333.

159 **From the age of one:** Levitin, Daniel J., J. A. Grahn, and J. London. "The Psychology of Music: Rhythm and Movement." *Annual Reviews in Psychology* 69 (2018): 51–75.

159 **In one illustrative study:** Cameron, D. J., J. Bentley, and Jessica A. Grahn. "Cross-Cultural Influences on Rhythm Processing: Reproduction, Discrimination, and Beat Tapping." *Frontiers in Psychology* 6 (2015): 366. https://doi.org/10.3389/fpsyg.2015.00366.

159 **And when strangers tap:** Valdesolo, Piercarlo, and David DeSteno. "Synchrony and the Social Tuning of Compassion." *Emotion* 11 (2011): 262–66.

159 **Listening to music that brings:** Fukui, Hajime, and Kumiko Toyoshima. "Chill-Inducing Music Enhances Altruism in Humans." *Frontiers in Psychology* 5 (2014): 1215. https://doi.org/10.3389/fpsyg.2014.01215.

160 **archive of life patterns:** Savage, Patrick E., Stephen Brown, Emi Sakai, and Thomas E. Currie. "Statistical Universals Reveal the Structures and Functions of Human Music." *Proceedings of the National Academy of Sciences* 112, no. 29 (July 2015): 8987–92. https://doi.org/10.1073/pnas.1414495112. This study analyzed twenty musical parameters of 304 songs from Africa, Asia, the Middle East, Europe, North America, and South Africa.

160 **adolescents gravitate to music:** Snibbe, Alana C., and Hazel R. Markus. "You Can't Always Get What You Want: Educational Attainment, Agency, and Choice." *Journal of Personality and Social Psychology* 88 (2005): 703–20. https://doi.org/10.1037/0022 -3514.88.4.703.

160 **music of thirty-nine African cultures:** Brown, Steven, Patrick E. Savage, Albert M. S. Ko, Mark Stoneking, Y. C. Ko, J. H. Loo, and Jean A. Trejaut. "Correlations in the Population Structure of Music, Genes and Language." *Proceedings of the Royal Society B: Biological Sciences* 281, no. 1774 (2013): 20132072. https://doi.org/10.1098/rspb .2013.2072. Pamjav, Horolma, Zoltan Juhász, Andrea Zalán, Endre Nemeth, and Bayarlkhagva Damdin. "A Comparative Phylogenetic Study of Genetics and Folk Music." *Molecular Genetic Genomics* 287 (2012): 337–49. https://doi.org/10.1007 /s00438-012-0683-y. Callaway, Ewen. "Music Is in Our Genes." *Nature*, December 10, 2007. https://www.nature.com/news/2007/071210/full/news.2007.359.html.

161 **I can feel it now:** https://www.myscience.org/news/wire/berkeley_talks_transcript _how_an_awe_walk_helped_one_musician_reconnect_with_her_home-2019 -berkeley.

163 **I am still:** My experience aligns with Leonard Meyer's influential theorizing about music: that its primary function is to set up expectations and move the imagination in violations and fulfillments of those expectations. Meyer, Leonard B. *Explaining Music: Essays and Explorations.* Berkeley: University of California Press, 1973.

Chapter 8: Sacred Geometries

166 **"A great deal of art":** Murdoch, Iris. *The Sovereignty of Good.* London: Routledge, 1970, 83.

167 **In the movie these wonders:** There is no shortage of human efforts to own and commodify the awe-evoking wonders of life for material gain and status. Two of my favorites are these: For an eye-opening cultural history of how the wealthy commodified and collected marvels of the world, from mysterious species to other cultures' artifacts, see: Daston, Lorraine, and Katharine Park. *Wonders and the Order of Nature 1150–1750.* New York: Zone Books, 2001. For coverage of how the landscape painting movement of the American sublime is an aesthetic justification of the westward expansion of the United States, and the colonizing and displacement of Indigenous peoples, see: Wilton, Andrew, and Tim Barringer. *American Sublime: Landscape Painting in the United States 1820–1890.* Princeton, NJ: Princeton University Press, 2002.

168 **As he tells me this:** Melville, Herman. *Moby-Dick.* Lexington, KY: Createspace, 2015, 80.

168 **Art allows us:** Murdoch, Iris. *The Sovereignty of Good.* London: Routledge, 1970, 83.

168 **The archaeological record suggests:** Dutton, Dennis. *The Art Instinct: Beauty, Pleasure, and Human Evolution.* London: Bloomsbury, 2009. Henshilwood, C. S. "Emergence of Modern Human Behavior: Middle Stone Age Engravings from South

Africa." *Science* 295, no. 5558 (2002): 1278–80. For carbon dating evidence tracing cave painting back to over 65,000 years ago, see: Hoffmann, Dirk, et al. "U-Th Dating of Carbonate Crusts Reveals Neandertal Origin of Iberian Cave Art." *Science* 359 (2018): 912–15. https://doi.org/10.1126/science.aap7778.

169 **Today, the passions we feel:** Schindler, Ines, Georg Hosoya, Winfried Menninghaus, Ursula Beermann, Valentin Wagner, Michael Eid, and Klaus R. Scherer. "Measuring Aesthetic Emotions: A Review of the Literature and a New Assessment Tool." *PLoS ONE* 12, no. 6 (2017): e0178899. https://doi.org/10.1371/journal.pone.0178899.

169 **The question we take on:** Gopnik, Blake. "Aesthetic Science and Artistic Knowledge." In *Aesthetic Science: Connecting Minds, Brains, and Experience*, edited by Art Shimamura and Steve Palmer. New York: Oxford University Press, 2012. Dennis Dutton and my colleague Keith Oatley have referred to this as the paradox of the arts, that they are obviously acts of the imagination but nevertheless evoke emotions that can feel truthful and informative of the most moral issues of our lives.

169 **"quiet revolutionary":** Sutton, Peter C. *Pieter de Hooch, 1629–1684*. Hartford, CT: Wadsworth Atheneum, 1998.

170 **Susanne Langer:** Langer, Susanne. *Feeling and Form*. New York: Charles Scribner's Sons, 1953, 374.

171 **Our language-based theories:** Nisbett, Richard E., and Timothy D. Wilson. "Telling More Than We Can Know: Verbal Reports on Mental Processes." *Psychological Review* 84, no. 3 (1977): 231–59. https://doi.org/10.1037/0033-295X.84.3.231. This revelatory article would make the point that our theories and words and concepts often do not map onto the more unconscious, automatic, intuitive ways in which we make sense of the world.

171 **Within the study of the brain:** For work on visual art and the brain, see: Kawabata, Hidekai, and Semir Zeki. "Neural Correlates of Beauty." *Journal of Neurophysiology* 91 (2004): 1699–1705. Nadal, Marcos, and Marcus T. Pearce. "The Copenhagen Neuroaesthetics Conference: Prospects and Pitfalls for an Emerging Field." *Brain and Cognition* 76 (2011): 172–83. Chatterjee, Anjan. *The Aesthetic Brain: How We Evolved to Desire Beauty and Enjoy Art*. New York: Oxford University Press, 2014. Starr, Gabrielle G. *Feeling Beauty: The Neuroscience of Aesthetic Experience*. Cambridge, MA: MIT Press, 2013. Pelowski, Matthew, Patrick S. Markey, Michael Forster, Gernot Gerger, and Helmut Leder. "Move Me, Astonish Me . . . Delight My Eyes and Brain: The Vienna Integrated Model of Top-Down and Bottom-Up Processes in Art Perception (VIMAP) and Corresponding Affective, Evaluative, and Neurophysiological Correlates." *Physics of Life Reviews* 21 (2017): 80–125.

172 **the neurochemical signals arrive:** Pelowski, Markey, Forster, Gerger, and Leder. "Move Me, Astonish Me . . . Delight My Eyes and Brain." Starr, *Feeling Beauty*.

173 **These champions of small awe:** Auden, W. H., and Norman Holmes Pearson. *Poets of the English Language*. Vol. 4. New York: Viking Press, 1950, 18.

173 **There are geometries:** Beardsley, Monroe C., Susan L. Feagin, and Patrick Maynard. *Aesthetics*. Oxford, UK: Oxford University Press, 1997.

174 **This first series of photos:** Fisher, Rose-Lynn. *Bee*. New York: Princeton Architecture Press, 2010. See also: www.rose-lynnfisher.com.

175 **more than one thousand photos:** Fisher, Rose-Lynn. *The Topography of Tears*. New York: Bellevue Literary Press, 2017. For a slideshow of this series, visit https://www.newyorker.com/tech/annals-of-technology/slide-show-the-topography-of-tears.

175 **measures of our body's physiology:** Kreibig, Sylvia D. "Autonomic Nervous System Activity in Emotion: A Review." *Biological Psychology* 84 (2010): 394–421.

177 **This book has:** Haeckel, E., O. Briedbach, I. Eibl-Eibesfeldt, and R. P. Hartmann. *Art Forms in Nature: The Prints of Ernst Haeckel*. Munich: Prestel, 1998. These

scientific illustrations would inspire many movements in visual design, including the Jugendstil and art nouveau movements.

178 **There is no better guide:** Gopnik, Adam. "The Right Man: Who Owns Edmund Burke?" *New Yorker*, July 22, 2013.

178 **The book has oddities:** This view is obviously naive and must reflect some sort of personal bias of Burke's. Emotion and olfaction share many common neural pathways, which in part accounts for how powerful, and awe-inspiring, scents can be. Soudry, Y., Cedric Lemogne, D. Malinvaud, S. M. Consoli, and Pierre Bonfils. "Olfactory System and Emotion: Common Substrates." *European Annals of Otorhinolaryngology, Head and Neck Diseases* 128, no. 1 (2011): 18–23. https://doi.org/10.1016/j.anorl.2010.09.007. Epub January 11, 2011. PMID: 21227767.

179 **When what we encounter:** Zajonc, Robert B. "Feeling and Thinking: Preferences Need No Inferences." *American Psychologist* 35 (1980): 151–75.

179 **studies of faces, scents:** Art critic John Berger, in his influential book *Ways of Seeing*, gives us reason to be skeptical of our feelings of comfort, pleasure, and beauty. For several hundred years, Berger shows, men like Renoir and Degas painted the female nude. In such art it is the male gaze that looks upon the woman, who is controlled and confined within society's regard. In this case art teaches us to find comfort in a way of seeing that preserves subjugating gender dynamics within a patriarchal status quo. Berger, John. *Ways of Seeing*. London: Penguin Books, 1972.

179 **In visual art, we like:** Palmer, Stephen E., Karen B. Schloss, and Jonathan S. Gardner. "Hidden Knowledge in Aesthetic Preferences: Color and Spatial Composition." In *Aesthetic Science: Connecting Minds, Brains, and Experience*, edited by Art Shimamura and Steve Palmer, 189–222. New York: Oxford University Books, 2012.

180 **enables new "possibilities of feeling":** Langer, Susanne K. *Mind: An Essay on Human Feeling*. Baltimore: Johns Hopkins Press, 1967. Shimamura, Art, and Steve Palmer, eds. *Aesthetic Science: Connecting Mind, Brain, and Experience*. New York: Oxford University Press, 2012. For a more recent history of this idea and others about the evocative powers of art: Berger, Karol. *A Theory of Art*. New York: Oxford University Press, 2000.

181 **to evoke mystical feeling:** Kandinsky, Wassily, and M. T. H. Sadler. *Concerning the Spiritual in Art*. New York: Dover, 1977, 2.

181 **Psychedelic artists like Alex Grey:** What is true of painting is true of all forms of visual design: that in engaging with perceptions of vastness and mystery, we as participants feel a sense of being connected to something larger than the self. For example, Haussmann's wide, airy, and light-filled boulevards and large public squares in Paris integrated Parisians into a larger sense of identity from the 1850s on.

181 **study of Mesoamerican art:** Stone, Rebecca. *The Jaguar Within: Shamanic Trance in Ancient Central and South American Art*. Linda Schele Series in Maya and Pre-Columbian Studies. Austin: University of Texas Press, 2011.

183 **what some call shamanism:** Winkelman, Michael. *Shamanism*. 2nd ed. Santa Barbara, CA: Praeger Press, 2010.

183 **art activates the dopamine network:** Nadal, Marcos, and Marcus T. Pearce. "The Copenhagen Neuroaesthetics Conference: Prospects and Pitfalls for an Emerging Field." *Brain and Cognition* 76 (2011): 172–83. Chatterjee, Anjan. *The Aesthetic Brain: How We Evolved to Desire Beauty and Enjoy Art*. New York: Oxford University Press, 2014.

183 **When paintings decorate the walls:** An, Donghwy, and Nara Youn. "The Inspirational Power of Arts on Creativity." *Journal of Business Research* 85 (2018): 467–75. https://doi.org/10.1016/j.jbusres.2017.10.025. Antal, Ariane B., and Ilana N. Bitran. "Discovering the Meaningfulness of Art in Organizations." *Journal of Cultural*

Management and Cultural Policy / Zeitschrift für Kulturmanagement und Kulturpolitik 4, no. 2 (2018): 55–76. https://doi.org/10.14361/zkmm-2018-0203.

183 **One impressive study:** Van de Vyver, Julie, and Dominic Abrams. "The Arts as a Catalyst for Human Prosociality and Cooperation." *Social Psychological and Personality Science* 9, no. 6 (2018): 664–74. https://doi.org/10.1177/1948550617720275.

184 **One recent study from Denmark:** Nielsen, Stine L., Lars B. Fich, Kirsten K. Roessler, and Michael F. Mullins. "How Do Patients Actually Experience and Use Art in Hospitals? The Significance of Interaction: A User-Oriented Experimental Case Study." *International Journal of Qualitative Studies on Health and Well-Being* 12, no. 1 (2017): 1267343. https://doi.org/10.1080/17482631.2016.1267343.

184 **In cities judged from photos:** Seresinhe, Chanuki I., Tobias Preis, and Helen S. Moat. "Quantifying the Impact of Scenic Environments on Health." *Scientific Reports* 5 (2015): 1–9. https://doi.org/10.1038/srep16899.

184 **cities with pathways for walking:** Jackson, Laura. "The Relationship of Urban Design to Human Health and Condition." *Landscape and Urban Planning* 64 (2003): 191–200. https://doi.org/10.1016/S0169-2046(02)00230-X.

184 **Simply being near cathedrals:** Shariff, Azim F., Aiyana K. Willard, Teresa Andersen, and Ara Norenzayan. "Religious Priming: A Metanalysis with a Focus on Prosociality." *Personality and Social Psychology Review* 20 (2016): 27–48. One study from Chile found that people were more cooperative with a stranger when in a chapel than when in a lecture hall. The obvious interpretation has to do with the religious significance of a chapel and its priming people to be kinder. It's also plausible, though, that these effects on saintly tendencies had to do with feelings of awe evoked by the design of the chapel. Ahmed, Ali, and Osvaldo Salas. "Religious Context and Prosociality: An Experimental Study from Valparaíso, Chile." *Journal for the Scientific Study of Religion* 52, no. 3 (2013): 627–37. https://doi.org/10.1111/jssr.12045.

186 **box we put prisoners in:** Crile, Susan. *Abu Ghraib: Abuse of Power.* Rome: Gangemi Editore, 2007.

186 **In relevant studies:** Mocaiber, Izabela, Mirtes G. Pereira, Fatima S. Erthal, Walter Machado-Pinheiro, Isabel A. David, Mauricio Cagy, Eliane Volchan, and Leticia de Oliveira. "Fact or Fiction? An Event-Related Potential Study of Implicit Emotion Regulation." *Neuroscience Letters* 476, no. 2 (2010): 84–88. In another study, anger-inducing treatment (harassment) was framed as a live theater performance or as an aptitude test developed by a recruitment firm. When viewing the same social event as an act of theater, participants showed attenuated peripheral physiological reactions. Wagner, Valentin, Julian Klein, Julian Hanich, Mira Shah, Winfried Menninghaus, and Thomas Jacobsen. "Anger Framed: A Field Study on Emotion, Pleasure, and Art." *Psychology of Aesthetics, Creativity, and the Arts* 10, no. 2 (2016): 134–46. https://doi.org/10.1037/aca0000029.

190 **we find art that progresses:** Stamkou, Eftychia, Gerben A. van Kleef, and Astrid C. Homan. "The Art of Influence: When and Why Deviant Artists Gain Impact." *Journal of Personality and Social Psychology* 115, no. 2 (2018): 276–303. https://doi.org/10.1037/pspi0000131.

190 **More surprising and awe-inspiring:** Berger, Jonah, and Katy Milkman. "What Makes Online Content Viral?" *Journal of Marketing Research* 49, no. 2 (2012): 192–205.

Chapter 9: The Fundamental IT

193 **"As I lay there thinking":** Neihardt, John G. *Black Elk Speaks (Complete).* Lincoln and London: University of Nebraska Press, 2014, 30.

NOTES

193 **"Twant me, 'twas the Lord":** Larson, Kate Clifford. *Harriet Tubman: Portrait of an American Hero.* New York: Little, Brown and Company, 2004, 190.

194 **numbers of the religiously unaffiliated:** Fahmy, Dahlia. "Key Findings about Americans' Belief in God." Pew Research Center, April 15, 2018. https://www.pewre search.org/fact-tank/2018/04/25/key-findings-about-americans-belief-in-god/. "In U.S., Decline of Christianity Continues at Rapid Pace." Pew Research Center, October 17, 2019. https://www.pewforum.org/2019/10/17/in-u-s-decline-of-christianity -continues-at-rapid-pace/.

194 **people today are deeply spiritual:** Following precedent in the scientific study of religion, I will use the word "religion" to refer to the organized, formal institutions and dogma of religion, and "spiritual" to refer to the experience of what a person deems to be Divine.

194 **a deep human universal:** Wright, Robert. *The Evolution of God.* New York: Little, Brown and Company, 2009. Robert Wright charts the universality of God in human societies, from hunter-gatherer groups to the present day, and the evolutionary arguments for this universal tendency.

195 **the trauma of racism:** This phenomenon is known as epigenetics. It reveals how trauma is passed on from one generation to the next by altering the myelination of our cells and proteins that allow for the expression of our genes. Carey, Nessa. *The Epigenetics Revolution.* New York: Columbia University Press, 2012.

195 **For thousands of years:** Eliade, Mircea. *The Sacred and the Profane: The Nature of Religion.* Orlando, FL: Harcourt Brace Jovanovich, 1987.

195 **Here is Lao Tzu:** Tzu, Lao, and Charles Johnston. *The Tao Te Ching: Lao Tzu's Book of the Way and of Righteousness.* Vancouver: Kshetra Books, 2016, 11–12.

196 **thousands of years old:** Pollan, Michael. *Second Nature: A Gardener's Education.* New York: Grove Press, 1991.

197 **"The perception of this law":** Emerson, Ralph Waldo. The Divinity School Address: Delivered Before the Senior Class in the Harvard Divinity School Chapel at Cambridge, Massachusetts, July 15, 1838. New York: All Souls Unitarian Church, 1938.

198 **dean of Grace Cathedral:** Malcolm Clemens Young has also written an account of how Henry David Thoreau's nature writings resemble the spiritual journaling of his times, and reveal, as with Young's experience, a sense of encountering the Divine in nature. Young, Malcolm C. *The Spiritual Journal of Henry David Thoreau.* Macon, GA: Mercer University Press, 2009.

199 **James was raised:** Richardson, Robert D. *William James: In the Maelstrom of American Modernism.* New York: Houghton Mifflin, 2006.

200 **"But it feels like":** Bronson, Bertrand H. *Johnson Agonistes and Other Essays.* Vol. 3. Berkeley: University of California Press, 1965, 52.

200 **listened to talks:** Tymoczko, Dmitri. "The Nitrous Oxide Philosopher." *Atlantic Monthly,* May 1996.

200 **Gifford Lectures in 1901:** James, William. *The Varieties of Religious Experience: A Study in Human Nature: Being the Gifford Lectures on Natural Religion Delivered at Edinburgh in 1901–1902.* New York; London: Longmans, Green, 1902.

201 **Religion is about our experience:** James defines mystical awe in terms of these qualities: The state is *ineffable*; it cannot be captured with language. It is *noetic*, involving profound realizations about human existence and the nature of reality. It is *transient* and rooted in fleeting feelings. And it is *passive*; our sense of self and agency diminish during mystical awe.

201 **We can find these feelings:** Van Cappellen, Patty. "Rethinking Self-Transcendent Positive Emotions and Religion: Perspectives from Psychological and Biblical Research." *Psychology of Religion and Spirituality* 9 (2017): 254–63.

201 **Or for Mark Twain:** Kripal, Jeffrey J. *The Flip: Epiphanies of Mind and the Future of Knowledge*. New York: Bellevue Literary Press, 2019. In this book Kripal surveys a wide range of extraordinary experiences that shaped the spiritual beliefs of well-known scholars over the ages.

202 **guided by Divine forces:** For a fascinating account of how evangelical Christians hear the voice of God, see: Luhrmann, Tanya. *When God Talks Back: Understanding the American Evangelical Relationship with God*. New York: Alfred Knopf, 2012.

202 **known collectively as yōkai:** Foster, Michael D. *The Book of Yokai*. Berkeley: University of California Press, 2015.

202 **ancient cognitive systems:** Boyer, Pascal. "Religious Thought and Behaviour as By-Products of Brain Function." *Trends in Cognitive Science* 7, no. 3 (2003): 119–24. Boyer, Pascal. *Religion Explained: The Evolutionary Origins of Religious Thought*. New York: Basic Books, 2001. Taves, Ann, Egil Asprem, and Elliott Ihm. "Psychology, Meaning Making, and the Study of Worldviews: Beyond Religion and Non-religion." *Psychology of Religion and Spirituality* 10, no. 3 (2018): 207–17.

202 **We attribute unusual experiences:** Barrett, Justin. "Exploring the Natural Foundations of Religion." *Trends in Cognitive Science* 4, no. 1 (2000): 29–34.

202 **When alone in an eerie:** Our attachment to adult figures is grounded in touch, soothing, comfort in the face of threat, and the formation of beliefs about how vast, powerful figures—caregivers—attend to our needs. It is sound to conjecture that our attachment experiences are a platform for the emergence of beliefs about the Divine. Given certain cultural and family contexts, this thinking goes, God becomes a noncorporeal attachment figure, a "secure base" in our adult lives. Cherniak, Aaron D., Mario Mikulincer, Phillip R. Shaver, and Pehr Granqvist. "Attachment Theory and Religion." *Current Opinion in Psychology* 40 (2021): 126–30. Granqvist, Pehr, and Lee A. Kirkpatrick. "Religion, Spirituality, and Attachment." In *APA Handbook of Psychology, Religion, and Spirituality*. Vol. 1, *Context, Theory, and Research*, edited by Kenneth I. Pargament, Julie J. Exline, and James W. Jones, 139–155. American Psychological Association, 2013. https://doi.org/10.1037/14045-007. This article shows that feelings of being securely attached to God account for some of religion's benefits, such as reduced distress. Bradshaw, Matt, Christopher G. Ellison, and Jack P. Marcum. "Attachment to God, Images of God, and Psychological Distress in a Nationwide Sample of Presbyterians." *International Journal for the Psychology of Religion* 20, no. 2 (2010): 130–47. https://doi.org/10.1080/10508611003608049.

203 **Carmelite nuns recall:** Beauregard, Mario, and David Leary. *The Spiritual Brain: A Neuroscientist's Case for the Existence of the Soul*. New York: HarperCollins, 2007. Newberg, Andrew. *Neurotheology: How Science Can Enlighten Us about Spirituality*. New York: Columbia University Press, 2018. See also: Sheldrake, Rupert. *Science and Spiritual Practices*. Berkeley: Counterpoint Press, 2018.

203 **This experience of mystical awe:** This we learn from Jess Bryon Hollenbeck's book *Mysticism: Experiences, Responses, and Empowerment*, in her tour of the place of mystical awe in the religions of the world that emerged some 2,500 years ago, and the cultural and spiritual traditions of the diverse Indigenous societies in North and South America that are 10,000 years old, or older. Hollenbeck, Jess Bryon. *Mysticism: Experiences, Responses, and Empowerment*. University Park, PA: Penn State University Press, 1996.

204 **soul in terms of patterns:** Halpern, Paul. *Synchronicity: The Epic Quest to Understand the Quantum Nature of Cause and Effect*. New York: Basic Books, 2020.

204 **Extraordinary experiences:** In 1996, social psychologist Paul Rozin published a generative paper that anticipated this thinking. He drew upon an idea found in evolutionary thinking, that of preadaptation: that evolved forms like emotions are put to

new uses to meet the ever-changing contexts of our complex social lives. The world's expert on disgust, Rozin applied this thinking to the ways in which culture elaborates upon elements of "core disgust" into new moral and religious forms. Core disgust, or distaste, evolved to ensure that we avoid ingesting toxic substances. We recoil at noxious smells and tastes of rotten food, and expel the substance from our mouths and stomachs. This core structure of distaste, in Rozin's thinking, is pre-adapted to extend to, or elaborate into, moral disgust. Our perceptions that trigger distaste, of what is toxic and fetid, feed into representations of moral disgust of a religious or moral quality—sins of the body, dirty minds, the filthy rich, wretches to be saved, rotten character. The primal urge of core distaste to expel, clean, and purify ritualizes into, for example, purification practices, such as bathing in rivers in India during religious festivals, washing the hands and mouth prior to entering temples in Japan, and baptisms in the United States. Rozin, Paul. "Towards a Psychology of Food and Eating: From Motivation to Model to Meaning, Morality and Metaphor." *Current Directions in Psychological Science* 5 (1996): 18–24.

204 **Out of mystical awe:** Another example of moral emotions being put to religious and spiritual uses is found in Karen Armstrong's sweeping history of the emergence of many religions during the Axial Age, some 2,500 years ago. In her book *The Great Transformation*, Armstrong argues that throughout the Middle East, the Mediterranean, and Asia, with an increase of commerce and trade, traditional communities were breaking down. There was a an increase in violence. In response to these challenges, people began to write down their core beliefs and engage in rituals and practices together, in founding Judaism, Christianity, Hinduism, Buddhism, Taoism, Confucianism, and classical Greek thought. Armstrong identifies how compassion, empathy, attending to suffering, forgiveness, and gratitude—all emotional processes shaped by our hypersocial evolution—are central to the emergence of these religious traditions. Armstrong, Karen. *The Great Transformation: The Beginning of Our Religious Traditions.* New York: Anchor Books, 2007.

205 **near-death experiences:** Holden, Janice M., Bruce Greyson, and Debbie James. *The Handbook of Near-Death Experiences: Thirty Years of Investigation.* Santa Barbara, CA: Praeger, 2009.

209 **bodily feeling of the Divine:** Krishna, Gopi. *Living with Kundalini: The Autobiography of Gopi Krishna.* Edited by Leslie Shepard. Boston and London: Shambhala, 1993, 3.

209 **Such rituals bring about:** Casper ter Kuile, a graduate of Harvard Divinity School, believes we can find mystical awe by returning to ritual. In his wonderful book *The Power of Ritual*, ter Kuile composts religious traditions and finds these pathways to mystical awe:

> Read sacred texts.
> Create sabbaths in your life, from work, technology, social life.
> Find opportunities for what one might call prayer—mindful quiet forms of reflecting.
> Eat with others.
> Walk in nature.

ter Kuile, Casper. *The Power of Ritual: How to Create Meaning and Connection in Everything You Do.* New York: Harper One, 2020.

209 **Muslims practicing the salat:** Van Cappellen, Patty, and Megan E. Edwards. "The Embodiment of Worship: Relations among Postural, Psychological, and Physiological Aspects of Religious Practice." *Journal for the Cognitive Science of Religion* 6, no. 1–2 (2021): 56–79.

210 **meditating or practicing yoga:** For a treatment of the benefits of yoga, and its scientific study, see: Broad, William J. *The Science of Yoga.* New York: Simon & Schuster, 2012.

210 **sense of spiritual engagement:** In one review of 145 studies involving 98,000 individuals, people who reported a sense of spirituality were less likely to be depressed. Smith, Timothy B., Michael E. McCullough, and Justin Poll. "Religiousness and Depression: Evidence for a Main Effect and the Moderating Influence of Stressful Life Events." *Psychological Bulletin* 129 (2003): 614–36. https://doi.org/10.1037/0033 -2909.129.4.614. Mystical awe is also good for our health. In an illustrative study, gay men with AIDS who regularly read spiritual texts, prayed, engaged in spiritual discussions, and attended services showed higher levels of killer T cells, part of the body's immune response. Ironson, Gail, and Heidemarie Kremer. "Spiritual Transformation, Psychological Well-Being, Health, and Survival in People with HIV." *International Journal of Psychiatry in Medicine* 32, no. 3 (2009): 263–81. Summing up these kinds of studies, one review found that religiously oriented people are less likely to die at any time in life. McCullough, Michael E., William T. Hoyt, David B. Larson, Harold G. Koenig, and Carl Thoresen. "Religious Involvement and Mortality: A Meta-analytic Review." *Health Psychology* 19, no. 3 (2000): 211–22. https://doi .org/10.1037//0278-6133.19.3.211.

210 **And greater humility:** Van Cappellen, Patty, Maria Toth-Gauthier, Vassilis Saroglou, and Barbara L. Fredrickson. "Religion and Well-Being: The Mediating Role of Positive Emotions." *Journal of Happiness Studies* 17 (2016): 485–505. Van Cappellen, Patty, Maria Toth-Gauthier, Vassilis Saroglou, and Barbara L. Fredrickson. "Religiosity and Prosocial Behavior among Churchgoers: Exploring Underlying Mechanisms." *International Journal for the Psychology of Religion* 26 (2016): 19–30.

210 **Groups that cultivated these tendencies:** Norenzayan, Ara, Azim Shariff, Will M. Gervais, Aiyana K. Willard, Rita A. McNamara, Edward Slingerland, and Joseph Henrich. "The Cultural Evolution of Prosocial Religions." *Behavioral and Brain Sciences* 39 (2015): e1. https://doi.org/10.1017/S0140525X14001356.

210 **More intelligent design:** Taves, Ann. *Religious Experience Reconsidered: A Building-Block Approach to the Study of Religion and Other Special Things.* Princeton, NJ: Princeton University Press, 2009. Norenzayan, Shariff, Gervais, Willard, McNamara, Slingerland, and Henrich. "The Cultural Evolution of Prosocial Religions." Wilson, David S. *Darwin's Cathedral: Evolution, Religion, and the Nature of Society.* Chicago: University of Chicago Press, 2002. Bellah, Robert. *Religion in Human Evolution: From the Paleolithic to the Axial Age.* Cambridge, MA: Harvard University Press, 2011.

210 **The toxicities of communities:** In his excellent book on morality, Joshua Greene suggests that such tribalism is the central moral problem facing our species today. Greene, Joshua. *Moral Tribes: Emotion, Reason, and the Gap between Us and Them.* New York: Penguin Press, 2013.

211 **experiences with entheogens:** Lee, Martin A., and Bruce Shlain. *Acid Dreams: The Complete Social History of LSD: The CIA, the Sixties, and Beyond.* New York: Grove Press, 1985. Steven, Jay. *Storming Heaven: LSD and the American Dream.* New York: Grove Press, 1987. Pollan, Michael. *How to Change Your Mind: What the New Science of Psychedelics Teaches Us about Consciousness, Dying, Addiction, Depression, and Transcendence.* New York: Penguin Press, 2019.

212 **After taking a small boat:** It is interesting to speculate that this crab species' signaling of vast size in its claw may stun other crabs into submission, thus elevating its own rank and chances of survival and reproduction. Perhaps this is an even deeper evolutionary origin of rudimentary awe than we have considered thus far, for example in Jane Goodall's description of a chimpanzee's behavior during the waterfall dance.

213 **scholars of mysticism:** Hood, Ralph W., Jr., Ghorbani Nima, Paul J. Watson, Ahad F. Ghramaleki, Mark N. Bing, H. K. Davison, Ronald J. Morris, and W. P. Williamson. "Dimensions of the Mysticism Scale: Confirming the Three-Factor Structure in the United States and Iran." *Journal for the Scientific Study of Religion* 40 (2001): 691–705. Hood's measurement derived from reading Walter Stace's excellent surveys of religious mysticism across religions: Stace, Walter T. *Mysticism and Philosophy.* New York: St. Martin's Press, 1960. Stace, Walter T. *The Teachings of the Mystics.* New York: Mentor, 1960.

213 **during times of transformation:** Caspi, Avshalom, and Terrie E. Moffitt. "When Do Individual Differences Matter? A Paradoxical Theory of Personality Coherence." *Psychological Inquiry* 4, no. 4 (1993): 247–71. https://doi.org/10.1207/s15327965 pli0404_1.

213 **People who are open:** Connelly, Brian S., Deniz S. Ones, and Oleksandr S. Chernyshenko. "Introducing the Special Section on Openness to Experience: Review of Openness Taxonomies, Measurement, and Nomological Net." *Journal of Personality Assessment* 96, no. 1 (2014): 1–16. https://doi.org/10.1080/00223891.2013.83 0620.

214 **The defining emotion of openness:** Shiota, Michelle N., Dacher Keltner, and Oliver P. John. "Positive Emotion Dispositions Differentially Associated with Big Five Personality and Attachment Style." *Journal of Positive Psychology* 1 (2006): 61–71.

214 **Bob Jesse quietly assisting:** Griffiths, Roland R., William A. Richards, Una McCann, and Robert Jesse. "Psilocybin Can Occasion Mystical-Type Experiences Having Substantial and Sustained Personal Meaning and Spiritual Significance." *Psychopharmacology* 187, no. 3 (2006): 268–83; discussion 284–92. https://doi.org/10.1007 /s00213-006-0457-5. Epub July 7, 2006. PMID: 16826400.

215 **Psychedelic experiences make us less:** Hendricks, Peter J. "Classic Psychedelics: An Integrative Review of Epidemiology, Therapeutics, Mystical Experience, and Brain Network Function." *Pharmacology and Therapeutics* 197 (2019): 83–102. Chi, Tingying, and Jessica A. Gold. "A Review of Emerging Therapeutic Potential of Psychedelic Drugs in the Treatment of Psychiatric Illnesses." *Journal of the Neurological Sciences* 411 (2020): 116715. Johnson, Matthew W., Albert Garcia-Romeu, Mary P. Cosimano, and Roland R. Griffiths. "Pilot Study of the 5-HT2AR Agonist Psilocybin in the Treatment of Tobacco Addiction." *Journal of Psychopharmacology* 28, no. 11: (2014): 983–92. Hendricks, Peter S., Christopher B. Thorne, C. B. Clark, David W. Coombs, and Matthew W. Johnson. "Classic Psychedelic Use Is Associated with Reduced Psychological Distress and Suicidality in the United States Adult Population." *Journal of Psychopharmacology* 29, no. 3 (2015): 280–88.

215 **the magic ingredient is awe:** Hendricks, Peter S. "Awe: A Putative Mechanism Underlying the Effects of Classic Psychedelic-Assisted Psychotherapy." *International Review of Psychiatry* 30, no. 4 (2018): 331–42. https://doi.org/10.1080/09540261.2018 .1474185.

215 **psychedelics consistently deactivate the DMN:** For relevant empirical work, see: Carhart-Harris, Robin L., et al. "Neural Correlates of the Psychedelic State as Determined by fMRI Studies with Psilocybin." *Proceedings of the National Academy of Sciences* 109, no. 6 (2012): 2138–43.

215 **Psychedelics lead people to feel:** Vollenweider, Franz X., and Katrin H. Preller. "Psychedelic Drugs: Neurobiology and Potential for Treatment of Psychiatric Disorders."

Nature Reviews Neuroscience 21 (2020): 611–24. https://doi.org/10.1038/s41583-020 -0367-2.

216 **These compounds lead us to be:** Hendricks. "Awe: A Putative Mechanism Underlying the Effects of Classic Psychedelic-Assisted Psychotherapy."

216 **Over lunch one day:** For an interesting discussion of pilgrimages and their evolutionary roots in our tendencies to walk together, and a broader discussion of looking at spiritual practices through the lens of science, see: Sheldrake, Rupert. *Science and Spiritual Practices*. Berkeley: Counterpoint Press, 2018.

217 **to champion nationwide toilet access:** At the time of ESI's founding, only the well-to-do had toilets and sanitation. Now 31 percent of Indians do.

217 **From such a modest room:** Of course, I'm biased to place such historical significance in the Berkeley free speech protests, but for a history of those protests, how they were shaped by the civil rights movement, and how they spread to the antiwar protests, see: Rosenfeld, Seth. *Subversives: The FBI's War on Student Radicals and Reagan's Rise to Power*. New York: Farrar, Strauss and Giroux, 2012.

218 **For Trupti, our greatest illusion:** This observation about scarcity reminded me of the scientific studies of my friend Tom Gilovich at Cornell with Leaf van Boven, which show that when we focus on materialism, we get less happy; when we focus on experience, we get happier. Van Boven, Leaf, Margaret C. Campbell, and Thomas Gilovich. "The Social Costs of Materialism: On People's Assessments of Materialistic and Experiential Consumers." *Personality and Social Psychology Bulletin* 36 (2010): 551–63.

Chapter 10: Life and Death

223 **"What do you think":** Whitman, Walt. *Song of Myself: 1892 Edition*. Glenshaw, PA: S4N Books, 2017, 10.

224 **Childbirth is the most undervalued:** For outstanding treatments of the role of childbirth in human evolution and society, see: Hrdy, Sarah B. *Mother Nature: A History of Mothers, Infants, and Natural Selection*. New York: Ballantine, 1999. Epstein, Randi Hutter. *Get Me Out: A History of Childbirth from the Garden of Eden to the Sperm Bank*. New York: W. W. Norton, 2010.

225 **In this astonished state:** Zebrowitz, Leslie. *Reading Faces: Windows to the Soul?* Boulder, CO: Westview Press, 1997.

226 **Common to the narratives were references:** Feldman, Ruth, Katharina Braugh, and Frances A. Champagne. "The Neural Mechanisms and Consequences of Paternal Caregiving." *Nature Reviews Neuroscience* 20 (2019): 205–24. For an excellent summary, see: Siegel, Daniel. *The Developing Mind*. 3rd ed. New York: Guilford Press, 2020.

228 **This shift in life expectancy:** Hawkes, Kristen, James F. O'Connell, and Nicholas G. Blurton-Jones. "Hazda Women's Time Allocation, Offspring Provisioning, and the Evolution of Long Postmenopausal Life Spans." *Current Anthropology* 38, no. 4 (1997): 551–77. Hawkes, Kristen. "Grandmothers and the Evolution of Human Longevity." *American Journal of Human Biology* 15, no. 3 (2003): 380–400.

229 **worked as a midwife:** To learn more about Nancy Bardacke's work, see: https://www .mindfulbirthing.org/. She summarizes this work in a book, as well: Bardacke, Nancy. *Mindful Birthing: Training the Mind, Body, and Heart for Childbirth and Beyond*. New York: HarperCollins, 2014.

229 **In the right circumstances:** The wonders of childhood and raising children are fueled by two vast forces of human development: intersubjectivity and play. For mothers, these forces are found often in soothing, touch, and "motherese"—that language of sounds and intonation oriented toward captivating an infant's attention—and positive emotional displays like smiling. For fathers, they are found in wild forms of exploratory play, such as throwing the baby in the air or moving them around in space as if they had just jumped off Half Dome in Yosemite in one of those exhilarating flight suits.

229 **In one illustrative study:** Colantino, Joseph A., and Elizabeth Bonawitz. "Awesome Play: Awe Increases Preschooler's Exploration and Discovery." In *Proceedings of the 40th Annual Conference of the Cognitive Science Society*, 1536–41. Edited by Timothy M. Rogers, Marina Rau, Jerry Zhu, and Chuck Kalish. Madison, WI: Cognitive Science Society, 2018.

230 **as children develop:** Anderson, Craig L., Dante D. Dixson, Maria Monroy, and Dacher Keltner. "Are Awe-Prone People More Curious? The Relationship between Dispositional Awe, Curiosity, and Academic Outcomes." *Journal of Personality* 88, no. 4 (2020): 762–79. https://doi.org/10.1111/jopy.12524.

230 **It's no wonder:** Twenge, Jean M. "Increases in Depression, Self-Harm, and Suicide among U.S. Adolescents after 2012 and Links to Technology Use: Possible Mechanisms." *Psychiatric Research & Clinical Practice*. Published online March 27, 2020. https://doi.org/10.1176/appi.prcp.20190015.

230 **Rachel Carson saw:** Popova, Maria. *Figuring*. New York: Pantheon Press, 2019.

230 **young people were being deprived:** Carson, Rachel. "Help Your Child to Wonder." *Woman's Home Companion*, July 1956.

230 **"Help Your Child to Wonder":** Carson, Rachel. *The Sense of Wonder: A Celebration of Nature for Parents and Children*. New York: Harper Perennial, 1998.

232 **Take in the ground:** For a visual treatment of this science, see: Schwartzberg, Louie, dir. *Fantastic Fungi*. 2019. Los Gatos, CA: Netflix, 2019.

233 **young men dying of AIDS:** Halifax, Joan. *Being with Dying. Cultivating Compassion and Fearlessness in the Presence of Death*. Boulder, CO: Shambala Publications, 2008.

234 **Be open to suffering:** Goetz, Jennifer, Emiliana Simon-Thomas, and Dacher Keltner. "Compassion: An Evolutionary Analysis and Empirical Review." *Psychological Bulletin* 136, no. 3 (2010): 351–74.

234 **"flickerings of that innermost flame":** Woolf, Virginia. *The Essays of Virginia Woolf*. Edited by Andrew McNeillie. London: Hogarth Press, 2008, 161.

234 **Seeking to understand those "flickerings":** Norton, Loretta, Raechelle M. Gibson, Teneille Gofton, Carolyn Benson, Sonny Dhanani, Sam D. Shemie, Laura Hornby, Roxanne Ward, and G. B. Young. "Electroencephalographic Recordings during Withdrawal of Life-Sustaining Therapy until 30 Minutes after Declaration of Death." *Canadian Journal of Neurological Science* 44, no. 2 (2017): 139–45.

234 **beheaded at the guillotine:** Taylor, Adam. "How Long Does the Brain Remain Conscious after Decapitation?" *Independent*, May 6, 2019. https://www.independent.co.uk/life-style/health-and-families/health-news/decapitation-survive-speak-anne-boleyn-henry-viii-conscious-brain-a8886126.html.

234 **These are narratives of people:** Pearson, Patricia. *Opening Heaven's Door: What the Dying Are Trying to Say about Where They're Going*. New York: Atria, 2014.

235 **Japanese families honor the deceased:** Koren, Leonard. *Wabi-Sabi: For Artists, Designers, Poets, and Philosophers*. Point Reyes, CA: Imperfect Publishing, 2008.

Chapter 11: Epiphany
237 **"Whilst this planet":** Darwin, Charles. *On the Origin of Species by Means of Natural Selection*. London: Murray, 1859, 489.

237 **Charles Darwin's emotions:** Browne, Janet. *Charles Darwin.* Vol. 1, *Voyaging.* New York: Alfred Knopf; London: Jonathan Cape, 1995. *Charles Darwin.* Vol. 2, *The Power of Place.* New York: Alfred Knopf, 2002.

237 **Caring for his ten-year-old daughter:** Goetz, Jennifer, Emiliana Simon-Thomas, and Dacher Keltner. "Compassion: An Evolutionary Analysis and Empirical Review." *Psychological Bulletin* 136, no. 3 (2010): 351–74.

238 **vast story of mammalian evolution:** Darwin, Charles. *The Expression of Emotions in Man and Animals.* 3rd ed. New York: Oxford University Press, 1998.

238 **Reading his descriptions:** For a table of Darwin's descriptions, see: Keltner, Dacher. *Born to Be Good: The Science of a Meaningful Life.* New York: W. W. Norton, 2009, 18–20.

238 **Frank's office is:** Gosling, Sam. *Snoop: What Your Stuff Says about You.* New York: Basic Books, 2001.

239 **MacArthur genius award:** Sulloway, Frank J. *Freud, Biologist of the Mind: Beyond the Psychoanalytic Legend.* New York: Basic Books, 1979.

239 **He wrote the bestselling book:** Sulloway, Frank J. *Born to Rebel: Birth Order, Family Dynamics, and Revolutionary Genius.* New York: Pantheon, 1996.

240 **"I frequently went":** Darwin. *On the Origin of Species by Means of Natural Selection,* 489.

241 **"It is interesting to contemplate":** Darwin. *On the Origin of Species by Means of Natural Selection,* 489–90.

243 **Literary studies speak of epiphanies:** Kim, Sharon. *Literary Epiphany in the Novel, 1850–1950.* New York: Palgrave Macmillan, 2012.

245 **the idea of systems:** Capra, Fritjof, and Pier Luigi Luisi. *The Systems View of Life: A Unifying Vision.* Cambridge, UK: Cambridge University Press, 2014. For an early philosophical statement about systems thinking, see: von Bertalanffy, L. *General Systems Theory.* New York: Braziller, 1968.

245 **Various forms of life:** Nowak, Martin A. "Five Rules for the Evolution of Cooperation." *Science* 314 (2006): 1560–63.

247 **a systems view of life:** Lent, Jeremy. *The Patterning Instinct: A Cultural History of Humanity's Search for Meaning.* Amherst, NY: Prometheus Books, 2016. In this ambitious book, Jeremy Lent details how our capacity to perceive patterns emerged in many of our awe-inspiring social tendencies—moving in unison, mimicry, collective behavior. We became a pattern-perceiving species.

248 **Our survival depended:** Lieberman, Matthew D. *Social: Why Our Brains Are Wired to Connect.* Oxford, UK: Oxford University Press, 2013.

248 **Many Indigenous peoples:** My colleague Richard Nisbett has argued that cultures divide in terms of their systems thinking, which is more prevalent in East Asian cultures than in the West, shaped so by classical Greek philosophy and the Age of Enlightenment, and its privileging of reductionistic analysis. Nisbett, Richard. *The Geography of Thought: Why We Think the Way We Do.* New York: Free Press, 2003.

248 **the centrality of systems thinking:** Wulf, Andrea. *The Invention of Nature: Alexander von Humboldt's New World.* New York: Vintage Books, 2015.

248 **Experiences of awe open:** For a fascinating account of how extraordinary perceptual experiences lead people to new systems of thought, often of a spiritual or religious quality, see: Kripal, Jeffrey J. *The Flip: Epiphanies of Mind and the Future of Knowledge.* New York: Bellevue Literary Press, 2019.

249 **shift us from the illusions:** Bai, Yang, Laura A. Maruskin, Serena Chen, Amie M. Gordon, Jennifer E. Stellar, Galen D. McNeil, Kaiping Peng, and Dacher Keltner. "Awe, the Diminished Self, and Collective Engagement: Universals and Cultural Variations in the Small Self." *Journal of Personality and Social Psychology* 113, no. 2 (2017): 185–209.

249 **complex systems of interdependent adaptations:** Wilson, Edward O. *The Meaning of Human Existence*. New York: Liveright Publications, 2014.

249 **systems-like patterns of agency:** Valdesolo, P., and Jesse Graham. "Awe, Uncertainty, and Agency Detection." *Psychological Science* 25 (2014): 170–78. http://dx.doi.org/10.1177/0956797613501884.

250 **Being cultural animals:** Keltner, Dacher, and James J. Gross. "Functional Accounts of Emotion." *Cognition & Emotion* 13, no. 5 (1999): 467–80.

Index

INDEX

INDEX

WITHDRAWN